Managing Legal and Ethical Social Work Practice

by

Marilyn J. Samuels, LL.B.

and

Elayne M. Tanner, M.S.W., R.S.W.

IRWIN LAW

MANAGING A LEGAL AND ETHICAL SOCIAL WORK PRACTICE
© Irwin Law Inc., 2003

Published in 2003 by
Irwin Law Inc.
347 Bay St.
Suite 501
Toronto, ON
M5H 2R7
www.irwinlaw.com

ISBN: 1-55221-067-7

National Library of Canada Cataloguing in Publication Data
Tanner, Elayne
   Managing a legal and ethical social work practice / Elayne,
Tanner, Marilyn Samuels.

Includes index.
ISBN 1-55221-067-7

   1. Ontario. Social Work and Social Service Work Act, 1988.
2. Social workers—Legal status, laws, etc.—Ontario. I. Samuels,
Marilyn (Marilyn J.) II. Title.

KE0618.S62T35 2002   344.71301'7613613   C2002-904745-5
KF3721.T35 2002

The publisher acknowledges the financial support of the Government of Canada through the Book Publishing Industry Development Program (BPIDP) for our publishing activities. The publisher also acknowledges the Government of Ontario through the Ontario Media Development Corporation's Ontario Book Initiative.

Cover Design © 2003 Worldwide Entertainment Productions
Photography © 2000 Jordan Bernstein – Worldwide Entertainment Productions.
WorldwideEnt.ca

Printed and bound in Canada

1   2   3   4   5   07   06   05   04   03

We would like to dedicate this book to Kim Ann Popen, Sara Podniewicz and Jordan Heikamp, whose tragic deaths provided the impetus for the passage of the Social Work and Social Service Work Act in Ontartio. We challenge all social workers and social service workers to embrace the ideals that come with this legislation. In doing so we honour and give meaning to the brief lives of these children. This will be their legacy.

Foreword

Elayne Tanner and Marilyn Samuels have written a book for social workers that is timely, important, interesting, and at times troubling in the issues it raises. For this they are to be commended.

Managing a Legal and Ethical Social Work Practice is timely for all Canadian social workers since we are now in an era in which our practice is not only governed by a moral commitment to our Codes of Ethics but also, in a more compelling way, by the legal requirements of professional legislation in its various forms across the nation. Recent court cases in Canada, Great Britain, and the United States have made it clear that social work practice is very much under public scrutiny. What we do and what we do not do is of considerable interest to the public at large through the scrutiny of the courts and the media. This, of course, is a sign of growing respect for our profession, but a respect that demands a demonstrably high standard of practice by those who bear the title of social worker.

Managing a Legal and Ethical Social Work Practice is an important book because it touches on a range of daily practice issues that, in many instances, are much more complex than we have thought them to be in the past. For example, issues like confidentiality and disclosure have become such intricate concepts that colleagues acting from the very best of intentions can find themselves in serious difficulty if they do not understand the legal demands of practice.

The book is interesting because it touches on a range of practice components for which there are not always ready answers and for which a range of opinions exist. The authors help us to understand the spectrum of issues involved in some of these difficult practice scenarios through a rich use of case examples from our own and other related professions as well as from other jurisdictions.

Managing a Legal and Ethical Social Work Practice is also a troubling volume as it brings into focus the many issues and responsibilities that accompany contemporary social work practice for which, at times, there are no clear answers. It is hoped that clarity will emerge as such issues and responsibilities are tested by various professional Colleges and the courts.

As the authors point out, although their material is relevant for persons in independent practice, it also has important ramifications for agency practices and for the policies on which many of us have depended for answers to uncertain questions of practice. Some of these policies and practices may well need to be revised in light of current legislation. The overall message of this important book is that contemporary social work practice is much more risky from a legislative perspective than we have ever considered before.

Fortunately, Tanner and Samuels have written a book that may be likened to the type of travel guides we all purchase when we are going to a place we don't know. It presents in a clear fashion the interpretation of two colleagues, one a social worker and the other a lawyer, on the implications for practice of contemporary social work legislation. Throughout, the authors urge us always to seek both collegial as well as legal advice. While their book offers a rich coterie of advice it, of course, does not profess to be the final word. That is the role of the Colleges and courts.

Of particular help are the various suggestions throughout the volume on how to avoid difficulties or *minefields* in our practice and what to do when things go wrong. One of the authors' important recommendations is the need for malpractice insurance. This is something that a few years ago was scarcely considered, yet it is now, perhaps, something that we should all have. Indeed, ethical practice may soon require that we carry such insurance not only for our own protection, but also for the protection of our clients. I found the sections on confidentiality, recording, and relationship issues especially insightful and wondered, looking back on my own teaching, if we give sufficient attention to these areas in our lectures and texts.

Tanner and Samuels correctly identify areas of our practice that have not yet been fully addressed by legislation and could thus be problematic for some practitioners. For example, the difficulties faced by persons who practise in smaller communities, which indeed is the reality of much of our country, in dealing with issues of relationship and confidentiality, are very complex and need to be studied carefully. As well, the authors raise the important question of who is a client. When I, as a Professor, talk to a troubled student who has asked to see me and I provide an appropriate referral, should this be viewed as a professional social work relationship that is covered by existing legislation? Some of these brief interviews may be very intense, replete with all the dynamics of longer-term relationships even though our role is to help the person to get the help he or she needs. In the same way, how are we to view some intake interviews, which may only last a few minutes but which require highly honed skills of social work knowledge and technique?

One of the most helpful sections in this volume is on recording, an area the complexities of which we have begun to appreciate but about which little has been written. The authors stress the need for standardized forms for releases and confidentiality. More importantly, they provide templates as exemplars of good practice. There are very few written examples of what good records should look like as well as examples of the content and wording that are potentially problematic. As far as I know, this is one of the first Canadian social work books that has presented this kind of concrete materials to practitioners.

Managing a Legal and Ethical Social Work Practice is well written and makes a timely contribution to our profession. Naturally, not everyone will agree with some of the authors' conclusions and recommendations. However, this is the way dialogue develops, ideas are tested, knowledge is promulgated, and clarity emerges; a much better way than having to wait until social workers are in difficulty with their respective legislative bodies to learn about what they should or should not be doing. I commend these two colleagues and wish them well with this endeavour. They have written an important practitioner-oriented text of which many such are greatly needed in Canada.

Francis J. Turner
Professor Emeritus

Summary Table of Contents

Detailed Table of Contents

Preface

This book is a practical handbook for social workers and social service workers, Ontario's newest regulated professions. It outlines in layman's terms the application of Ontario's *Social Work and Social Service Work Act, 1998* to the lives of the province's social workers and social service workers. In this book we explain in simple, non-legal language the rights and obligations of social workers and social service workers under the legislation. We also point out some of the potential minefields that social workers and social service workers may find themselves in and ways to avoid these risky aspects of practice.

Social workers in other provinces, as well as Ontario health professionals, will also find this book useful since the social work statutes of other provinces and Ontario's *Regulated Health Professions Act, 1991*, are similar to Ontario's *Social Work and Social Service Work Act, 1998*. Furthermore, this book will serve as a helpful reference tool for members of the Ontario legal community who advise social workers on the application of the Act.

As noted in Ontario Regulation 383/00, entitled Registration (reprinted as appendix III), social workers must have a minimum of a Bachelor of Social Work degree obtained through a university education, while social service workers must have a Social Service Worker's diploma obtained through a college education. As a result of these educational differences, the major distinction between social workers and social service workers lies in the scope of practice. The only difference in the scope of practice noted in the *Standards of Practice Handbook* (reprinted as appendix II) is that the social worker is able to provide diagnostic services, while the social service worker is denied this right. With this in mind, references to social workers in this book are meant to include social service workers as well.

We caution that the legislation is still evolving. Although every effort was made to make this book as accurate as possible, it is conceivable that some changes in the law may have occurred by the time this book is published or used. Laws change, legislation can be amended, and courts can alter or reinterpret longstanding precedents. Although we believe the information in this book is factual, it is not meant to replace independent legal advice. Readers who are members of the Ontario College of Social Workers and Social Service Workers should seek guidance from the College, their professional or legal representatives, or both when in doubt about the application of the law to their work. The opinions expressed in this book are meant to guide the reader's thinking and analysis and are not specific diagnostic rules to apply directly to one's own practice.

The forms and waivers provided in this book are meant to serve as templates for readers to adapt to their specific needs. These documents are provided without any warranty, implied or explicit, that they are appropriate forms or waivers for use in a reader's practice. Any form or waiver that constitutes a legal document between a social worker and his or her client should be reviewed by legal counsel to ensure that it conforms to all applicable laws and social work practices. The authors are not responsible for any actions taken by the reader with regard to his or her practice and are not responsible for any losses incurred by the reader as a result of his or her use of information or materials in this book.

The authors acknowledge that the scope of this book has some limitations. Our desire was to write a practical book that all social workers could use on a daily basis. We anticipate that this book can be used as an informative reference source when social workers are faced with questions about ethics or standards of practice. We have not canvassed all of the extensive case law that exists in some of the areas we write about. Certain legal cases are included as illustrative examples, but this book by no means provides a complete review of the law.

A unique feature of this book is its examination of the *Social Work and Social Service Work Act, 1998* from two different perspectives. The book is co-authored by a social worker and a lawyer. The social work perspective makes it relevant to the College member and easily applicable to daily practice, while the legal viewpoint assures the College member that he or she is working within the law of the Act. If Ontario social workers are not both aware of and careful to work within the mandate of the Act they may find themselves in a tenuous legal position. For the first time, all social workers in Ontario are at risk of being held accountable by a regulatory College for their actions. Complaining to the College about alleged malpractice by a social worker is a much easier process than launching legal proceedings, and thus far more likely to occur. Furthermore, if a complaint to the College is found to be valid and disciplinary proceedings are undertaken, the social worker in question faces an increased likelihood of becoming the target of a successful civil suit.

Because provincial social work statutes are very similar to one another, and there does not exist another guidebook such as this, provincial legislation outside Ontario is also covered in this book, in order to benefit social workers across the country.

Although they are governed by legislation different from that which governs Ontario social workers, namely the *Regulated Health Professions Act, 1991*,[1] nurses, registered massage therapists, dentists, physiotherapists, pharmacists, and other health professionals in Ontario who must work within the same ethical and professional constraints that social workers face, will find important guidance in this book. Although the *Regulated Health Professions Act, 1991* has been in effect for more than a decade, there are no other suitable Canadian-based references for Ontario's health professionals who do not have legal training.

The reader may question why most of the legal cases included in this book relate to disciplines other than social work. This is because to date there have been few legal actions in Canada against social workers. There are two reasons for this. First of all, because most social work counselling and psychotherapy is conducted in private settings, and thus is not subject to outside scrutiny, it has always been very difficult to construct a firm evidentiary basis for suing a social worker. Secondly, the unregulated nature of the profession has created additional legal impediments. But now that social workers are subject to legislative control, using the court system to hold them to account is much easier.

In its *Standards of Practice Handbook* (reprinted as appendix II), the College sets out eight principles specifying the minimum standards of professional practice and conduct that members are required to meet. These principles are accompanied by interpretive text, and in this book we elaborate on the interpretations supplied by the *Handbook* and provide practical advice for meeting the College's standards. This book, used as a reference tool, will provide guidance for social workers confronted by legal issues that arise in daily practice as well as in less common circumstances. For some situations, however, we cannot offer definitive answers, but we do provide points to consider that can help one clarify one's professional position. It is far better to avoid legal pitfalls in the first place than to try to unravel legal problems created by an uninformed, ill-prepared approach. As Francis Turner remarked, "In a way it is a status achievement for social work that we too are open to litigation from clients who believe that they have been abused. Such risks have the effect of making us more precise, specific, careful, and humble, all desirable attributes in any professional person."[2] With the advent of the new legislation, these are not only desirable attributes but also necessary skills for every member of the College. Social work and social service work now take their place as true professions. Congratulations, social workers and social service workers! You have arrived!

---

1. S.O. 1991, c. 18.
2. Francis J. Turner, *Psychosocial Therapy* (New York, New York: The Free Press, 1978) at 67.

Chapter 1

Overview: The Legislation and Its Impact

A. Introduction

The professions of social work and social service work have come of age. On August 15, 2000, the *Social Work and Social Service Work Act, 1998* came into full force and effect.[1] This Act created a new professional College to regulate the activities of social workers and social service workers in Ontario. Ontario, usually a leader in passing new legislation, was the last province in Canada to enact legislation regulating social workers. For the first time in Ontario, these professionals will be regulated and held accountable by legislation rather than by personal choice, just as physicians, nurses, psychologists, and other professionals have been for many years.

The new legislation affects not only the individual social worker or social service worker and the profession as a whole but the public as well. The Act is designed to accomplish the following:

1. Provide a standard by which the public can judge the qualifications of individuals calling themselves social workers or social service workers, and verify the qualifications of those individuals through the Ontario College of Social Workers and Social Service Workers.
2. Provide a process through which the public can complain to the College about a member's alleged misconduct or incompetence.
3. Increase the credibility of social workers and social service workers, not only in the eyes of the general public, but also in the eyes of other professionals.

---

1.   [*SWSSW Act*], S.O. 1998, c. 31.

1

If an individual in Ontario wants to use the title social worker or social service worker, membership in the College is now mandatory. Once a member of the College, the individual is subject to all of the rules and regulations of the College. This represents a dramatic change in the professional lives of Ontario's social workers.

As Elaine Vayda and Mary Satterfield state, "The hallmarks of an autonomous profession include public accountability and the provision of protection through the establishment of minimum professional standards and mechanisms for review and discipline."[2] Why is this necessary for the profession of social work? And why has it taken so long to establish? The answers to these questions lie, in part, in the history of social work. When social work emerged as a profession in the 1920s, "Nearly all workers were employees of government or private social agencies. Clients sought services from the agency/employer rather than the worker. The agencies were accountable for any problems so they exercised great care in their hiring and supervising of social work employees."[3] In this environment, there was no need for legislation or further supervision of social workers.

Allison Taylor declares, "Social work sprang from the philanthropic ideal of giving practical assistance and support to the less fortunate."[4] Given the altruistic ambitions of social workers, why would anyone question their actions? Part of the problem was the fact that the role of a social worker was (and is) so difficult to define. As Taylor states:

> social work . . . lacks the common and defined purpose found in medicine — the model from which it borrows most — and thus, a solid professional identity.
>
> Modern social work appears to bend to whatever social, penal and economic ideologies are dominant. Its purpose is unclear, it has no independent goals or standards, and its responses are reactive and crisis-driven.[5]

Taylor also observes that "Social work does not enjoy a good reputation, even among those who have never had recourse to its services . . . . Most people have little real understanding of what social workers do, but there persists a strong suspicion that they do more harm than good, or are at best ineffectual at great public expense."[6]

---

2.   E. Vayda and M. Satterfield, *Law for Social Workers: A Canadian Guide* (Toronto: Carswell, 1989) at 313.

3.   R.L. Barker and D.M. Branson, *Forensic Social Work: Legal Aspects of Professional Practice* (New York: Haworth Press, 1993) at 77.

4.   A. Taylor, "Hostages to fortune: the abuse of children in care," in G. Hunt, ed., *Whistleblowing in the Social Services: Public Accountability & Professional Practice* (London: Arnold, 1998) at 45.

5.   *Ibid.*, at 45.

6.   *Ibid.*, at 46.

These portrayals of social workers certainly cover a broad scope — from philanthropic idealist to social danger at the public's expense. The Ontario Act's purpose is to address these concerns by setting minimum standards that social workers must meet, no matter in what setting or capacity their work is done.

B.   The Early History of Social Work

Social work as a profession developed in the twentieth century. Before then, of course, people engaged in philanthropic and voluntary work, but there was no professional title to apply to their activities. In 1914, the University of Toronto School of Social Work was founded. Since this school was, until the 1980s, Canada's largest school of social work and the only Canadian school offering doctoral studies in the field, it undeniably had a powerful influence on the development of social work in this country. The school developed with two differing focuses. The first was that of social work practice, and "was made up largely of female part-time sessional appointments with a frame of reference to the field and a growing American influence. The other identified with social science and comprised largely male full-time university appointments with a frame of reference to the university and a British pedagogical heritage."[7] The full-time professors had much more influence and thus the field of social work was, to a large extent, male, British, and scientifically based. For this reason, social casework played a secondary role in social work, despite the fact that World War I, the Great Depression, and World War II all created tremendous social turbulence during the three decades after the founding of the University of Toronto School of Social Work.

The social work perspective, which rests on a holistic view of the individual, was, however, developing. In 1926, Ethel Taylor spoke of "understanding individuals as whole personalities and the adjustments of these individuals to socially healthy lives."[8] In 1927, the Canadian Association of Social Workers (CASW) was established and in 1964 the Ontario Association of Professional Social Workers was incorporated. As the *CASW National Scope of Practice Statement* notes, "Social work pioneers were among the first to address the significance of deeply connected relationships that constitute the social context of people's lives. Out of this rich heritage, social work is recognized for its familiar 'person-in-environment' perspec-

---

7.   J. Graham and A. Al-Krenawi, "Contested Terrain" (2000) 17 *Canadian Social Work Review* at 245.

8.   Francis J. Turner, *Psychosocial Therapy* (New York, New York: The Free Press, 1978) at 7.

tive, which characterizes the unique relationship-centered focus of the profession."[9] This perspective gave rise to the concept that "the central mission is to have social workers engaged in activities that will improve social well-being structures and enhance individual, family and community social functioning at local, national and international levels."[10] It was with this onerous task in mind that the Ontario Association of Professional Social Workers, which later became the Ontario Association of Social Workers, began its task of advocating for legislation to regulate the social work profession.

C.   The Need for Legislation

In 1976, Ontarians were shocked to learn of the death by abuse of Kim Anne Popen, an infant. The judicial inquiry into the incidents leading up to her death resulted in the publication in 1982 of an official report.[11] One tragic piece of information that emerged was the apparent negligence of the attending social worker, who failed to adequately supervise the child or check the provincial child abuse registry, which contained the name of the abuser later responsible for Kim Anne's death. An important part of the report was a recommendation that legislation should be enacted making social workers legally accountable for their professional actions. According to the report, there was a need to put in place a system of checks and balances to ensure that social workers used their extensive powers responsibly.

In 1982, in part driven by this impetus and in anticipation of legislation to regulate the profession, the Ontario College of Certified Social Workers was created. It was a non-statutory entity separate from the Ontario Association of Professional Social Workers. Membership in the College was voluntary, and although the College served as the professional regulatory body for Ontario social workers, its non-statutory status robbed it of any true power. By 1985, the Ontario Association of Professional Social Workers had established an initiative known as Project Legislation to work towards making social work a regulated profession. That same year, the *Child and Family Services Act*[12] was enacted to limit the power of social workers. The need to regulate the profession to protect the public from inadequate social work practices was becoming more and more evident.

The Code of Ethics adopted by the College at the time of its creation set forth standards for the knowledge, skills, and attitudes expected of profes-

---

9.   *CASW National Scope of Practice Statement* (2000) at 1.
10.   *Ibid.*, at 2.
11.   *Judicial Inquiry into the Care of Kim Anne Popen by the Children's Aid Society of the City of Sarnia and the County of Lambton* (Toronto: Queen's Printer, 1982).
12.   R.S.O. 1990, c. C.11, as am.

sional social workers. The Code gave the profession added prestige and defined the boundaries of social workers' responsibility to clients, their profession, and society as a whole. The College involved itself in areas such as continuing education, competency, practice skills, and professional ethics. There was, however, a problem inherent in the structure of the College — its voluntary membership. For this reason, the College could, of course, have an impact on the behaviour of only those social workers who chose to join it. The College could investigate allegations of misconduct against members and, if the allegations were deemed valid, recommend disciplinary action. A social worker who decided to disregard the standards set by the College could simply choose not to join it or, if already a member, could leave the College and thus avoid any disciplinary consequences. In addition, membership status had no impact on an individual's ability to use the title of social worker. In fact, anyone, regardless of education or ability, could legally call himself or herself a social worker. This fact seriously jeopardized the credibility of the profession and of those who, although they may not have been members of the College, did meet the criteria for membership.

In 1994, six-month-old Sara Podniewicz died at the hands of her parents, Michael Podniewicz and Lisa Olsen. This family was involved with the Catholic Children's Aid Society of Toronto at the time. Michael had already spent time in jail for the brutal beating of another of their children, a boy, which had resulted in severe and permanent brain damage. It was determined that the children's aid society had made many errors in handling Sara's case and that these had led to the baby's death. Although neither the children's aid social workers nor their supervisors were charged in the cases of Sara and her brother, these cases led the public to more closely question the role and responsibilities of social workers.

In 1997 another tragic case in Toronto, that of Jordan Desmond Heikamp, who died when he was five weeks old, came to light. The cause of Jordan's death was determined to be inappropriate care and feeding. In an unusual development, the Catholic Children's Aid Society social worker assigned to the case was charged with criminal negligence causing death. Although all charges against this worker were eventually dropped, this case again brought home the importance of setting standards for social worker accountability, not only to protect the public but also as a benchmark for assessing adequacy of care. Social workers asked themselves how they could attain an acceptable level of professionalism and promote social work as an honourable profession if no minimum standards of care were in place. Ultimately these concerns led to the passage of the *Social Work and Social Service Work Act, 1998*. As noted earlier, social work encompasses a broad spectrum of activities. The new Act, unlike those statutes that omit particular areas of social work practice, covers all fields of practice and so the professional body gains strength as a profession and as an agent of change, both by its number of members and by the diversity of the knowledge base.

D.   The Implications of the Legislation

The new legislation has many implications for the public, the individual social worker, and the profession of social work. It allows for public confidence in the established academic qualifications of social workers and the professional standards required of social workers. It also gives the public a proper channel through which to lodge complaints against members of the College who allegedly have not complied with College standards. Because people wanting to call themselves social workers or social service workers now have to be members of the College, anyone using these titles is now subject to legal challenge for alleged professional misconduct or incompetence. For this reason, the credibility of social workers in the eyes of the public and other professionals will, in time, be enhanced. As an authority on social work ethics remarks, "One of the defining characteristics of a profession is its members' willingness to provide a mechanism through which the general public can hold the profession accountable."[13] This increased status will result in two additional benefits: members of the College will be consulted when future legislative and public policy changes in the area of social work are being considered, and it also increases the likelihood of third-party coverage of the fees charged by members of the College for professional services.

Third-party payment is the term used when an entity such as an insurance company or employee benefit plan pays for counselling or other social work services on behalf of a client. In the past, insurance companies and the like were more willing to pay for counselling and other services provided by psychologists than for services provided by social workers, even though social workers tend to be less expensive. When government cutbacks led to the closing or amalgamation of several social service agencies in Ontario in the 1990s, leaving many members of the public without access to publicly funded services, and many social workers without publicly supported employment, more and more people turned to private-sector counsellors for help, and many social workers decided to enter private practice. The public wanted their insurers to pay for these services, and both the public and the insurers wanted guarantees that the private-sector counsellors were competent. The legislation regulating social workers and social service workers does address the issue of competence and as such will enable insurers to make third party payments confidently. As Dan Andreae, president of the Ontario Association of Social Workers at the time the legislation was enacted, stated, "all social workers stand to benefit in many ways from the

---

13.   F.G. Reamer, *Ethical Standards in Social Work: A Critical Review of the NASW Code of Ethics* (Washington, DC: NASW Press, 1998) at 13.

enactment of this legislation, whether practicing in social and health services, educational settings or in private practice."[14]

Another important feature of the Act is that it is to be reviewed in 2005, five years after its passage. If inconsistencies, inaccuracies, or weaknesses in the Act are noted, it is the duty of members of the College to convey this information to the College for possible changes when the Act is reviewed.

E.   Two New Social Work Functions

The 1998 statute has opened the door to two new functions for members of the College. First, social workers are now authorized to act as evaluators under the *Health Care Consent Act, 1996*.[15] An evaluator is a person authorized to determine whether an individual is capable of making his or her own decisions regarding his or her personal daily care or admission to a care facility. In addition, social workers are now authorized to perform capacity assessments under the *Substitute Decisions Act, 1992*.[16] A capacity assessment is an assessment of a person's ability to manage his or her own property or provide his or her own personal daily care.

F.   Licensing versus Registration

One important fact to note is that Ontario social workers are "registered"'under the Act but not licensed. Although the titles "social worker," "social service worker," "registered social worker," and "registered social service worker" now have legal implications and can be used only by members of the College, individuals who do not meet the criteria for membership can substitute a title such as counsellor or psychotherapist and legally carry on their practice. The title is legislated but the work is not. Licensing, " . . . the least understood credential because of confusing terminology and the mixed purposes and function for which it was envisioned,"[17] would have protected the work that is done by social workers as well as the title. No one, for example, is allowed to perform the duties of a medical physician or a licensed psychologist without the prescribed qualifications. As Donald Brieland and John Lemmon remark, "The registration/certification approach

---

14.   D. Andreae, "Social Work Legislation — A Reality" (1999) 26 *OASW Newsmagazine* 1 at 1-2.
15.   S.O. 1996, c. 2, Sched. A.
16.   S.O. 1992, c. 30.
17.   W. Pryzwansky and R. Wendt, *Professional and Ethical Issues in Psychology* (New York, NY: W.W. Norton & Company, 1999) at 103.

was recognized as inadequate for the development of necessary standards, and professional concern shifted toward advocacy of licensure. Licensing provides greater protection than certification because it defines who can practice and because a license can be revoked for cause."[18] Where members of the Ontario College are concerned, however, registration does define who can practise under the title and registration can be revoked, so these concerns may not be valid.

It is also worth noting that the terms used for the three forms of legal regulation — registration, certification, and licensing — have different meanings in different jurisdictions. In places where registration, the "weakest form of legal regulation," prevails, "the state merely lists people who falsely claim to be in the registry. However, the state has no authority to punish those who call themselves social workers, as long as they do not claim to be registered."[19] Other jurisdictions rely on licensing, "which is the strongest form of legal regulation because it explicates education, knowledge, and skill requirements, and uses the state's regulatory powers to ensure that the worker's behavior complies with the required standards."[20] The reader will note that the term registration as it is currently defined for Ontario social workers and social service workers means that those who want to call themselves social workers or social service workers must be registered members of the College, but those who want to perform the functions of social work or social service work are free to do so as long as they do not misrepresent themselves as social workers or social service workers.

G.   Accountability and Responsibilities

Social work has been given a long-awaited opportunity to legitimize itself as a true profession. Social workers now have an obligation to be seen carrying out their responsibilities in a professional, ethical, and legal manner while recognizing their accountability to their College and respecting its goals. They must extend themselves to increase their professionalism and broaden their scope of practice while acting as advocates for the profession and broadening the vast body of social work knowledge through research and professional writing.

When social workers were beginning to enter private practice, concerns were voiced that the move to private practice was an abandonment of the profession's original mission of protecting the underprivileged and disenfran-

---

18.   D. Brieland and J. Lemmon, *Social Work and the Law* (St. Paul: West Publishing Company, 1977) at 578.
19.   Barker and Branson, above note 3, at 73.
20.   *Ibid.*

chised. Some have even suggested that individuals who have opted for private practice have done so to escape "the regulations and policies of social agencies."[21] Private practice, however, can (and must) be carried out in a manner that recognizes social work's moral obligations and maintains the profession's ethical standards. Now is the time for social workers to reject labels that others have applied to the profession — "bleeding hearts," "do-gooders," "busybodies," and so forth — and represent themselves as competent practitioners capable of pursuing a wide range of mental health, political, and research activities.

The guidance offered within will allow registered social workers and social service workers to understand the implications of the new legislation to their work and how to conduct themselves within the legislation's limits. Although nothing can insulate members of the College from legal challenges, "the practitioner's best hopes are in always adhering to professional standards of conduct. This means that the worker must first know what those standards are. Ignorance of the standards is in itself practicing at a substandard level. Next, the worker must choose to meet those standards."[22] The new legislation enhances the credibility of the profession. It is up to the social worker to acquire the skills and expertise necessary for maintaining this credibility.

Many members of the College do not recognize the importance of the new legislation and its impact on their lives and work. It is imperative that they understand the legal implications of the Act and take the necessary measures to protect themselves. Disciplinary hearings, appeals, and civil actions all require the hiring of legal representatives, and even if a member of the College is not deprived of his or her ability to work as a social worker, the financial cost of defending himself or herself can be very high. There are also further financial costs as well as non-monetary professional costs. A member whose professional certificate is revoked by the College cannot apply for reinstatement for at least one year. The College also has the option of extending the revocation period to up to two years. Other powers given to the College by the Act include placing restrictions on the areas in which a social worker is entitled to practise (for instance, preventing a member found guilty of inappropriate behaviour with a child from working with children in any setting); publicly admonishing, reprimanding, or counselling a member, and noting the action in the member's permanent record; levying a fine of up to $5,000; publishing the member's name and a description of the inappropriate behaviour in the official College publication and any other publication

---

21. B. Carniol, *Case Critical: Challenging Social Work in Canada* (Toronto, ON: Between the Lines, 1990) at 83.

22. *Ibid.*, at 30.

deemed appropriate; and requiring the member to pay the entire cost of a hearing, appeal, or reinstatement proceeding, including the College's costs.

Although members of the College need to be aware of their new legal vulnerability under the Act, "legal vulnerability should be placed in an appropriate perspective. Despite the very great increase in suits against social workers, the plain truth is that the vast majority of social workers will not be sued and that, for most of those who are, the legal system — and insurance — can provide reasonable protection."[23] The increased legal accountability should not deter social workers from fully participating in their profession.

---

23.   D. Bersharov, *The Vulnerable Social Worker: Liability for Serving Children & Families* (Washington, DC: National Association of Social Workers, 1985) at 168.

Chapter 2

The Role of the Ontario College
of Social Workers and
Social Service Workers

A.   Introduction

The Ontario College of Social Workers and Social Service Workers was created by the *Social Work and Social Service Work Act, 1998*.[1] The College is an incorporated entity and is the sole regulatory body of the social work profession in Ontario. As a corporation, the College has all the powers of a natural person. It can hire and fire employees, start and defend actions, and borrow money. It is exempt from the *Business Corporations Act* and thus does not have to hold annual general meetings, nor does it issue shares.

As in any other regulated profession, the primary purpose of the College is to serve and protect the public interest.[2] When the Honourable Janet Ecker, Minister of Community and Social Services, introduced the legislation in November 1998, she spoke of two key objectives for the legislation. One was to provide recognition for the social work profession and the other was to ensure that the public would receive high-quality ethical services from social workers. One of the tenets of a regulated profession is public accountability, which comes from self-governance. For that reason, the Act dictates that the Council, which governs the College and its committees, must do so with the public interest in mind. This provides not only the accountability required of a regulated profession but also the openness to scrutiny by the public of the College's activities, which the public expects in return for allowing the profession to govern itself.

The Act outlines 10 objects or goals of the College:

   1.   To regulate the practice of social work and the practice of social service work and to govern its members.

---

1.   *Social Work and Social Service Work Act, 1998* [*SWSSW Act*], S.O. 1998, c. 31.
2.   *Ibid.*, s. 3(1).

2. To develop, establish and maintain qualifications for membership in the College.
3. To approve professional education programs offered by educational institutions for the purpose of applications for membership in the College.
4. To approve ongoing education programs for the purpose of continuing education for members of the College.
5. To provide for the ongoing education of members of the College.
6. To issue certificates of registration to members of the College and to renew, amend, suspend, cancel, revoke and reinstate those certificates.
7. To establish and enforce professional standards and ethical standards applicable to members of the College.
8. To receive and investigate complaints against members of the College and to deal with issues of discipline, professional misconduct and incompetency and incapacity.
9. To promote high standards and quality assurance with respect to social work and social service work and to communicate with the public on behalf of the members.
10. To perform the additional functions prescribed by the regulations.[3]

The College has a statutory duty to carry out these objects and the courts will nullify any action taken by the College that is inconsistent with these objects. The legislation mandates that the College must approach any matters it deals with both in the context of carrying out these objects and with the general duty of protecting the public. An examination of these objects shows that nearly half of them deal with ensuring the competence of the members both on joining and on a continuing basis. This quality assurance, as it is commonly called, demonstrates that the College is as interested in maintaining the competence and educational qualifications of its members as it is in disciplining them.

The function of the College is therefore far different from that of the Ontario Association of Social Workers. Whereas membership in the College is mandatory if a social worker wants to use the title social worker, membership in the Association is voluntary. The Association is interested in providing services to its members and it acts as an advocate on behalf of its members. The College, on the other hand, is required to look at everything it does with the public interest as its paramount priority.

B.   The Structure of the College

The College carries out its objects through a council that functions much the same as a board of directors. The council comprises 21 members: 7

---

3.   *Ibid.*, s. 3(2).

elected social workers, 7 elected social service workers, and 7 appointed public members. The 14 elected members must be members of the College and are elected by their fellow members. The Lieutenant Governor in Council appoints the remaining members, who cannot be social workers or social service workers. The council manages the affairs of the College. It reports to the Minister of Community and Social Services, whose Ministry controls the College and by extension the profession.

A social worker becomes a member of the College as soon as he or she registers with the College. Subject to the by-laws, every member of the College in good standing is entitled to vote at an election of members of the council.[4] To be in good standing and entitled to vote, a member must have paid his or her membership fee and not have had his or her certificate of registration suspended.[5]

According to section 13(1) of the Act, every person who holds a certificate of registration is a member of the College subject to any terms, conditions, or limitations to which the certificate is subject. The College maintains jurisdiction over all its members regardless of whether they commit their alleged professional misconduct in Ontario or not. If a member wants to resign his or her membership, he or she must submit the resignation in writing to the registrar of the College, who then cancels the registration. A person, who resigns, however, is still subject to the jurisdiction of the College for any professional misconduct, incompetence, or incapacity that occurred during the time the person was a member of the College.[6] Hastily resigning from the College in anticipation of a complaint does not protect a social worker against action by the College if the behaviour giving rise to the complaint occurred while the social worker was a member of the College.

The Act provides that the terms of members of the council cannot exceed three years, although a person may be a member of the council for more than one term. Regardless of how many terms they serve, members of the council may not serve for more than 10 consecutive years.

All meetings of the College are open to the public as well as to all members. The College must notify the public and the members of its meetings; this is usually accomplished by publishing an announcement in a local newspaper. In certain circumstances, however, the Act allows the council to exclude the public and members of the College from a meeting. The council can close its meetings if the members of the council are satisfied, for example, that a person involved in a civil or criminal proceeding may be prejudiced, the safety of a person may be jeopardized, litigation affecting the

---

4.   *Ibid.*, s. 6(1).
5.   *Ibid.*, s. 6(2).
6.   *Ibid.*, s. 13(3).

College will be discussed, or instructions will be given to or opinions received from solicitors for the College.[7]

The council appoints a registrar, who is an employee of the College and acts as its chief executive officer. The registrar has many duties, including but not limited to the registration of applicants, maintaining the register of members, suspending and reinstating members, receiving complaints, and appointing investigators for disciplinary matters and matters involving the possible incapacity of a member.

In addition to managing the affairs of the College, the council also has the authority to establish committees to carry out the specific objects of the College. It is the function of these committees that is of particular importance to the member as these are the committees that have the most impact on the member's professional activities. These committees, which are mandated by section 14 of the Act, are the bodies that actually govern the members, and for this reason they will be discussed in greater detail in the following chapters. The committees mandated by the Act include an Executive Committee, a Registration Appeals Committee, a Complaints Committee, a Discipline Committee, and a Fitness to Practise Committee. These committees must have a minimum of three members, at least one-third of whom must be elected members of the council. The remaining two-thirds of the committee can but do not necessarily have to be members of the College who are appointed by the committee chair to conduct reviews and investigate complaints. Elected members can sit on more than one committee, but any member who sits on the Complaints Committee cannot also be a member of the Discipline or Fitness to Practise committee.

Fairness to a member who is the subject of a complaint dictates that it is inappropriate for another member to both investigate the complaint and be responsible for determining the member's guilt or innocence. As will be discussed in more detail later in this book, it is the Complaints Committee which, following an investigation into a disciplinary matter, decides whether to refer the matter to the Discipline Committee. Presumably the members of the Complaints Committee will never refer a matter to the Discipline Committee without believing that the related complaint has merit, and in such circumstances a member sitting on both committees may already have reached a conclusion about the matter before it reaches the Discipline Committee.

The administration of the College is overseen by the Executive Committee. It is the Executive Committee that directs the Discipline and Fitness to Practise committees to hold a hearing into the conduct of a member on receiving a recommendation for a hearing from the Complaints Committee. The Executive Committee can also make an interim order suspending or

---

7.   *Ibid.*, s. 8(2).

restricting a certificate of registration pending the decisions of either of those committees. It has the power, as well, to reinstate, without a hearing, a certificate of registration that has been suspended or revoked for any reason. In addition, the Executive Committee approves requests from the registrar for appointment of an investigator to look into allegations of a member's professional misconduct, incompetence, or incapacity.

C.   Regulations and By-laws

To facilitate the day-to-day running of the College and help it carry out its objects, the Act provides that the council may make regulations and by-laws. Richard Steinecke in his guide to the *Regulated Health Professions Act* describes the difference between regulations and by-laws in the following manner:

> Matters are put in the regulations and by-laws for two reasons; one because the provisions are too detailed for inclusion in the statute itself and two because frequent amendments are likely to occur. Regulations and by-laws can be changed without going to the legislature. The major difference between a by-law and a regulation is that a by-law is made directly by the College while the Cabinet must approve a regulation. For that reason, by-laws generally deal with the administrative and internal matters of the College, while regulations deal with matters of broader public concern.[8]

In addition to the statutory committees required by the Act, the College has also established three non-statutory committees, namely the Elections Committee, the Standards of Practice Committee, and the Nominating Committee. The Elections and Nominating committees were established to oversee the annual elections of College members to the council. The Standards of Practice Committee produced the *Standards of Practice Handbook*, which now forms part of the criteria for judging the conduct of a social worker's actions and behaviour.

The Act lists at least 18 areas in which the College can make regulations. The full list can be found in section 36(1). The regulations cover a wide range of activities, all of which have an impact on a social worker's professional life. The following are some of the areas covered by the regulations:

1.   Prescribing classes of certification, imposing terms and conditions on certificates, establishing rules for the issuance, suspension, or revocation of certificates.

---

8.   R. Steinecke, *A Complete Guide to the Regulated Health Professions Act* (Aurora, ON: Canada Law Book, 1995), at 2-26.

2. Prescribing standards, qualifications, and educational requirements for the issuance of certificates, and prescribing ongoing educational requirements.
3. Requiring and providing for the inspection and examination of a member's premises and books and records. Requiring members to keep records and prescribing the contents of those records.
4. Prescribing what constitutes a conflict of interest in the practice of social work.
5. Defining professional misconduct.
6. Advertising and promoting the profession of social work.
7. The reporting and publication of committee decisions.
8. Regulating or prohibiting the use of terms, titles, and designations by members of the College in respect of their practices.
9. Giving notice of meetings and hearings that are to be open to the public.

Under paragraph 2 of section 36(1), a regulation may authorize the registrar to assess the qualifications or competency of potential members by examination or other means. It is anticipated that future membership applicants will have to write an entrance examination to gain admission to the College.

As noted above, the by-laws deal predominantly with the actual mechanics of running the College. The College has the power to make by-laws that, among other things, prescribe a code of ethics and standards of practice, require members to pay annual registration fees, establish fees for mandatory continuing education courses, establish penalties for late payment of fees, and require members to have professional liability insurance.

The College has made two regulations since its establishment: Ontario Regulation 384/00, dealing with professional misconduct, and Ontario Regulation 383/00, dealing with registration. The registration regulation will be examined in chapter 3. The professional misconduct regulation will be discussed primarily in chapter 8.

D. Title Protection

The Act protects the titles "social worker," "social service worker," "registered social worker," and "registered social service worker." Only individuals who are members of the College are permitted to use any of these titles. Notwithstanding an individual's qualifications or education, he or she cannot use these titles if he or she is not a member of the College. Anyone using a protected title without being a member is guilty of an offence and on conviction is liable to a fine of not more than $5,000 for a first offence and not more than $10,000 for a subsequent offence.[9] If a member knowingly makes a false representation for the purpose of having a certificate of registration issued or knowingly assists another person in making a false misrepresentation, he or she is guilty of an offence and on conviction is liable to a fine of not more than $10,000. The College can enforce these restrictions either by commencing a private prosecution if the conduct is considered a violation of a provincial offence or by applying to a judge of the Ontario Superior Court of Justice for an order directing the person to comply with the provision. Failure to comply with a court order can result in the person being held in contempt of court. A contempt of court order could result in imprisonment or the imposition of a heavy fine.

The College enjoys immunity with respect to its actions. No one can initiate an action against the College, the council, a committee of the College, a member of the council, a member of a committee of the College, or any officer, employee, or agent of the College for any act done in good faith in the performance of a duty or power under the Act, a regulation, or by-law.[10] Good faith is simply something done with an honest intention and an absence of malice.

E.   Confidentiality

The College has a duty of confidentiality under section 50 of the Act. Confidentiality is particularly important when the College is dealing with sensitive mental health information or allegations of a member's misconduct. Indiscriminate disclosure of confidential information can have a detrimental effect on a member's reputation and also dissuade witnesses or other individuals from coming forward with information.

Requests for information from the College can arise under various circumstances. For example, a client who is suing a social worker may seek to obtain any information the College has on that member. A law enforcement agency or a public inquiry such as the Jordan Heikamp inquest may also seek information about a particular member. The College may be required to disclose information if it is subpoenaed or if an investigation determines that a child is in need of protection (which creates the necessity for a report to the children's aid society).

In addition to keeping information confidential, the Act also protects the College and anyone doing College work from being summoned to give oral

---

9.   *SWSSW Act*, above note 1, s. 55(1).
10.   *Ibid.*, s. 49.

evidence or to produce documents. The College and anyone else engaged in the administration of the Act is required to keep confidential any information he or she obtains in the course of carrying out his or her duties. This includes investigators appointed by the College to investigate complaints brought against a member as well as independent expert witnesses, lawyers, and consultants acting on behalf of the College. Section 50(1) states that this information may not be communicated to any other person except

    a)   as may be required in connection with the administration of this Act and the regulations or by-laws or any proceeding under this Act or the regulation or by-laws;

    b)   to his or her counsel;

    c)   with the consent of the person to whom the information relates;

    d)   to a police officer to aid an investigation undertaken with a view to a law enforcement proceeding or from which a law enforcement proceeding is likely to result; or

    e)   to the extent that the information is available to the public under this Act.

No one engaged in the administration of the Act, including an investigator, is allowed under section 50(1)(d) to disclose information about a nonmember. Moreover, section 50(1)(d) does not require a person engaged in the administration of the Act to disclose information to a police officer unless the information is required to be produced under a warrant. Does this mean that the College can pass information to the police if, during a College investigation, it discovers evidence of criminal activity by a member? Section 50(1)(d) would seem to suggest that the College can share information with the police, thereby creating, in effect, a joint investigation where information and resources are shared. The difficulty with this sharing of information is that a College investigation into a member's misconduct can be transformed into a criminal investigation without any of the safeguards an individual enjoys in a criminal investigation. For example, a member of the College is required under the Act to cooperate with a College investigation, whereas a suspect in a criminal investigation has the right to remain silent.

It is not possible to compel any person engaged in the administration of the Act to give testimony regarding information obtained in the course of his or her duties or in any civil proceeding, other than a proceeding under the Act or an appeal or a judicial review relating to a proceeding under the Act. Neither the records of a discipline or fitness to practise hearing nor any documents prepared for a discipline or fitness to practise hearing are producible in a civil proceeding.

An Ontario case illustrates this point. *Forget* v. *Sutherland* involved a physician who was sued by a patient for sexual abuse.[11] The patient had also complained to the College of Physicians and Surgeons. The civil suit was set-

---

11.   (1999), 174 D.L.R. (4th) 174 (Ont. Div. Ct.), aff'd 188 D.L.R. (4th) 296 (Ont. C.A.).

tled with an agreement from Dr. Sutherland that he would pay damages to the patient. The patient then provided a second sworn statement to the College changing her version of what had happened, which led the College to stop the discipline proceedings against Dr. Sutherland. The physician in turn refused to pay the settlement, arguing that the original statement (complaint) the patient had originally provided to the College had been fraudulent. The issue before the Divisional Court was whether the physician could rely on the second statement to support his refusal to pay the settlement. The court held that the sworn statement had been "prepared for" the complaint and discipline hearing before the College and was therefore inadmissible in a civil court even though there had been no discipline hearing.

The majority of the Court of Appeal upheld the decision of the Divisional Court and in doing so commented as follows:

> The purpose of s. 36(3) [similar to s. 50 of the Social Work Act] is to encourage the reporting of complaints of professional misconduct against members of a health profession, and to ensure that these complaints are fully investigated and fairly decided without any participant in the proceedings — a health professional, a patient, a complainant, a witness or a College employee — fearing that a document prepared for the College proceedings can be used in a civil action.[12]

Documents covered by section 50 of the Act are therefore inadmissible as evidence. They cannot even be produced voluntarily.

Any person who contravenes the confidentiality provisions of the Act is guilty of an offence and on conviction is liable to a fine of not more than $25,000.

F.   Conclusion

Self-governance gives a profession status in the eyes of the public and sends a message to the public that members of the profession have special knowledge and skills. As we have seen, the primary purpose of regulation is to protect the public interest. Protection is necessary because some of the services provided by social workers, such as counselling or psychotherapy, can harm the public. Regulation advances the public interest in a number of important ways. It protects the public from unqualified and incompetent social workers. A statement by an Ontario court judge in *Levkoe and the Queen* illustrates this point. Although the case involved a pharmacist who was licensed under the *Regulated Health Professions Act*, the judge's comments are relevant to the present discussion:

---

12.   *Ibid.*, 188 D.L.R. (4th) 296 at 307.

> To grant a licence to a member of a given profession is to confer on him or her a monopoly to practice that profession that is to make unlawful, or to prohibit, under pain of punishment, the practice of that profession by anyone who is not licensed. The purpose of licensing is, or course, to protect the public from unqualified persons in an activity, which the Legislature had deemed detrimental or even, in some cases, dangerous if undertaken by the unqualified.[13]

Registration gives the public some assurance, when choosing a social worker, that the chosen social worker has a certain level of education, knowledge, and skill. It encourages social workers to maintain and increase their level of skill through continuing educational programs and through the complaints, discipline, and fitness to practise processes.

Shannon McCorquodale identifies the following as some of the characteristics of a regulated profession:

1. A governing body with representatives of the public as well as the profession.
2. Registration that identifies the standards and procedures for evaluating applicants.
3. A complaint review process wherein structure and procedures are identified by which complaints may be received and investigated and a review conducted.
4. Discipline wherein a hearing of the complaint can be conducted. This stage of the complaint review process requires a more formal structure, legal representation of the parties, examination and cross-examination, witnesses and expert witnesses.
5. Appeal process wherein decisions of the regulatory body may be appealed. The form of the appeal process is dependent upon the legislation of the provincial setting of the regulatory body. There may be appeal procedures for each of the regulatory decisions.
6. "Continuing competency" is the element requiring professionals to maintain their professional knowledge and skills, and to meet specified standards for maintaining the relevance of their professional knowledge.
7. "Standards" is the responsibility to develop and publish standards, and the provision of consultation with regard to the interpretation of those standards.[14]

The standards referred to in the final item in this list provide the critical roadmap for social workers. These standards of practice, usually based on a code of ethics, help social workers know what their regulatory body considers to be sound and ethical practice. Social workers who practise in accordance with the standards and the code of ethics will be less likely to have any discipline-related dealings with the College.

---

13.   (1977), 37 C.C.C. (2d) 356 at 361 (Ont. Div. Ct.).
14.   S. McCorquodale, "The Role of Regulators in Practice," in F.J. Turner, ed., *Social Work Practice: A Canadian Perspective* (Scarborough, ON: Prentice-Hall Canada, 1999) 462 at 467.

Chapter 3

Registration with the College

A.   The Act

Registration with the College is usually a routine exercise if the applicant meets the criteria for registration outlined in the *Social Work and Social Service Work Act, 1998*.[1] Section 18(1) of the Act states that the registrar shall issue a certificate of registration for social work if the applicant

a) applies for it in accordance with the regulations and the by-laws;

b) produces documentation satisfactory to the Registrar that shows that the applicant,

    i)   has obtained a degree in social work from a social work program accredited by the Canadian Association of Schools of Social Work, a degree from a social work program or an equivalent program approved by a body prescribed by the regulations or a degree from a social work program or an equivalent program prescribed by the regulations, or

    ii) has a combination of academic qualifications and practical experience that is substantially equivalent to the qualifications required for such a degree, as prescribed by the regulations;

c) has paid the fees prescribed by the by-laws; and

d) meets any other requirements prescribed by the regulations for registration.[2]

It is important to note that section 18(1) does not apply to social service workers, whose registration requirements are set out in section 18(2).

Registration as a social worker or social service worker is normally a straightforward administrative procedure. The applicant simply fills out the appropriate form and pays the prescribed fees, following which the College

---

1.   *Social Work and Social Service Work Act, 1998* [*SWSSW Act*], S.O. 1998, c. 31.
2.   *Ibid.*, s.18(1).

processes the application and issues the certificate of registration. Under section 18(3) of the Act, however, the registrar can refuse to issue a certificate if he or she has reasonable grounds to believe that

a)   the past conduct or actions of the applicant afford grounds for the belief that the applicant will not perform his or her duties as a social worker or social service worker, as the case may be, in accordance with the law, including but not limited to this Act, the regulations and the by-laws; or

b)   the applicant does not fulfill the requirements under this Act for the issuance of the certificate.[3]

It is usually easy to ascertain whether the applicant has the academic qualifications or the equivalent experience to meet the criteria for registration. The onus is on the applicant to prove that he or she meets the criteria. Under normal circumstances the registrar accepts the application at face value.

The registrar may refuse to issue a certificate of registration under section 18(3) (a). In order to do so the registrar must have "reasonable grounds" to believe that the applicant will not perform his or her duties in accordance with the Act because of past conduct or actions.[4]

Before issuing a certificate, the registrar must be satisfied that the applicant is mentally competent to practise social work or social service work; will perform his or her duties with decency, integrity, and honesty, and in accordance with the law, including but not limited to the Act, the regulations, and the by-laws; and has the requisite knowledge, skill, and judgment needed to practise social work or social service work.[5]

In addition, the registrar is required by the Act to refuse to issue a certificate of registration if the applicant previously had a certificate of registration that was revoked because of a decision of the Discipline Committee or the Fitness to Practise Committee and never reinstated. This prevents a person from attempting to circumvent a committee decision by simply reapplying for a certificate.

Lastly, the registrar can, if he or she believes it necessary, issue the certificate with terms, conditions, or limitations attached.[6] If the registrar intends to refuse to issue a certificate or impose terms, conditions, or limitations on it, he or she must serve notice on the applicant. Whatever the registrar intends to do must be stated in the notice. The registrar is not required to give notice if he or she is simply refusing to issue a previously revoked certificate.

Section 19 of the Act allows an applicant seeking a certificate of registration to obtain a copy of any documents relevant to the application that are

3.   *Ibid.*, s. 18(3).
4.   *Ibid.*, s.18(3)(a).
5.   *Ibid.*, s. 18(3)(b).
6.   *Ibid.*, s.18(5).

held by the College. This section is interesting because it implies that the College has the power to seek out additional information on an applicant before deciding whether to issue a certificate. Section 19(2) provides that the registrar can refuse to give out any information or documentation that may in the registrar's opinion jeopardize the safety of any person. This provision allows a person to speak candidly about an applicant without fear that the applicant will learn about that person's dealings with the College.

It is important to keep in mind, however, that if the registrar refuses to issue a certificate of registration and the applicant appeals the decision, in the interests of fairness to the applicant the information in question will likely be ordered disclosed. There is a real balancing act between the right of an applicant to know the reason why his or her application was refused and the well-being of a third party involved in the application process. An applicant has the right to ask the Registration Appeals Committee to review his or her application if the registrar refuses to issue a certificate or issues it with terms, conditions, or limitations attached. The applicant has 60 days from the date he or she receives the notice referred to above to request a review. The request must be in writing and served on the registrar.

The members of the Registration Appeals Committee can refuse to review the registrar's decision if they believe that the applicant's request is frivolous, vexatious, or an abuse of process.[7] If the committee agrees to review the decision, it must ensure that the applicant has an opportunity to look at all of the documents the committee intends to use for the review. The applicant also has the right to make written submissions. The committee does not have to hold a hearing.

After considering the request, the submissions, and any other documents that the committee considers relevant, the committee may make an order doing one or more of the following:

1. Directing the Registrar to issue the appropriate certificate of registration.
2. Directing the Registrar to issue the appropriate certificate of registration and to make it subject to specified terms, conditions or limitations.
3. Directing the Registrar to vary specified terms, conditions or limitations in the Registrar's proposal.
4. Directing the Registrar to refuse to issue a certificate of registration.[8]

The committee is required to give its decision in writing to the registrar within 60 days from the time it considers the applicant's request. The decision must then be served on the applicant.[9]

The failure of the committee to give reasons for its decision can be grounds for a court to overturn the decision. The case of *White* v. *Nova Sco-*

---

7.   *Ibid.*, s. 21 (2).
8.   *Ibid.*, s. 21(6).
9.   *Ibid.*, s. 21 (7).

tia Assn. of Social Workers demonstrates this point.[10] The Social Worker's Act which governed the Nova Scotia Association of Social Workers made licensing compulsory for those practising social work in Nova Scotia. The applicant applied for membership in the Association. The applicant was subsequently advised by the Registrar of the Board of Examiners that since her "current employment does not meet the requirements of the definition of the practice of social work under the Act", her application was not accepted.

The Social Worker's Act provided for an appeal of the Registrar's decision. The applicant requested a review of the decision denying her registration. At the review hearing various documents were tendered and evidence given in support of the application by the applicant. The Board subsequently confirmed the decision to refuse registration, giving the following as its reasons:

> The Board of Examiners finds that the applicant employed as the coordinator at the Senior Citizens' Secretariat in Halifax is not practicing social work as defined in section 5(2) of the Act. It is the decision of the Board that the applicant has not demonstrated the specialized knowledge, values and skills required as a basic level or practice of the social work provision.[11]

The social worker then brought an application for an order quashing the decision of the Board of Examiners of the Nova Scotia Association of Social Workers and for a further order requiring the board to register the applicant as a member of the Association. The rationale for the board's decision had been that the applicant, who was employed as a coordinator at the Senior Citizens' Secretariat, was not practising social work as defined in the relevant statute. In her application the applicant argued that the Board had failed to provide adequate "reasons" for refusing registration in its review decision and merely stated a conclusion that mirrored the statutory language.

The Nova Scotia Supreme Court, in allowing the appeal, stated: It is trite law to state that an administrative tribunal must give reasons for its decision, and in this case it failed to do so. The court found that the board's decision was nothing more than a conclusion, and that although it was required to give reasons for its decision it had not done so. The Board's error was not that it misinterpreted the phrase "the practice of social work," but that it failed to give reasons why the applicant was found not to be a person practising social work.[12] The matter was referred back to a differently constituted Board for a re-hearing.

Section 22 of the *Social Work and Social Service Work Act, 1998* requires the registrar to keep a register of all members of the College. The register will usually contain the following:

---

10.   [1997] N.S.J. No. 200 (S.C.) (QL).

11.   *Ibid.*, at p. 3.

12.   *Ibid.*, at p. 6.

1. The name of each member and the class of his or her certificate of registration.
2. Any terms, conditions, or limitations imposed on a member's certificate of registration.
3. A notation of every revocation, cancellation, or suspension of a member's certificate of registration.
4. Information required by a section 14(1) committee.
5. Information that the by-laws prescribe.[13]

The register is kept at the College and is open to anyone for inspection during normal business hours. On payment of a reasonable photocopying charge anyone can get a copy of any part of the register. The register can be consulted by College staff when dealing with a member involved in the complaints process or by members of the public seeking information about the conduct or qualifications of a member of the College. It is unclear whether the registrar must disclose information in the register if he or she has reasonable grounds to believe that disclosure may jeopardize a member's safety. This is an issue that should particularly concern child protection workers, who often have to remove children from abusive homes, thereby putting themselves at risk from irate parents.

The registrar has the authority to impose an administrative suspension for failure to pay the membership fees, to pay a penalty imposed under the Act, or to provide information required by the by-laws. The registrar must give a member facing suspension notice in writing of his or her intention to suspend the member. The notice should state the member's default and what is required to correct the default.

The registrar can suspend a member's certificate 60 days after giving the member notice of the default and the registrar's intention to suspend the member. This enables the member to correct the default by paying the fees, paying the penalty, or providing the required information. As soon as the default is corrected, the suspension is lifted.

B. The Registration Regulation

Ontario Regulation 383/00, the first regulation passed by the College, deals extensively with registration and the procedure involved in applying for membership. To apply for membership, an applicant, as mentioned above, submits a completed application form and the required membership fees to the registrar.

---

13. *SWSSW Act*, s. 22(2).

In addition to completing the application form and providing standard information such as name and address, the applicant must disclose the following:

    i)   Every finding of professional misconduct, incompetence or incapacity and every other similar finding, including a finding of professional misconduct, incompetence or incapacity made by a professional association or other body that has self-regulatory responsibility.

    ii)   Every current proceeding in relation to professional misconduct, incompetence or incapacity and every other similar proceeding, including a proceeding relating to professional misconduct, incompetence or incapacity held by a professional association or other body that has self-regulatory responsibility.[14]

In addition the applicant must disclose every finding of guilt in relation to a criminal offence, an offence under the *Controlled Drugs and Substances Act*[15] or the *Food and Drugs Act*,[16] or any other offence relevant to the applicant's suitability to practise social work or social service work, as the case may be.

The applicant must be able to speak and write in either English or French with reasonable fluency. The applicant must also be a Canadian citizen or permanent resident of Canada, or be authorized under the federal *Immigration Act*[17] to engage in the practice of social work.

The regulation also provides that any false or misleading statement, representation, or declaration in the application will result in the applicant being deemed not to have satisfied the requirements for a certificate of registration of any class.[18] Case law suggests that there must be clear evidence, however, that the statement, representation, or declaration is false or misleading. Presumably if an applicant made a false or misleading statement on his or her application, it would be unlikely that the applicant could satisfy the registrar that he or she would practise social work with decency, integrity, and honesty.

An applicant who, after applying for but before being issued a certificate of registration, is found guilty of an offence, or is the subject of a finding of or a proceeding relating to professional misconduct or incompetence, must notify the registrar.

The above requirements are also conditions of maintaining a certificate of registration, once a certificate of registration has been issued to the applicant. Additionally, the member must provide to the College, on an ongoing basis, satisfactory evidence of his or her competence to practise social work. The

---

14.   O. Reg. 383/00, s. 5(2)(1).

15.   S.C. 1996, c.19.

16.   R.S.C. 1985, c. F-27.

17.   R.S.C. 1985, c. I-2.

18.   O. Reg., above note 14, s. 5(3).

type of evidence required is set out in guidelines approved by the council and distributed to the members.[19]

Initially the regulation provided for two classes of certificate, general and provisional. The requirements for each are specified in the regulation. The regulation allowed a provisional certificate of registration to be issued to an individual who had been "employed in the role of a social worker" but did not have the academic qualifications required for a general certificate of registration. Provisional certificates of registration were necessary in order to accommodate individuals who would not otherwise qualify for admission to the College. Upon application, provisional certificates were granted to individuals who had been principally working in social work performing the role of a social worker, for at least 5 of the 7 years immediately preceding the date of the application. It was also necessary for the applicant's employer to provide evidence documenting the applicant's current duties and responsibilities and confirming that the applicant practised social work safely and ethically and was paid for the services performed.

Lastly, the applicant had to give the College a signed undertaking (promise) that he or she would successfully complete, to the registrar's satisfaction, additional training approved by the College in social work ethics and social work standards of practice, within three years after the day the College notifies the applicant of the additional training.[20]

A provisional certificate of registration will expire on the day that is three years after the day the College notifies the member of the additional training. If the member completes the additional training within the time allowed, he or she will be entitled to a general certificate of registration, provided all other requirements for a general certificate are met.

Individuals seeking a provisional certificate of registration had until November 21, 2002, to apply to the College. This provision has been commonly called the "Grandfather clause."

C. General Certificates of Registration

In addition to the registration requirements already discussed, there are special requirements that apply to general certificates of registration. Section 7(1) of the regulation sets out the requirements:

    1)   The applicant must produce documentation satisfactory to the registrar that shows the applicant,

        i)   has obtained a degree in social work from a social work program accredited by the Canadian Association of Schools of Social

---

19.   O. Reg., above note 14, s. 6(3).
20.   *Ibid.*, s. 9(2).

Work, or a degree from a social work program or an equivalent program offered in Canada and approved by Council as equivalent to a social work program accredited by the Canadian Association of Schools of Social Work,

ii) has obtained a degree from a social work program or an equivalent program outside Canada and approved by Council as equivalent to a social work program accredited by the Canadian Association of Schools of Social Work; or

iii) has a combination of academic qualifications and practical experience that the Registrar determines is substantially equivalent to the qualifications required for a degree in social work from a social work program accredited by the Canadian Association of Schools of Social Work.

Section 7.1 is identical in wording to section 18.1 of the Act. Section 7 (1) (iii) permits individuals who do not have the required educational qualifications to be admitted to the College if their academic qualifications and practical experience are "substantially equivalent" to the qualifications required for a degree in social work. It is the registrar who determines the issue of what is substantially equivalent. This provision is more narrowly framed than the provisional certificate provisions in that the registrar is required to determine if the combination of an individual's education and experience is substantially the same as that of a university graduate of a social work program. For provisional certificates of registration the registrar's primary focus is on evaluating the individual's work experience.

One further point of importance for individuals contemplating applying to the College: it is anticipated that applicants will eventually be required to write an examination approved by council before gaining admission to the College.

Once registered under either certificate, the certificate holder is permitted to use the title "Social Worker" or "Registered Social Worker," and the designation "RSW," in connection with his or her practice of social work. Social service workers would use the title "Social Service Worker" or "Registered Social Service Worker" and the designation "RSSW" in connection with his or her practice of social service work.

D.   Conclusion

It is clear from the provisions of the Act and the registration regulation that the registrar should register prospective members who meet certain minimal requirements. For the most part, therefore, prospective members have their applications processed and approved as a matter of administrative routine. Moreover, members retain their membership forever unless they run afoul of a provision in the Act that requires the College to strip them of their membership.

With registration comes the benefit of being able to publicly call oneself a "Registered Social Worker," but this privilege also imposes accountability on social workers. It has been stated that qualified registrants have a right to "preserve their livelihood" as registered social workers, and it therefore falls to the College to ensure that the registration requirements and the ability to call oneself a social worker are jealously guarded.[21]

---

21.   *Doiron* v. *Duplisea* (1998), 170 N.S.R. (2d) 15 (C.A.).

Chapter 4

The Complaints Process

A.   The Registrar's Role

A new complaint usually goes to the registrar first. It is natural to assume —
although this power is not specified in the Act — that the registrar reviews
the complaint after receiving it to determine whether there is enough information for the complaint to proceed. If in the registrar's opinion there are reasonable and probable grounds to believe that a social worker has committed
an act of professional misconduct, or is incompetent or incapacitated as
alleged in the complaint, he or she has the option to have the complaint formally investigated. These powers of investigation are discussed more fully in
chapter 7. Although some complaints of a less serious nature, for example
minor fee disputes, could be resolved by the intervention of the registrar,
there appears to be no formal provision in the Act, however, that would allow
the registrar to initiate steps to resolve the complaint at this point. It appears
that the only power the registrar has is to refer the complaint to the Complaints Committee.

B.   Form and Content of the Complaint

The complaint must be in writing before the College will act[1] and has to
relate to the provision of services by a social worker. The Complaints Committee will not take action unless the complaint is in the form prescribed by
the College by-laws.[2] The College's By-law No. 1 outlines the necessary
contents of a complaint. It must contain the name, address, and telephone

---

1.   *Social Work and Social Service Work Act, 1998* [*SWSSW Act*], S.O. 1998, c. 31, s. 24(1).
2.   *Ibid.*, s. 24 (3)(a).

number of the complainant and the member of the College who is the subject of the complaint, as well as details regarding the conduct or actions of the member sufficient to identify the complainant's concerns. This would normally include the following: date(s), time(s) and place(s) of the event or events giving rise to the complaint and a description of the member's actions or conduct.

Conduct outside of a member's professional obligations cannot be the subject of a complaint unless it can be directly related to the member's ability to provide the services of a social worker. But even when the College receives a complaint in writing and the complaint relates to provision of social work services, the Act states that it is not required to consider and investigate the complaint if, in its opinion, the complaint does not relate to professional misconduct, incompetence, or incapacity on the part of a member or if it believes that the complaint is frivolous, vexatious, or an abuse of process.[3] The language of this provision of the Act suggests that the committee can dismiss a complaint without obtaining a response to the complaint from the member in question. In reality, the committee is likely to conduct at least a preliminary investigation into the complaint just to ensure that there is evidence, if necessary, to prove that the complaint was considered in the event the complainant disagrees with the disposition of it.

The committee is not required to take any action unless the following occurs:

a) a complaint in the form prescribed by the by-laws has been filed with the Registrar;

b) the member of the College whose conduct or actions are being investigated has been notified of the complaint and given at least 30 days in which to submit in writing to the committee any explanations or representations the member may wish to make concerning the matter; and

c) the committee has examined all the information and documents that the College has that are relevant to the complaint.[4]

Although the Act states that the complaint must be in writing, it does not give any guidance on what actually constitutes a complaint. It is widely accepted by the regulators of other health professionals that a complaint is an expression of concern about the service provided or other aspects of the professional relationship.[5] To determine the level of concern it may be necessary to look to the intent of the complainant. Specific concerns about a member

---

3.   *Ibid.*, s. 24(2).
4.   *Ibid.*, s. 24(3).
5.   Government of Ontario, Health Professions Legislation Review, *Striking a New Balance: A Blueprint for the Regulation of Ontario's Health Professions* (Toronto: Health Professions Legislation Review, 1989).

or his or her practice will usually be sufficient to constitute a complaint; vague generalities about a member's practice will not. If the complaint lacks particularity, the committee will ask the complainant for additional information or for clarification of the information already provided.

Although the Act makes clear that the member must receive notice of the complaint, the committee is not required to provide a copy of the actual complaint to the member. The committee can provide a summary, although it must ensure that the summary contains enough information about the allegations in the complaint to allow the member to prepare a meaningful response.[6] Usually, however, the committee provides a complete copy of the complaint, to which the member, as noted above, has at least 30 days to respond in writing. Failure of the committee to give a member notice may invalidate its decisions regarding a complaint.

A member's failure to respond to a complaint could be interpreted as professional misconduct. For that reason, it is imperative for a member who is the subject of a complaint to respond to the complaint, even if it is baseless. Although a member may feel justified in not responding to a baseless complaint, to simply ignore a complaint is foolhardy.

It is possible for the committee to investigate a complaint before giving notice to the member who is the subject of the complaint, but the committee must be careful not to prejudice the member's case by reaching a decision about the veracity of the complaint before hearing from the member, or by waiting too long to notify the member.

C.   The Origin of a Complaint

An important point to be aware of is that complaints do not have to originate with a member's clients. Although complaints usually do originate this way, the College itself has the authority not only to initiate complaints but actually to solicit a complaint if it becomes aware of information that it believes ought to be considered by the Complaints Committee. It is therefore quite proper for the College to approach a member's client, advise the client of the complaints process, and ask him or her to register a complaint.

Complaints do not have to come from a person directly affected by the member's conduct. Anyone with information about a member's alleged misconduct may register a complaint, including the client's family, friends, and physicians. A complaint received from a non-client can create problems for the College, however. What if the client does not want to be involved in the complaint process or refuses to cooperate with the College's investigation?

---

6.   *SWSSW Act*, above note 1, s. 24(4).

Theoretically the College can still investigate the complaint without the client's cooperation, though practically speaking this would make the investigation more difficult for the College.

D.   Withdrawal of a Complaint

Another problem the committee can face arises when a complainant withdraws the complaint. There is no requirement that the committee must proceed with a complaint if the complainant is unwilling to proceed. In certain circumstances, however, it is highly likely that the committee will proceed, irrespective of the complainant's wishes. If a complaint is serious enough — if there is an allegation of sexual abuse, for example — or if the committee wants to send a message to the profession, it is likely that the committee will continue to pursue the complaint. Any suggestion that a member has used a financial inducement or otherwise exerted undue influence to get a client to withdraw a complaint will likely result in the committee pursuing the complaint even more vigorously.

Because the College's primary purpose is protecting the public interest, the Complaints Committee has the jurisdiction to continue pursuing a complaint even in the absence of the complainant. Nor does it matter to the College that a complainant has a civil suit outstanding against the member in question — the complaint can go forward at the same time as the civil suit. The College does not judge the merits of a complaint based on the existence or not of a civil action.

E.   Investigating the Complaint

The Complaints Committee's duty is to investigate complaints, not determine their veracity. As mentioned in chapter 2, the Complaints Committee must have at least three members, one-third of whom are elected members. At the time of writing, the committee has six members. The committee chairperson selects the panel that will investigate the complaint. A panel usually has three members, which is the quorum for investigating a complaint.

The committee will obtain witness statements, relevant documents, and a complete response from the member. It is important to note that a College investigator is allowed to investigate only the complaint itself. He or she cannot look into issues unrelated to the specifics of the complaint. An investigator can, however, investigate similar events involving other clients to determine whether the allegations being investigated are part of a pattern of conduct.

It is important that the member control, to the extent possible, what is being disclosed during an investigation, since any other types of misconduct discovered could become the subject of a further new complaint. If, for example, the investigator discovers evidence of a sexual relationship with a client while he or she is investigating some other totally unrelated complaint, then that information will be provided to the College. The College will then launch a new complaint against the member.

Because a copy of a member's written response to a complaint may be given to the complainant, it is important to prepare a carefully written response that is complete and not inflammatory. We recommend engaging the services of a lawyer to review a response before it is delivered to the committee. Obtaining a lawyer's input is important because a properly drafted response can persuade the committee to dispose of a complaint without referring it for further action.

Depending on the Complaints Committee workload, it will investigate by way of correspondence or by telephone or face-to-face interviews conducted by College staff, who then submits a written report to the committee. Sometimes time constraints do not allow the College to interview all of the relevant parties in person. It is likely, however, that a complaint involving an allegation of serious misconduct such as sexual abuse will prompt the College to arrange face-to-face interviews with the complainant and other witnesses.

If the committee cannot obtain adequate information through the efforts of College staff and committee members themselves it may ask the registrar to appoint an investigator pursuant to section 32 of the Act. The registrar's powers of investigation are discussed more fully in chapter 7, but an investigator appointed by the registrar under this section has broad sweeping powers to attend at the member's place of business to personally investigate the complaint, and in the course of this can seize any documents relevant to the complaint. These are powers that the Complaints Committee does not possess.

The committee does not have to thoroughly investigate a complaint, but only has to make a reasonable effort to consider all the records and documents it believes are relevant in order to make a reasoned determination of how to handle the complaint. The courts, however, can review the adequacy of their efforts.

F.   The Complaint Committee's Decision

Once the committee has examined all of the information and documents the College has that are relevant to the complaint, it must, according to section 24(5) of the Act, do one of five things:

    a)   direct that the matter be referred, in whole or in part, to the Discipline Committee or the Fitness to Practise Committee;

b)   direct that the matter not be referred under clause (a);
c)   require the person complained against to appear before the Complaints Committee to be cautioned;
d)   refer the matter for alternative dispute resolution if the Committee considers it appropriate to do so and the complainant and the member agree; or
e)   take any action it considers appropriate in the circumstances and that is not inconsistent with this Act, the regulations or the by-laws.[7]

When deciding whether to refer a complaint to the Discipline or Fitness to Practise committee, the Complaints Committee examines the allegations to determine whether a *prima facie* case for referral exists (this is discussed in more detail in chapter 5). Only if the allegations warrant a referral does the Complaints Committee look at the sufficiency of the evidence. A complaint will not be referred if the evidence is inadequate to satisfy the burden of proof that the Discipline or Fitness to Practise committee will have to meet for a finding of professional misconduct or incapacity.

The burden of proof is not beyond a reasonable doubt, as it is with criminal trials. Since the outcome of disciplinary hearings can have serious implications on a member's career and professional reputation, the case law accepts that the burden of proof should be more certain than the civil burden of proof, which is on a balance of probabilities. This civil burden of proof is discussed more fully in chapter 14. The leading case in Canada describing this certainty is *Re Bernstein and the College of Physicians and Surgeons of Ontario.*[8] One of the judges hearing this case wrote: "I hold that the degree of proof required in disciplinary matters of this kind is that the proof must be clear and convincing and based upon cogent evidence which is accepted by the Tribunal."[9]

Except in the case of a referral to the Discipline or Fitness to Practise committee under section 24(5)(a), the Complaints Committee must deliver its decision in writing to the registrar, and must provide reasons for its decision. Although a section 24(5)(a) referral does not require reasons, the committee must nevertheless specify what allegations are being referred. It is not permissible for the committee to simply say that it is referring "the complaint." In court, a referral that does not contain specific allegations of professional misconduct or incapacity is open to attack from the member's lawyer. Specifying the allegations serves two purposes — it alerts the member to the exact allegations that must be addressed and limits the college to proceeding with only those exact allegations. Because the wording of a referral is so important, the Complaints Committee will often send its file to a lawyer retained by the college to draft the allegations before referring the complaint. This

---

7.   *Ibid.*, s. 24(5).
8.   (1977) 76 D.L.R. (3d) 38 (Ont. Div. Ct.).
9.   *Ibid.*, at p. 76.

ensures that the required element of specificity is present in the referral document.

The other provisions of section 24(5) also need explanation. Section 24(5)(c) states that the Complaints Committee has the power to compel a member to appear before the committee to be cautioned. Cautioning occurs at the College during normal business hours and generally involves a discussion with the member about the appropriateness of the conduct that formed the basis for the complaint. The Complaints Committee can also decide not to refer the complaint to the Discipline Committee if they believe no further action is warranted.

The Act makes alternative dispute resolution available for handling a complaint if the Complaints Committee considers it appropriate. Alternative dispute resolution is a process whereby an impartial third party — a mediator — intervenes to help the parties settle the issues between them. With the mediator's help, the parties themselves present ideas to resolve the issues between them and reach their own solutions. A competent mediator will strive to advance all of the parties' interests equally. He or she will ensure that all of the parties are heard and that the process is conducted fairly.

Alternative dispute resolution is available in College proceedings if both the member and the complainant agree to it. An agreement to employ alternative dispute resolution brings the formal complaints process to an end. Exiting the formal complaints process benefits both the member and the complainant. For one thing, it avoids the expense and uncertainty of a formal discipline hearing. The process is no longer adversarial and the parties are not required to testify under oath, as is the case in a formal hearing. And by giving the member input into resolving the complaint, alternative dispute resolution allows for a more creative solution and a potentially less professionally embarrassing outcome than would result from a formal discipline hearing.

Section 24(5)(e) is a catchall provision that allows the committee to take any action it deems appropriate as long as that action does not conflict with the Act, regulations, or College by-laws. This provision gives the committee leeway to fashion a result that may be more appropriate than a referral to a discipline hearing or fitness to practise hearing. Such alternative dispositions can include obtaining an undertaking from the member, implementing changes in the member's practice, requiring the member to upgrade his or her education, or referring the complainant to an agency outside the College that can handle the complaint more appropriately. The committee does not, however, have the power to order the member to pay a sum to the College or the complainant, nor can it require third parties such as the police to take action.[10]

---

10. *Modi* v. *Ontario Health Professions Board* (1996), 27 O.R. (3d) 762 (Ont. Ct. Gen. Div.).

Once the registrar receives the Complaint Committee's written decision, he or she must give the member and the complainant a copy.[11]

In reaching its decision, the Complaints Committee does not have to hold a hearing or allow anyone, including the complainant or the member, to make oral or written submissions.[12] There appears to be no provision in the Act providing for a review of complaints that are dismissed at this stage.

Timely disposal of a complaint is always the most desirable result, hence the requirement in the Act that the Complaints Committee "shall use its best efforts" to dispose of a complaint within 120 days of its being filed with the registrar.[13]

Complaints relating to sexual abuse have been a problem for many professional bodies. Often a sexual abuse complainant will make a complaint and then have second thoughts about proceeding, or will want the College to proceed slowly while he or she receives the emotional support necessary to continue with the complaint. The Complaints Committee must be careful not to allow the complaint to drag on too long without a decision or resolution of the complaint because the courts do not accept a complainant's fragile emotional psyche as a valid excuse for delay. This is particularly important in cases where the investigation commences before the member is notified. An example of this point is the case of *McIntosh* v. *College of Physicians & Surgeons of Ontario*.[14] In that case Dr. McIntosh was accused of having sexual relations with the complainant when she was 16 years old and his patient. The complainant, now an adult, sent a letter of complaint to the College of Physicians and Surgeons in August of 1991. On January 22, 1992, she wrote to the College and asked that the matter not proceed but be left "open" because she had personal reasons for not proceeding with this action. On December 5, 1995, notwithstanding that the complaint had been abandoned by the complainant, the College decided to proceed with the complaint. On September 1996, despite Dr. McIntosh's complete denial of any sexual relationship with the woman and notwithstanding that he outlined a history of harassment by the complainant of Dr. McIntosh and his family, the Complaints Committee referred the matter to the Discipline Committee without giving reasons. Dr. McIntosh then applied for judicial review of the Complaints Committee decision.

The court held that the Committee had an obligation to consider and investigate the complaint in a timely manner, certainly within the six-month interval from receiving the complaint and the complainant's efforts to halt the process. The court was critical of the College's responses to the com-

---

11.   *SWSSW Act*, above note 1, s. 24(7).
12.   *Ibid.*, s. 24 (8).
13.   *Ibid.*, s. 24 (9).
14.   (1998) O.J. No. 5222 (Ont. Ct. Gen Div.) (QL).

plainant's attempts to turn it on and off at her whim and the fact that Dr. McIntosh had not been aware of the complaint for over 4 years. The court, in finding that it was the intent of the legislation (Regulated Health Professions Act) that complaints be disposed of expeditiously, quoted with approval from *Sekleski* v. *Sullivan* (unreported case of the Health Professions Board) the following:

> The fact that a client or a patient whose treatment or care is in question . . . refuses to assist in an investigation does not absolve the College or the Committee from its obligation in the interest of the protection of the public, to conduct an investigation . . .[15]

In holding that notice is an essential part of natural justice, the court found that failing to give notice for over four years to Dr. McIntosh and then not dealing with the complaint within the time frame provided for in the legislation did not meet the standard of procedural fairness. To allow the complainant to turn the investigation on and off from time to time is not appropriate. Once the complaint is made, the complainant should no longer have control of the proceedings and the investigation must continue into the complaint whether or not the complainant asks that it be halted.[16] The court allowed Dr McIntosh's application and made an order preventing the College from proceeding with the complaint.

G.   Avoiding and Responding to Complaints

The following summary from Peter Jenkins's book entitled *Counselling, Psychotherapy and the Law* provides helpful advice on how to avoid and respond to complaints.

> Avoiding complaints:
>> a)   ensure clients have adequate information about
>>> i)   the nature of the counselling, therapeutic or training service that you are going to provide
>>> ii)   codes of ethics and standard of practice which are relevant
>>> iii)   complaint systems, both informal and formal
>> b)   review arrangements for getting feedback on the service from clients
>> c)   review and update documentation, consent forms, etc.
>
> Responding to a potential complaint:
>> a)   acknowledge the legitimacy of the client's complaint and of the feelings involved wherever possible

---

15.   *Ibid.*, at p. 6.
16.   *Ibid.*, at p. 6.

b) avoid defensive reactions to criticism and complaint
c) react speedily to explore the problem and negotiate a solution
d) seek expert advice, if warranted, from other professionals as soon as possible
e) rely on your own personal support systems to help you with the emotional effects of responding to a complaint
f) record all significant contact with clients where a pattern of conflict, misunderstanding or complaint emerges, including phone contact, copies of letters, notes of meetings.[17]

A member who is in the position of having to respond to a complaint needs to remember that not all complaints result in discipline hearings. In 2000, the college received 14 complaints. By 2001, that number had risen to 25 (in a College with 8,160 members). It is expected that the number will continue to rise as the College grows and people become more aware of their rights. Of the 25 complaints in 2001, 11 were formally investigated by the Complaints Committee. The complaints fell into 4 areas: custody/access, confidentiality and disclosure, child welfare, and third party capacity assessments. The majority of the complaints were in the first two areas.

These early statistics demonstrate that the majority of the complaints received are resolved during the early stages of the Complaints Committee handling of the complaint. For this reason it is critical for a member of the College not only to respond to a complaint in a timely fashion, but also to ensure that the response is carefully drafted and is as complete as possible. As already mentioned, the response should be reviewed by a lawyer before it is submitted to the College. If aspects of the complaint are valid, the member should acknowledge them. If remedial action is warranted, the member should implement it. If changes in how the member performs a certain activity are necessary, the member should make those changes and use the response to advise the College that the changes have been made. In the response the member should demonstrate concern for the complainant, but be careful not to admit liability. The member should also try to disentangle any feelings of being personally attacked from the professional issues that need to be addressed. Likewise, the member should try to avoid defensiveness, as difficult as that can be. It is in the member's best interest to take the time and effort to put his or her best foot forward so that the complaint can be disposed of without a formal investigation or referral to a Discipline or Fitness to Practise hearing.

---

17. P. Jenkins, *Counselling, Psychotherapy and the Law* (London: Sage Publications, 1997) at 276.

Chapter 5

Disciplinary Proceedings

One of the most important functions of a self-governing profession is the disciplining of its members for professional misconduct or incompetence. Allegations of misconduct or incompetence against Ontario social workers are heard by the College's Discipline Committee. The College's complaints and disciplinary procedures must comply with the procedural provisions set out in the *Social Work and Social Service Work Act, 1998*.[1] As we saw in chapter 2, either the Executive Committee pursuant to their authority found in section 25(1) of the Act or the Complaints Committee acting through the Executive Committee can refer a matter to the Discipline Committee. The Executive Committee has the authority to refer any matter involving allegations of misconduct or incompetence that comes to its attention, whether there has been a formal complaint or not. The Complaints Committee can only refer complaints that have been formally lodged and only after the complaints provisions of the Act have been complied with.

A.   Notice of Hearing

Once a complaint is referred to the Discipline Committee a notice of hearing containing specific allegations of the misconduct or incompetence is prepared. This notice of hearing is the formal beginning of the disciplinary process. Specificity is important for two reasons. One, it enables the member to know exactly what case he or she has to meet, and two, it confines the Discipline Committee to proceeding only on a clearly defined set of allegations.

A notice of hearing that does not contain specific allegations may be subject to a court challenge that results in a disciplinary decision being over-

---

1.   *Social Work and Social Service Work Act, 1998* [*SWSSW Act*], S.O. 1998, c. 31.

turned. *Shewchuk-Dann* v. *Alberta Assn. of Social Workers* illustrates this point.[2] This case was an appeal from a judgment confirming a decision of the council of the Alberta Association of Social Workers that the appellant was guilty of conduct unbecoming a social worker. The key ground for appeal was the argument that the appellant had not been given adequate notification of the complaint against her. The council had not, at any point, advised the appellant that it was laying specific charges against her as a result of the allegation. The complaint was a three-page statement of facts by a former employee which was never provided to the Appellant. In fact the college had refused to provide it when asked by the Appellant. The appellant did not know when she arrived for the hearing what charges she faced. The court held that the hearing was fundamentally unfair to the appellant and breached the rules of natural justice because of the lack of specificity in the allegations. The appeal was allowed and the order of the council was vacated.

B.   Interim Orders

Before a disciplinary hearing begins, the Executive Committee has the power to protect the public by making an interim order suspending the member's certificate of registration pending the outcome of the hearing[3]. Because a suspension before a hearing can have significant consequences for the member, the committee must first satisfy itself that the member's conduct exposes his or her clients to harm. Case law indicates that the committee should, in making this determination, consider the seriousness of the allegations against the member, how long ago the conduct in question occurred, whether the conduct occurred once or several times, whether non-College restrictions on the member's practice (such as bail conditions) are already in place, how cooperative the member has been during the investigation, and any expert opinions solicited by the College on whether the member poses a threat to the public. Because of the potentially severe effect of an interim order, the committee must notify the member that it intends to make the order; this is to give the member an opportunity to submit a written response opposing the order.

If a member receives notice that the committee intends to make an interim order, he or she should engage the services of a lawyer to help draft the response. A well-drafted response is critical because there is no other avenue that the member can pursue to dissuade the committee from making the order. It is not uncommon for a discipline hearing to occur many months after a member receives notification that he or she will be the subject of a for-

---

2.   [1996] A.J. No. 61 (C.A.) (QL).
3.   *SWSSW Act*, above note 1, s.25(3).

mal hearing, so orders of this type should be avoided if at all possible. An order suspending a member's certificate of registration before the hearing and any finding of guilt can have serious financial consequences to the member. In drafting a response, the member should make a statement denying all of the complainant's allegations as well as statements that point out any weaknesses in the College's information, supply evidence supporting the member's case, provide reasons why the College should not be concerned that further incidents will occur, and explain any safeguards the member has put in place to protect his or her clients since the allegations were made. For example, an allegation that a form of specialized therapy harmed a client might prompt the member to give the College an undertaking that he or she will not use that form of therapy with any other client until the hearing is held.

If the committee makes an interim order, it is required to proceed with the hearing as quickly as possible and to give the hearing precedence over other pending matters. Interim orders are discussed again in chapter 6 dealing with Fitness to Practise hearings.

C.   The Hearing

As was noted in chapter 2, the council appoints the members of the Discipline Committee in accordance with the College's by-laws. The committee chairperson appoints a panel of members to hear a particular discipline matter. The panel must have at least three members. If a panel has more than three members, at least three of them must be present for the entire hearing; otherwise, the validity of the hearing is jeopardized. When the chairperson appoints the panel, he or she must ensure that none of the appointees have previously been involved in the investigation in another capacity.

The Supreme Court of Canada has held that professional disciplinary tribunals must adhere to a high standard of justice when the right to continue in one's profession or employment is at stake.[4] A disciplinary suspension can have a serious impact on a career.

The legal concepts of natural justice and fairness play an important role in how a hearing is conducted and in how the panel members arrive at their decision. Three fundamental principles are at play in a discipline hearing:

> The first principle is that of neutrality. The tribunal will always appear impartial and put the member's right to a fair hearing ahead of the tribunal's conve-

---

4.   *Kane* v. *Board of Governors of the University of British Columbia*, [1980] 1 S.C.R. 1105.

nience. The second principle involves the adversarial process, and the duty of the tribunal to decide the case on the evidence presented. They do not try to discover the truth on their own. The third principle is respect for the human rights of the participants as defined by human rights laws.[5]

It is critically important, and a fundamental principle of law, that the panel remains disinterested and unbiased, for an allegation of bias, if proven, against the panel will nullify the hearing. Bias or the reasonable apprehension of bias can occur when a panel prejudges the matter before it, interferes with the conduct of the hearing, or has some conflict of interest vis-à-vis a participant in the hearing. Whether there is an apprehension of bias will depend on whether an individual looking objectively at the circumstances of the case could reasonably suppose that the panel would not weigh the allegations in an impartial manner.[6]

Disciplinary proceedings are subject to the *Statutory Powers Procedure Act*, which provides that the subject of a hearing must be allowed representation by counsel and an opportunity to make a full answer and defence to the allegations against him or her.[7] The hearing must, in accordance with the doctrine of fairness, allow the member to know the case against him or her, to fully answer the charges, and to make representations on his or her own behalf. The College and the member whose conduct is being investigated are the parties to the hearing. The complainant is not a party and has no status in the proceeding other than as a witness.

Before the hearing begins, the member must be allowed an opportunity to examine any documents that will be given in evidence. This is called disclosure and is usually accomplished by giving the member or his or her lawyer copies of all of the relevant documents. The College must also disclose the identity of any witnesses who will be testifying at the hearing. Disclosure must take place at least 10 days before the hearing date.

Discipline Committee hearings are open to the public. The Discipline Committee, however, may make an order excluding the public, including other members of the College, from the hearing if it is satisfied that

a)   matters involving public security may be disclosed;

b)   financial or personal or other matters may be disclosed at the hearing of such a nature that the desirability of avoiding public disclosure of them in the interest of any person affected or in the public interest outweighs the desirability of adhering to the principle that hearings be open to the public;

---

5.   S. McCorquodale, "The Role of Regulators in Practice," in F.J. Turner, ed., *Social Work Practice: A Canadian Perspective* (Scarborough, ON: Prentice-Hall Canada, 1999) 462 at 467.

6.   *Misra* v. *College of Physicians and Surgeons of Saskatchewan* (1988), 52 D.L.R. (4th) 477 (Sask. C.A.).

7.   R.S.O. 1990, c. S.22, s. 10.

c)   a person involved in a civil or criminal proceeding may be prejudiced; or

d)   the safety of a person may be jeopardized.[8]

The committee can order a ban on the publication of a witness's identity where the witness fears for his or her safety or the witness's psychiatric records are to be disclosed. In sexual misconduct cases it is not uncommon for a witness to seek an order banning publication of his or her identity because of the sensitive or embarrassing nature of the evidence that will be disclosed.

It is important to recognize that a discipline hearing is an adversarial process similar to a criminal trial. The two sides — the prosecutor, acting for the College, and the member, usually represented by a lawyer — are both given an opportunity to present their case. One author summarizes the role of discipline committees in the adversarial process as follows:

a)   to ensure that both parties present their sides of the case fairly;

b)   to listen impartially to the evidence and arguments; and

c)   after the parties have completed their presentations, to decide the issues.[9]

The Discipline Committee panel hearing the case normally engages a lawyer to advise it on issues of law, procedure, and evidence. The lawyer is present throughout the hearing. The lawyer's function is not to make decisions for the panel, give advice on the merits of the allegations or penalty, or conduct the hearing. His or her only function is to assist the panel on points of law, procedure, and evidence when asked to do so by the chairperson. Because the panel members are not lawyers and may not be familiar with the law or the rules of evidence, the lawyer's advice can be very helpful to them in their efforts to reach legally appropriate decisions. This advice is given openly in the presence of all of the parties to the hearing. Legally appropriate decisions at the hearing stage make an appeal less likely.

A court reporter records all of the oral evidence given by witnesses at discipline hearings. The record, as it is called, is necessary for an appeal or judicial review. Transcripts are provided to the parties at their expense if requested. Documents and other items entered into evidence at a hearing are returned to the parties who supplied them (but again, only if requested). These items are never returned until the hearing is over.

The objects of a discipline hearing are to determine the facts, assess the extent to which the behaviour demonstrated by the member proves the allegations against him or her, and decide what penalty, if any, to impose. The

---

8.   *SWSSW Act*, above note 1, s. 28(7).
9.   R. Steinecke, *A Complete Guide to the Regulated Health Professions Act* (Aurora, ON: Canada Law Book, 1995), at 6-32.

Discipline Committee panel is required to provide a written decision (including a statement of its reasons for the decision) and to serve the decision on the parties and on the complainant, if there is one.[10] The committee may, at its discretion, withhold its reasons from the complainant if the hearing was closed.

The function of written reasons is to allow the member who has been adversely affected by the decision to know the underlying reasons for the decision. A decision that merely states the conclusions reached and not why those conclusions were reached will be successfully challenged in court. Adequate reasons should demonstrate that the parties' case has been heard and understood; inform the reviewing judge of the basis for the decision; and negate any perceptions of arbitrariness or unfairness on the part of the panel hearing the complaint.[11]

The committee's decision must be based solely on the evidence admitted during the hearing. Discipline Committee panel members who are themselves social workers sometimes find it difficult to set aside their own knowledge when making a finding of fact, but they must do so to ensure that the hearing is fair. No matter how obvious a fact may seem to the panel, a finding of fact must be based on evidence presented at the hearing. For this reason, it is common in discipline hearings for prosecutors to call social workers to give evidence on what the appropriate standard of practice should be.

Discipline Committee members who participate in a hearing can do so only if they have not been involved in any investigation of the case before the hearing begins, other than as members of the body (council or Executive Committee) that referred the matter to the Discipline Committee. Discipline Committee panelists are not permitted to contact directly or indirectly any person, including any party or representative of a party, except on notice to all of the parties. All of the parties must be allowed to attend the hearing and be given an opportunity to make submissions on any issues that arise outside the hearing room itself.

D.   Onus and Standard of Proof

The onus of proving the allegations rests with the prosecutor and the College. The allegations must be proved on a balance of probabilities. This means that if two plausible explanations are given at a hearing, the panel will decide in favour of the party with the more plausible explanation, even if that explanation is only slightly more plausible than the other explanation.[12]

---

10.   *SWSSW ACT*, above note 1, s. 28(15).
11.   *Bailey* v. *Saskatchewan Registered Nurses' Association* (unreported, April 20, 1988, Sask. Q.B.).
12.   R. Steinecke, above note 9, at 6-46.

The standard of proof in discipline cases under the *Regulated Health Professions Act, 1991*[13] was discussed in the case of *Re Bernstein and the College of Physicians and Surgeons of Ontario*.[14] Although Bernstein dealt with a physician's misconduct under the *Regulated Health Professions Act*, it has become, since it was decided in 1977, the test for all disciplinary proceedings under regulatory legislation.

One of the Ontario Divisional Court judges in *Bernstein* made the following comments:

> In my view discipline committees whose powers are such that their decisions can destroy a man's or a woman's professional life are entitled to more guidance from the Courts than the simple expression that "they are entitled to act on the balance of probabilities."

> The important thing to remember is that in civil cases there is no precise formula as to the standard of proof required to establish a fact.

> In all cases, before reaching a conclusion of fact, the tribunal must be reasonably satisfied that the fact occurred, and whether the tribunal is so satisfied will depend on the totality of the circumstances including the nature and consequences of the fact or facts to be proved, the seriousness of an allegation made, and the gravity of the consequences that will flow from a particular finding.[15]

Another judge wrote, "I hold that the degree of proof required in disciplinary matters of this kind is that the proof must be clear and convincing and based upon cogent evidence which is accepted by the tribunal."[16]

Much the same was said in another important disciplinary case, *Carruthers* v. *College of Nurses of Ontario*, which dealt with the alleged misconduct of a nurse.[17] Carruthers was a nurse working in a psychiatric intensive care unit. While helping another nurse restrain and give an injection to a violent female patient, Carruthers tried to distract the patient by kissing her. The tribunal found Carruthers guilty of failing to maintain the profession's standards of practice, of physically abusing the patient, and of engaging in disgraceful, dishonourable, or unprofessional conduct.

The court held that the tribunal could properly determine whether physical abuse occurred only by considering all of the circumstances, including

- the circumstances in which the conduct is alleged to have occurred
- the nature of the conduct
- the words or gestures which accompanied the conduct
- the nature and extent of the force applied

---

13.   S.O. 1991, c. 18.
14.   (1977), 76 D.L.R. (3d) 38 (Ont. Div. Ct.).
15.   *Ibid.*, at 61.
16.   *Ibid.*, at 76.
17.   (1996), 31 O.R. (3d) 377 (Div. Ct.), [1996] O.J. No. 4275 (QL).

- the intent, purpose, or motive of the member in engaging in the conduct
- the nature and extent of the consent, if any, to the conduct.[18]

The court upheld the tribunal's finding of physical abuse. The standard of proof was held to be "proof on a balance of probabilities based on clear, cogent and convincing evidence" with "appreciation of the nature and seriousness of the allegations made" and "an equivalent understanding of the gravity of the consequences to the appellant of any adverse finding."[19]

E. Finding Professional Misconduct or Incompetence

The Discipline Committee may find a member of the College guilty of professional misconduct if it believes that the member has engaged in conduct that, in the words of section 26(2) of the *Social Work and Social Service Work Act, 1998,*

a) contravenes this Act, the regulations or the by-laws;
b) contravenes an order of the Discipline Committee, the Complaints Committee, the council or the Registrar; or
c) is defined as being professional misconduct in the regulations.

Section 26(3) of the Act states that "The Discipline Committee may, after a hearing, find a member of the College to be incompetent if, in its opinion, the member has displayed in his or her professional responsibilities a lack of knowledge, skill, or judgment or disregard for the welfare of a person or persons of a nature or extent that demonstrates that the member is unfit to continue to carry out his or her professional responsibilities or that a certificate of registration held by the member under this Act should be made subject to terms, conditions or limitations."

A finding of incompetence usually does not include a component of unethical or dishonest behaviour. As the above quotation indicates, incompetence relates to the ability or condition of a member. For a member to be judged incompetent, the incompetence must be connected with the member's treatment or care of his or her client. There must be some evidence of a lack of skill, knowledge, or judgment, and the lack must be of sufficient seriousness to have warranted a discipline hearing.

Section 26(4) of the Act states that

If the Discipline Committee finds a member guilty of professional misconduct or to be incompetent, it shall make an order doing one or more of the following:

---

18. *Ibid.*, at 11.
19. *Ibid.*, at 18.

1. Directing the Registrar to revoke any certificate of registration held by the member under this Act.
2. Directing the Registrar to suspend any certificate of registration held by the member under this Act for a specified period, not exceeding 24 months.
3. Directing the Registrar to impose specified terms, conditions or limitations on any certificate of registration held by the member under this Act.
4. Directing that the imposition of a penalty be postponed for a specified period and not be imposed if specified terms are met within that period.

Revocation is the removal of the member from the profession, whereas suspension is the temporary removal of the member's certificate of registration. If the member's certificate of registration is revoked, it is the member's responsibility to reapply to the College once the prescribed period has elapsed. The Discipline Committee has discretion to fix as part of their decision the period of time that must elapse before a member can reapply for membership. If the Discipline Committee does not specify the period then a member must wait one year.[20] To be reinstated, a member has to satisfy the College that he or she ought to be readmitted to the profession. A suspended member is not a member of the College for the duration of the suspension. The suspension cannot last more than 24 months. At the end of the term of the suspension, the member is automatically reinstated and does not have to reapply for membership.

Section 26(5) of the Act states that

If the Discipline Committee finds a member guilty of professional misconduct, it may, in addition to exercising its powers under subsection (4), make an order doing one or more of the following:

1. Requiring that the member be reprimanded, admonished or counseled by the Committee or its delegate and, if considered warranted, directing that the fact of the reprimand, admonishment or counseling be recorded on the register for a specified or an unlimited period.
2. Imposing a fine in an amount that the Committee finds appropriate, to a maximum of $5,000, to be paid by the member to the Minister of Finance for payment into the Consolidated Revenue Fund.
3. Directing the finding and the order of the Committee to be published, in detail or in summary, with or without the name of the member, in the official publication of the College and in any other manner or medium that the Committee considers appropriate in the particular case.
4. Fixing costs to be paid by the member.

---

20. *SWSSW Act*, above note 1, s. 29(4).

The committee is also empowered to make an order requiring the successful completion of a specified course or courses of study.

F.   Penalty Considerations

As can be seen, the committee has some discretion in determining the penalty for a member convicted of professional misconduct or incompetence. When deciding what the penalty should be, the panel will consider the purpose of the College, which is to protect the public. Any penalty imposed must satisfy this purpose. In addition, penalties may be viewed as sending a message to other members of the profession about what is appropriate conduct; a penalty not seen as a deterrent may send the wrong message to the profession. A penalty should also be substantial enough to ensure that the member does not engage in the censured activity again, but not so severe as to discourage rehabilitation.

A review of the case law involving disciplinary decisions under the *Regulated Health Professions Act, 1991* indicates that a discipline committee should consider a number of factors when determining a penalty, including whether the conduct complained of was part of a pattern of similar conduct, involved a breach of trust, was motivated by financial gain, or could be considered immoral or dishonest. The case law indicates that conduct of the types just listed should be dealt with more severely than other types of conduct. Some leniency will usually be shown towards members whose conduct was the result of a substance abuse problem or psychiatric illness.

If the Discipline Committee determines that an allegation of professional misconduct or incompetence was unfounded it will, at the member's request, publish its conclusions in the College's official publication. And if the committee believes that the proceeding was unwarranted, it has the discretion to order the College to reimburse all or part of the costs incurred by the member.[21]

---

21.   *Ibid.*, s. 26(9).

Chapter 6

Incapacity and Fitness to Practise

A.   Introduction

One of the obligations of a professional regulatory body is to ensure that its members maintain a continuing level of competence in all areas. In addition to maintaining the requisite skill and knowledge a social worker must also be physically and mentally fit to practise. Incapacity deals with members who are sick, whether it is from psychological causes such as burnout, stress, secondary trauma, or addictions such as alcohol or drugs, or from physical causes such as disease. The *Social Work and Social Service Work Act, 1998* states that the Fitness to Practise Committee "may, after a hearing, find a member of the College to be incapacitated if, in its opinion, the member is suffering from a physical or mental condition or disorder such that . . . the member is unfit to continue to carry out his or her professional responsibilities."[1] Incapacity impairs a member's ability to carry out these responsibilities. His or her work-related performance diminishes in quality and as a result it is desirable and in keeping with the Act's goal of protecting the public interest that members found to be incapacitated should no longer be able to practise.

The definition of incapacity is broad and certainly open to a great deal of interpretation. Generally speaking, it is not the physical or mental condition or disorder that determines incapacity but the member's reaction to the condition or disorder. A member can have a disability or serious illness and still not be considered incapacitated. What makes a member incapacitated is an inability to judge whether the disability or illness is seriously impairing his or her ability to practise. Members who demonstrate no insight into their disability or illness are more likely to be deemed incapacitated than those who do.

---

1.   *Social Work and Social Service Work Act, 1998* [*SWSSW Act*], S.O. 1998, s. 27(2).

Frederic Reamer, an American authority on social work ethics, defines impairment as follows:

> Interference in professional functioning that is reflected in one or more of the following ways: (a) an inability and/or unwillingness to acquire and integrate professional standards into one's repertoire of professional behaviour; (b) an inability to acquire professional skills in order to reach an acceptable level of competence; and (c) an inability to control personal stress, psychological dysfunction, and/or excessive emotional reactions that interfere with professional functioning.[2]

Fitness to practise inquiries usually involve the third type of impairment listed by Reamer. Typically, the member's professional behaviour is being impaired by a psychiatric condition or substance abuse problem.

Whereas disciplinary proceedings focus on laying blame and punishing, fitness to practise proceedings are aimed at helping the member while protecting the public. The goals are to ensure that the member gets adequate treatment for his or her illness and, if possible, to continue practising, but under College supervision. It is thus unusual at the end of a fitness to practise hearing for the College to suspend or revoke the certificate of registration of a cooperative member who has demonstrated a desire to get better.

B.   Initiating a Fitness to Practise Hearing

A fitness to practise hearing can be initiated in one of two ways: from the results of a registrar's investigation, or by referral from the Complaints Committee. Under section 32 of the *Social Work and Social Service Work Act, 1998*, the registrar himself or herself also has the power to initiate an inquiry into a member's apparent incapacity. If the registrar believes on reasonable and probable grounds that a member is incapacitated, he or she can appoint an investigator to investigate whether the member truly is incapacitated. The registrar cannot, however, appoint an investigator without the approval of the Executive Committee. Presumably the registrar himself or herself has to informally investigate the situation before being in a position to conclude that there are reasonable and probable grounds for recommending the appointment of an investigator.[3] For a more detailed discussion of the registrar's overall powers of investigation see chapter 7.

As we have seen, the Complaints Committee is initially charged with investigating a complaint against a member. The committee may, after an

---

2.   F.G. Reamer, *Ethical Standards in Social Work: A Critical Review of the NASW Code of Ethics* (Washington, DC: NASW Press, 1998) at 134.

3.   *SWSSW Act*, above note 1, s. 32 (1).

investigation, recommend referring the complaint to the Fitness to Practise Committee. It will do this if it believes that the member is ill or behaving unusually. After receiving the recommendation from the Complaints Committee, the council or the Executive Committee may direct the Fitness to Practise Committee to hold a hearing on the member's alleged incapacity.[4] By using the word "may" section 25(2) of the Act would suggest that the council and the Executive Committee have the power to not order a hearing even if the Complaints Committee recommends one. The decision to hold a hearing requires a balancing of the member's right to privacy against the College's obligation to protect the public. It is probable that a hearing will be ordered only if the council or Executive Committee is satisfied that there is genuine reason to be concerned about the effect of the member's disability or illness on his or her ability to practise.

C.   The Investigation

During its investigation, the Complaints Committee will usually review all of the documentation supporting the allegations. It will then interview the member and possibly obtain witness statements from clients, co-workers, and relatives. It may also obtain, with the member's consent, copies of the member's medical records. In cases where there is some concern that a member's physical illness, for example, may be impairing his or her clinical judgment the Complaints Committee may also obtain copies of the member's client records. In addition to looking for medical evidence of a physical or mental illness, the committee might also look for evidence of unusual, bizarre, or inappropriate behaviour. Unusual or bizarre behaviour could establish that the member's illness is affecting his or her clinical judgment. The committee is therefore entitled to look at more than just medical evidence during its inquiries.[5]

Unlike the Procedural Code of the *Regulated Health Professions Act, 1991*[6] (RHPA), there is no provision in the *Social Work and Social Service Work Act, 1998* that allows the committee to order the member to undergo a physical or mental examination. Under the RHPA a member can be ordered to undergo a medical examination. The medical examination is conducted by a specialist in the illness or condition the member is alleged to be suffering from. For example, a psychiatrist would be used in the event the member was suffering from a mental illness or condition. Since the *Social Work and*

---

4.   *Ibid.*, s. 25(2).
5.   *Re Percheson and College of Physicians and Surgeons of Ontario* (1987), 37 D.L.R. (4th) 545 (Ont. Div. Ct.).
6.   S.O. 1991, c. 18., Procedural Code, s. 59.

Social Service Work Act, 1998 does not specifically authorize these examinations it is not within the power of the Complaints Committee to order a social worker to undergo one. The only medical evidence the Committee is able to rely on is the evidence gleaned from the member's medical records.

D.   Interim Orders

One of the concerns the College faces in dealing with the alleged incapacity of a member is balancing the rights of the member with the College's mandate to protect the public. Allowing a member to continue practising while an incapacity investigation is taking place can in some circumstances put the member's clients at risk. For that reason the Act provides that the council or Executive Committee can make an interim order directing the registrar to suspend a member's certificate of registration or impose terms, conditions, or limitations on the certificate if

a)   an allegation respecting the member has been referred to the Fitness to Practise Committee, and

b)   the council or the Executive Committee believes that the actions or conduct of the member in the course of his or her practice exposes or is likely to expose a person or persons to harm or injury.[7]

This interim order cannot be made until the member has been notified of the council's or Executive Committee's intention to make the order and has had at least 14 days to respond in writing.[8] Moreover, it will be made only if the council or Executive Committee is satisfied that the member's clients could be exposed to harm or injury if the member continued practising.

If the council or Executive Committee believes that the risk is great, it may ignore the 14-day requirement and immediately suspend the member's certificate without holding a hearing or affording the member an opportunity to respond orally or in writing.[9]

An interim order to suspend a member's certificate of registration continues in force until the member's case is disposed of by the Fitness to Practise Committee. This rule obviously has the potential to create significant financial hardship for the member. Accordingly, if an interim order is made, the College is required to give the member's case precedence and prosecute it expeditiously.

---

7.   *SWSSW Act*, above note 1, s. 25(3).
8.   *Ibid.*, s. 25(4).
9.   *Ibid.*, s. 25(5).

E.   The Hearing

The College and the member whose conduct is being investigated are the parties to the hearing. The complainant is not a party and has no status in the proceeding other than as a witness.

Before the hearing begins, the member must be allowed an opportunity to examine any documents that will be given in evidence. This is called disclosure and is usually accomplished by giving the member or his or her lawyer copies of all of the relevant documents.

Unlike discipline hearings, fitness to practise hearings are usually closed to the public, presumably because these hearings are not intended to be punitive and focus on very personal health issues.[10]

A fitness to practise hearing may be open to the public or other members of the College, however, if the member who is the subject of the proceeding requests an open hearing in writing before the hearing begins. The Fitness to Practise Committee can refuse the request if it believes that

a)   matters involving public security may be disclosed;

b)   financial or personal or other matters may be disclosed at the hearing of such a nature that the desirability of avoiding public disclosure of them in the interest of any person affected or in the public interest outweighs the desirability of acceding to the request of the person who is alleged to be incapacitated;

c)   a person involved in a civil or criminal proceeding may be prejudiced;

d)   the safety of a person may be jeopardized.[11]

Although fitness to practise hearings are similar to discipline hearings, there are some important differences. Because fitness to practise hearings focus on the member's health and not on punishment, the rules of evidence are more relaxed. The committee can accept documents without having to enter them into evidence and witnesses can testify to events that they did not personally observe. Hearsay evidence is also acceptable.

A court reporter records all of the oral evidence given by witnesses at fitness to practise hearings. Transcripts are provided to the parties at their expense if requested.[12] Documents and other items entered into evidence at a hearing are returned to the parties who supplied them (but again, only if requested). These items are never returned until the hearing is over.

The burden of proving that the member is incapacitated rests with the College, but because fitness to practise proceedings are not meant to be punitive,

---

10.   *Ibid.*, s. 28(9).
11.   *Ibid.*, s. 28(10).
12.   *Ibid.*, s. 28(12).

the burden is less restrictive than that which applies to discipline hearings. Just as the council appoints the members of the Discipline Committee, so it does for the Fitness to Practise Committee as well. The make-up of the committee and the procedure followed by the council to appoint committee members was discussed more fully in chapter 2. The Fitness to Practise Committee chairperson will then appoint a panel of members from among the committee members to hear a particular incapacity matter.[13]

Fitness to Practise Committee members who participate in a hearing can do so only if they have not been involved in any investigation of the case before the hearing begins, other than as members of the body (council or Executive Committee) that referred the matter to the Fitness to Practise Committee. Committee members are not permitted to contact either directly or indirectly any witnesses, party, or representative of a party, except on notice to all of the parties. All of the parties must be allowed to attend the hearing and be given an opportunity to participate and make submissions to the panel hearing the case. These procedures ensure not only a fair hearing but remove any suggestion of bias on the part of the committee members.

Most panels rely on independent advisors, usually lawyers, for advice in legal matters. If such advice is obtained, it is disclosed to the parties so that they can make submissions on the points of law addressed by the advice.[14] The role of the advisors was discussed more fully in chapter 5. A member of the Fitness to Practise Committee cannot rule on a matter unless he or she is present throughout the hearing and hears all of the evidence and legal arguments.[15]

F.   The Decision

Section 27(2) of the Act states that

> The Fitness to Practise Committee may, after a hearing, find a member of the College to be incapacitated if, in its opinion, the member is suffering from a physical or mental condition or disorder such that,
>
> a)   the member is unfit to continue to carry out his or her professional responsibilities; or
> b)   a certificate of registration held by the member under this Act should be made subject to terms, conditions or limitations.

The first decision the committee must make is to decide whether the member is incapacitated. A finding of incapacity is usually based on evidence

---

13.   *Ibid.*, s. 14.
14.   *Ibid.*, s. 28(5).
15.   *Ibid.*, s. 28(13).

from health professionals who have treated the member. Once a committee determines that a member is incapacitated, it must then decide what conditions or restrictions it should place on the member's certificate of registration. Section 27(3) of the Act states that

> If the Fitness to Practise Committee finds a member to be incapacitated, it shall make an order doing one or more of the following:
>
> 1)   Directing the registrar to revoke the member's certificate of registration.
> 2)   Directing the registrar to suspend the member's certificate of registration for a specified period, not exceeding 24 months.
> 3)   Directing the registrar to impose specified terms, conditions or limitations on the member's certificate of registration.
> 4)   Directing that the imposition of a penalty be postponed for a specified period and not be imposed if specified terms are met within that period.

The committee is required to provide a written decision (including a statement of its reasons for the decision) and to serve the decision on the parties.[16] The committee usually orders treatment followed by a return to practice under supervision. If, for example, a member's professional behaviour is affected by a substance abuse problem, the committee may order the member to undergo a treatment program in a facility approved by the College, with the member's certificate of registration suspended pending successful completion of the program. After completion of the program the member's certificate of registration could be reinstated with the condition that the member undergo regular drug testing for a further specified period. Another order might require regular psychiatric reports until the member's psychiatrist certifies that the member no longer needs psychiatric monitoring.

If the committee determines that an allegation of incapacity was unfounded it will, at the member's request, publish its conclusions in the College's official publication. And if the committee believes that the hearing was unwarranted, it may order the College to reimburse all or part of the costs incurred by the member.

As part of its decision the committee can also impose a waiting period before a member may apply to the registrar to have his or her certificate reinstated or the conditions placed on it removed. A member who wants to have his or her certificate reinstated or any conditions that were placed on it removed must apply in writing to the registrar. Upon receipt of the request from the member, the registrar must refer it to the Fitness to Practise Committee for their consideration. Under section 29 of the Act, the member must be able to prove to the Fitness to Practise Committee that there has been a

---

16.   *Ibid.*, s. 28(15).

change in circumstances justifying a reinstatement or removal of conditions. The procedure is similar to that of a fitness to practise hearing, although the evidence presented is usually limited to documentation.

A member also has the right to appeal a decision of the Fitness to Practise Committee to the Ontario Divisional Court.[17] The appeal can be brought on a question of law, fact, or both. The Act gives the court all the powers of the Fitness to Practise Committee, which means that it can make any order on appeal that the committee could have made in the first instance. Again, as in discipline decisions, an appeal from a fitness to practise order or decision does not operate a stay of that decision or order. The decision will take effect immediately notwithstanding the member's appeal.

17. *Ibid.*, s. 31(1).

Chapter 7

Investigations and Appeals

A.   The Registrar's Powers of Investigation

Although we briefly touched on the registrar's powers of investigation as they related to discipline and fitness to practise matters in chapters 5 and 6, respectively, these powers warrant further discussion here. When these powers are used they have a significant intrusive impact on a member's professional life. Under section 32 of the *Social Work and Social Service Work Act, 1998*,[1] the registrar has broad powers to investigate allegations of improper conduct against a member. Section 32(1) of the Act reads as follows:

> If the Registrar believes on reasonable and probable grounds,
>
> a)   that a member of the College has committed an act of professional misconduct or is incompetent or incapacitated,
> b)   that there is cause to refuse to issue a certificate applied for under this Act,
> c)   that there is cause to suspend or revoke a certificate issued under this Act; or
> d)   that there is cause to impose terms, conditions or limitations on a certificate applied for or issued under this Act,
>
> the Registrar may appoint one or more investigators to investigate whether such act has occurred, such incompetence or incapacity exists or there is such cause.

In a formal investigation, a member may be called on to answer an investigator's questions orally or in writing and to produce records and files for inspection. An investigation can therefore significantly disrupt a member's work. The most serious consequence of an investigation is that it may

---

1.   *Social Work and Social Service Work Act, 1998* [*SWSSW Act*], S.O. 1998, c. 31.

uncover evidence of wrongdoing or misconduct that can lead to a disciplinary hearing.

Before the registrar can appoint an investigator, there must, as we have seen, be "reasonable and probable grounds" for the appointment. The phrase "reasonable and probable grounds," which appears in section 32(1) of the Act, has been interpreted by the Supreme Court of Canada to mean "the point where credibility based probability replaces suspicion."[2]

If a decision or order of the College flowing from an investigation is appealed, the court may look at whether there were reasonable and probable grounds to appoint an investigator. The threshold for satisfying the reasonable and probable grounds test in disciplinary cases is lower than in criminal cases. It can be established by a combination of the following factors: specific details of the alleged offence, information from a reliable individual who is in a position to know what occurred, and some evidence of corroboration of the details obtained from another source.

A portion of section 32(1) also states that the registrar must believe that the member has committed an act of professional misconduct or is incompetent or incapacitated. This is a subjective requirement and therefore difficult to challenge. It is usually satisfied by the registrar simply recording his or her belief.

Executive Committee approval is the final requirement that must be satisfied before an investigator can be appointed. Executive Committee approval is a way to guard against improper initiation of an investigation. To obtain approval, the registrar writes a report for the Executive Committee.

The formal appointment of an investigator is usually made in writing. The wording of the appointment is critical. Wording that is too broad or vague could be successfully challenged in court. Wording that is too narrow places undue restrictions on the investigator's powers.

The registrar cannot appoint an investigator without the approval of the Executive Committee. Once approval is obtained, the Act empowers the investigator to "inquire into and examine the conduct or actions of the member to be investigated as the conduct or actions relate to the matter the Registrar sought to be investigated in appointing the investigator."[3] After showing the member the document containing the appointment, the investigator may enter the member's place of work or the premises of the member's employer at any reasonable time. While there, the investigator is empowered to examine anything he or she finds that is relevant to the investigation.[4] The investigator's power to obtain records overrides any rights of confidentiality that may be attached to those records.

---

2. *Hunter* v. *Southam Inc.* (1984), 11 D.L.R. (4th) (S.C.C.) 641 at 659.
3. *Ibid.*, s. 32(3).
4. *Ibid.*, s. 32(5).

If a member obstructs an investigator in the course of his or her duties, or destroys or hides evidence that is relevant to the investigation, he or she can be found guilty of an offence under section 55(2) of the Act and may be liable to a fine of not more than $10,000. It is always preferable for a member to cooperate with an investigator, because failure to do so may be interpreted as evidence of guilt and lend credence to the allegations against the member. Failure to cooperate may also constitute professional misconduct. The requirement that a member must cooperate with an investigator in the gathering of evidence against the member is one of the most distinctive characteristics of professional self-governance. Whereas in a criminal investigation a person has a right to remain silent, no such right exists in a professional investigation.

The member is afforded some protection, however, by section 8 of the *Canadian Charter of Rights and Freedoms*,[5] which states that "Everyone has the right to be secure against unreasonable search and seizure." The courts, including the Supreme Court of Canada, have determined that registrars' investigations can constitute a search or seizure. Because actions such as entering a member's premises and seizing files and documents may constitute an unreasonable search or seizure, a member under investigation should always obtain legal representation.[6] Consulting a lawyer at this stage not only assists the member in responding to the investigation but ensures that the college has satisfied the conditions necessary to prove that the search in question is a valid one. The most significant conditions are the registrar's belief and the presence of reasonable and probable grounds.

In addition to the power to search a member's place of work, an investigator can search any other place and examine anything that is relevant to the investigation at that place on obtaining a search warrant from a justice of the peace.[7] A justice of the peace will issue a search warrant if he or she is satisfied that the investigator has been properly appointed and that there are reasonable and probable grounds for believing that

a) the member being investigated has committed an act of professional misconduct or is incompetent or incapacitated; and

b) there is something relevant to the investigation at the place.[8]

The search warrant is executable only during daylight hours unless it specifies otherwise. The investigator is entitled to engage others to assist him or

---

5. *Canadian Charter of Rights and Freedoms*, Part I of the *Constitution Act, 1982*, being Schedule B to the *Canada Act 1982* (U.K.), 1982, c. 11.

6. R. Steinecke, *A Complete Guide to the Regulated Health Professions Act* (Aurora, ON: Canada Law Book, 1995), at p. 5.1.

7. *SWSSW Act*, above note 1, s. 33(1).

8. *Ibid.*

her and has the authority to enter a place by force if entry is refused (in which case the investigator is likely to ask the police for assistance). The investigator is required to produce identification and the search warrant at the member's request.

The potential impact of section 33(1) on a member cannot be overstated. Not only does the investigator have the right to search the member's place of work, but with a valid search warrant he or she can also search the member's place of residence or any other place that the member frequents if the investigator believes there is something relevant to the investigation to be found there. The investigator can, for example, search the member's locker at a health club if he or she believes documents relevant to the investigation are kept there.

The member can expect that the investigator will want to copy any documents he or she believes are relevant to the investigation, including electronic documents, appointment books, and dates of client's attendances, employment, and billing records. Copying is done at the College's expense. Because of the importance of keeping one's professional files and other professional papers intact, it is infinitely better to arrange, if possible, for the investigator to take copies rather than originals. The investigator, however, has the power to remove original files and documents if copying is not practicable or if the investigator believes that obtaining the originals is necessary for the investigation (for example, if the authenticity of a record is at issue).[9] An investigator who takes an original must give the member a copy within a reasonable time and must also return the original within a reasonable time.

Because the role of the investigator is to gather facts, not to determine guilt, it is unlikely that the investigator is obliged to give the member prior notice of his or her visit, to provide particulars of the allegations being investigated, or to tell the member what evidence has been gathered.

An investigator is entitled to interview any witnesses believed to be relevant to the investigation, including the member's employers, employees, colleagues, and teachers, as well as professionals who have referred clients to the member or been consulted by the member.

Once the investigation is completed, the registrar reports the results to one or more of five committees, as he or she sees fit. These committees are the Executive Committee, the Registration Appeals Committee, the Complaints Committee, the Discipline Committee, and the Fitness to Practise Committee.[10] Reports received by the Complaints Committee, Discipline Committee, or Fitness to Practise Committee will then be handled as outlined in the previous chapters on those topics.

---

9.   *Ibid.*, s. 34(2).
10.   *Ibid.*, s. 35.

B.   Appeals and Reinstatements

All decisions and orders of the Registration Appeals Committee, the Discipline Committee, and the Fitness to Practise Committee are reviewable by the Ontario Divisional Court.[11] Having an appeal process in place helps ensure that the College follows its own procedures and fairly and reasonably applies its rules and regulations. The court, however, will usually defer to the expertise of the Registration Appeals Committee and will not require that committee to exercise its discretion in a particular way. Decisions of the Discipline and Fitness to Practise committees, on the other hand, are more susceptible to review. Discipline and fitness to practise hearings can be very lengthy and complex. It is common for procedural, jurisdictional, or evidentiary issues to arise during the course of a hearing which the applicable panel must rule on. These rulings can have a significant impact on the outcome of the hearing, so it is not unusual for the party who got an adverse ruling to appeal that ruling to the court. Sometimes these appeals take place while the hearing is still ongoing.

For an appeal to the Divisional Court, a member or the member's legal representative must obtain a certified copy of the record of the committee proceeding being appealed from, including transcripts of evidence, copies of any documents received in evidence, and a copy of the order or decision in question. The College by-laws prescribe a fee for this service.

The powers of the Divisional Court on an appeal are far-reaching. Section 31(4) of the Act states that

> An appeal under this section may be made on questions of law or fact or both and the court may affirm or may rescind the decision of the committee appealed from and may exercise all powers of the committee and may direct the committee to take any action which the committee may take and that the court considers appropriate and, for the purpose, the court may substitute its opinion for that of the committee or the court may refer the matter back to the committee for rehearing, in whole or in part, in accordance with any directions the court considers appropriate.

Unusual for a regulated profession in Ontario, an appeal to the Divisional Court does not automatically stay a committee's decision or order. Most orders under the *Regulated Health Professions Act, 1991*,[12] for example, are automatically stayed when an appeal is launched. Appeals can take at least a year to be heard, and it is obvious that the unavailability of a stay can create hardship for a social worker who is unable to practise because his or her certificate of registration has been suspended or revoked. The rules of court, however, give the court discretion to impose a stay in appropriate cases. To

---

11.   *SWSSW Act*, above note 1, s. 31(1).
12.   S.O. 1991, c. 18.

obtain a stay, the member's lawyer must apply to the court. There is no guarantee, of course, that the court will order a stay.

In addition to the appeal process the Act provides a mechanism for a member asking the College to reinstate his or her certificate of registration. These provisions in section 29 apply equally to decisions and orders made by the Fitness to Practise Committee.[13]

The Act allows a member whose certificate of registration has been suspended or revoked to go before the Discipline Committee to ask for reinstatement after a certain amount of time has passed.[14] The member must first apply in writing to the registrar for a new certificate or removal of the suspension, as the case may be. The member may also ask for any conditions, terms, or limitations imposed by the Discipline Committee to be removed or modified.[15] The registrar then forwards the application to the Discipline Committee.

Section 29(3) of the Act states that a member cannot apply to the registrar for one year from the date of the Discipline Committee's decision and order. A longer waiting period can be imposed by the Discipline Committee as a condition of their original decision.

At the hearing, the member (or his or her lawyer) presents arguments in support of the application. The College is also a party to this hearing and can appear before the Discipline Committee if it wishes. Before the hearing begins, the member and the committee are required to disclose to each other the documents they intend to use at the hearing. If requested by the member, a record of the oral evidence given at the hearing will be made. The member can also ask for transcripts (at his or her expense). Although a record of the oral evidence is not required, a member should always ask for a record to be made in case he or she decides to appeal the committee's decision.

The Discipline Committee is required to provide its decision in writing, with reasons. The College then serves a copy of the decision on the member. To participate in the decision, a committee member must be present throughout the hearing and hear all of the evidence and arguments presented by the parties. A decision made by a panel that includes a member who was not present throughout the hearing is likely to be overturned on appeal.

The Act also includes a provision that allows an application for reinstatement to be handled without a hearing. Section 30 of the Act states that the council or the Executive Committee may make an order directing the registrar to issue the member a certificate of registration or remove a suspension.

The Act is silent on when or how the section 30 procedure can be invoked. It appears to be invocable at the discretion of the council or Executive Com-

---

13. *SWSSW Act*, above note 1, s. 29(14).
14. *Ibid.*, s. 29(1).
15. *Ibid.*, s. 29(2).

mittee and is probably available only for minor disciplinary problems. It is highly unlikely that a member guilty of serious misconduct could have his or her certificate of registration reinstated without a formal hearing. The other apparent difficulty with the reinstatement process is the one-year waiting period before a member can bring an application for reinstatement. From a member's point of view this makes an appeal more attractive as appeals can usually be heard within a year.

Chapter 8

Professional Misconduct

A.   Introduction

The degree to which the public can trust a profession is ultimately determined by its members' collective commitment to integrity. A code of ethical standards professionalizes an occupation by creating an implied social contract with the public that purports to balance professional privilege with responsibility and a commitment to consumer welfare.[1]

Integrity is considered a fundamental requirement for a member of any profession. If a member is dishonest in his or her dealings with clients, the College or third parties, all of whom have placed their trust and reliance on the social worker, then it cannot be said that the social worker has the requisite integrity to be a member of the profession.

B.   Ontario Regulation 384/00

The *Social Work and Social Service Work Act, 1998* provides that the Discipline Committee may find a member of the College guilty of professional misconduct if, after a hearing, the Committee believes that the member has engaged in conduct that "is defined as being professional misconduct in the regulations."[2] The applicable regulation, Ontario Regulation 384/00, is reprinted in its entirety as Appendix III. Passed by the College, it divides acts of professional misconduct into five broad categories, each of which is given its own section of the regulation. These are the categories:

---

1.   G.P. Koocher & P. Keith-Spiegel, *Ethics in Psychotherapy, Professional Standards & Cases* (New York, NY: Oxford University Press) 1998 at 27.

2.   *Social Work and Social Service Work Act, 1998* [*SWSSW Act*], S.O. 1998, c. 31, s. 26(2).

1. The practice of the profession and the care of, and relationship with, clients
2. Representations about members and their qualifications
3. Record keeping and reports
4. Business practices
5. Miscellaneous matters

Of the 36 acts of professional misconduct described in the regulation, 14 belong to the first category. The remaining categories include, respectively, four, four, five, and nine acts of professional misconduct. The acts are numbered sequentially from 1 to 36.

As can be seen from a review of the regulation, professional misconduct can have both an ethical and a legal component. In order to determine whether a particular behaviour is professional misconduct, it is necessary to determine whether the behaviour falls within the applicable definition. This involves interpreting the meaning of the wording of the definition. As we shall see this can sometimes be a very difficult task for the Discipline Committee. It is important to note at this point that as the standards of professional misconduct have been left to self-governing tribunals to interpret, courts will only intervene if the Committee's interpretation is unreasonable. Self-governing tribunals are thought to be better qualified to both establish the standards and then to judge any departures from those standards.

I.   The Practice of the Profession and the Care of, and Relationship with, Clients

The acts of professional misconduct in this section of the regulation relate to the practice of social work and the relationship between social workers and their clients. Some of the acts are self-explanatory, such as contravening a term, condition, or limitation imposed on the member's certificate of registration; discontinuing professional services that are needed except under certain circumstances; giving information about a client to a person other than the client or his or her authorized representative; breaching a term of an agreement with a client relating to the fees for professional services, and failing to supervise adequately a person who is under the professional responsibility of the member. Other acts have been or will be discussed elsewhere in this book and include: abusing a client physically, sexually, verbally, psychologically, or emotionally; practising the profession while under the influence of any substance or while suffering from an illness or dysfunction that impairs the member's ability to practise; and using information obtained during a professional relationship with a client or using one's professional position of authority to coerce, improperly influence, harass, or exploit a client or former client.

Some of the acts, however, require a further explanation or commentary. It is professional misconduct, for example, to fail to meet the standards of the profession[3]. But what are the standards of the profession and how are they measured? This is the difficulty that faces both a member in trying to abide by the standards and a Discipline Committee in trying to determine if a member has breached the standards. The standards of the profession have been defined as the standard that is reasonably expected of the ordinary competent practitioner in the member's field of practice.[4] It is important to note that not every error or mistake in judgment ought to be disciplined. A mere lapse in judgment that is not indicative of a pattern of conduct will not usually be prosecuted. The exception is sexual abuse of a client by a social worker. A review of the social work complaints process in Canada reveals that the primary areas of risk for clients include child protection decisions, court-ordered custody assessments, breaches of confidence, and sexual abuse. The latter is the area of most concern for regulatory bodies. For the most part, social workers see their clients in private. It is this privacy, coupled with the vulnerability of the client and the nature of the therapeutic relationship, that provides the best opportunity for sexual exploitation of the client. In recent years, many professional colleges have developed a "zero tolerance" policy concerning sex with patients and clients. At the same time, the courts have begun looking more closely at the duties and obligations of professionals to their patients and clients. What was once considered merely "sexual impropriety" is today condemned in the strongest terms as "sexual abuse" — behaviour that is considered a breach of trust and a breach of the professional's fiduciary duty to the patient or client,[5] in addition to being ethically improper.

It is professional misconduct to do anything to a client in the course of practising the profession in a situation in which consent is required by law, without such consent.[6] This act of professional misconduct, on the other hand, is an example of a clearly worded prohibited act. It is quite clear that a social worker who does anything to a client without his or her consent will have committed an act of professional misconduct. As we will see in later chapters, obtaining informed consent from a client is an integral part of the accepted standard of practice of the profession.

It is professional misconduct to abuse a client physically, sexually, verbally, psychologically, or emotionally, including sexually abusing a client

---

3.   O Reg. 384/00, s. 2.
4.   *Heurto* v. *College of Physicians & Surgeons* (1994), 117 D.L.R. (4th) 129 (Sask Q.B.), aff'd 133 D.L.R. (4th) 100 (C.A.).
5.   *Norberg* v. *Wynrib* (1992), 92 D.L.R. (4th) 449 (S.C.C.).
6.   O. Reg. 384/00, s. 3.

within the meaning of subsection 43(4) of the Act.[7] The issue of sexual misconduct is explored more fully in chapter 12, but this section refers to more than sexual contact with a client; it refers to all inappropriate behaviour towards a client. This could include rudeness or lack of civility by the social worker in correspondence, telephone calls, or in person. It could include yelling or screaming or speaking harshly or using insulting language.

It is professional misconduct to provide a professional service while the member is in a conflict of interest.[8] This is another example of an act that is not clearly defined. It can be argued that virtually every decision made by a practitioner has personal consequences and is therefore a conflict of interest. A practitioner who provides counselling to a client and recommends further counselling benefits from the fees paid by that client. A conflict of interest exists where a social worker's interest could reasonably give rise to the danger of influencing the social worker's professional duty. Regrettably this section provides no insight into what the interest might involve. There are several types of interests that could apply. Material interests are the financial benefits that a member might receive as a result of influencing a client to make a particular decision. Examples might include splitting fees with a third party in exchange for referrals, or accepting gifts from clients. Personal interests involve family and personal relationships. Personal interests tend to reduce the member's ability to act solely in the best interest of the client. Examples might include entering into a business relationship with a client or counselling a family member. Moral interests relate to the member's values and convictions and include his or her religious convictions. Examples might include difficulty dealing with a client considering an abortion or struggling with the aftermath of an extramarital affair. As can be seen, this is an area where the College could provide some guidance and ultimately draft a conflict of interest regulation similar to the regulations present for other professions in the Regulated Health Professions Act.

II.   Representations about Members and Their Qualifications

The four acts of professional misconduct listed under the heading of representations about members and their qualifications are designed to guard against misuse of the titles of social worker and social service worker. A member is required to identify himself or herself as a social worker when providing social work services. The same holds true for social service workers. The acts include inappropriately using a term, title or designation in respect of the member's practice.[9] Both the regulation and the Act are quite

---

7.   *Ibid.*, s. 5.
8.   *Ibid.*, s. 10.
9.   *Ibid.*, s. 15.

clear in prohibiting an individual from using a title he or she is not entitled to. In this instance a court would uphold the provision because the wording is clear and explicit. Simply put, unless an individual is registered with the College, he or she is simply not allowed to call himself or herself a social worker or a social service worker.

III.　Record Keeping and Reports

The four acts listed under the heading of record keeping and reports are as follows:

19. Falsifying a record relating to the member's practice.
20. Failing to keep records as required by the regulations and standards of the profession.
21. Making a record, or issuing or signing a certificate, report or other document in the course of practising the profession that the member knows or ought reasonably to know is false, misleading or otherwise improper.
22. Failing, without reasonable cause, to provide a report or certificate relating to a service performed by the member, within a reasonable time, to the client or his or her authorized representative after a client or his or her authorized representative has made a written request for such a report or certificate.[10]

A social worker who refuses or fails to provide a report after one has been requested by the client can jeopardize a patient's legal rights or interfere with his or her ability to get treatment. It also prevents the client from exercising his or her right to see what is in the social work record. For a more detailed discussion of the professional issues surrounding record keeping, see chapter 10.

IV.　Business Practices

The acts of misconduct described under the heading of business practices are most relevant to social workers in private practice. The acts include failing to inform the client, before or at the commencement of a service, of the fees and charges to be levied for the service, and for late cancellations or missed appointments, submitting an account or charge for services that the member knows is false or misleading, and charging a fee that is excessive in relation to the service performed. This is an area that can easily be abused by a social worker. Vulnerable clients in need of the services provided by the social worker are unlikely to refuse or question the social worker's fees or his or her recommendations for treatment.

10.　*Ibid.*, ss. 19-22.

V.   Miscellaneous Matters

The remaining acts of professional misconduct listed in the regulation are truly a hodge-podge of miscellaneous matters. Some of the sections are self-evident, such as the one stating that it is professional misconduct to contravene any provision of the Act or regulations or by-laws. Others are more difficult to understand, such as section 29, which states that the following is professional misconduct:

> Contravening a federal, provincial or territorial law or a municipal by-law if,
> i.   the purpose of the law or by-law is to protect public health, or
> ii.   the contravention is relevant to the member's suitability to practise.[11]

It can be argued that whether a member has contravened a federal or provincial law or a municipal by-law goes to the member's suitability to practise the profession. The difficulty is deciding which offenses are relevant to the member's suitability to practise. Offenses involving violence, abuse, or dishonesty such as fraud are easy to judge. Other offenses, impaired driving, for example, may be more difficult to judge. It is left to the Discipline Committee to look at the particular circumstances of each case before it to make the determination. The other difficulty surrounds the meaning of contravention. Does that only include a conviction, or can it also mean that a finding of guilt will suffice? A conditional discharge in a criminal matter, for example, means that the member has not been convicted of the offense, although a finding of guilt has still been made. A very different result occurs depending on the interpretation of contravention in this example.

Sections 31, 32, 33 and 34 of the regulation all deal with the member's obligations in relation to his or her dealings with the College. Some of the acts of professional misconduct include failing to comply with an order of a panel of the Complaints Committee, Discipline Committee, or Fitness to Practise Committee of the College, failing to comply with a written undertaking given to the College, failing to co-operate with a College investigation, and failing to take reasonable steps to ensure that all requested information is provided in a complete and accurate manner where a member is required to provide information to the College.

The rationale for these provisions is simple. In exchange for the privilege of having a monopoly over titles, designations and areas of practice, the member submits to the authority of the College over him or her. With the rights afforded a social worker under the Act comes the obligation to accept governance by the College, and a failure by the member to accede to this authority is professional misconduct under this regulation.

---

11.   *Ibid.*, s. 29.

All professional misconduct regulations have what is commonly referred to as a "catchall" provision. Social Work regulation 384/00 is no exception. Section 36 describes the last act of professional misconduct as follows:

> Engaging in conduct or performing an act relevant to the practice of the profession that, having regard to all circumstances, would reasonably be regarded by members as disgraceful, dishonourable or unprofessional.[12]

This section is designed to catch any improper behaviour that was not caught by the wording of the other sections in the regulation. The section is broad in scope and encompasses any conduct that is considered disgraceful, dishonourable, or unprofessional. The determination of this is made by the profession. The acceptability of the conduct reflects the values of the profession, not the values of the general public. It assumes, however, that there is a general consensus with the members of the profession as to what conduct is acceptable. More often than not this is not the case. What is acceptable in a large cosmopolitan urban centre may not be acceptable in a small rural centre. Although the section refers to conduct relevant to the practice of the profession, it can be argued that any conduct outside the actual practice of the profession might be included in this section if the conduct in question is thought to have affected the member's professional character or integrity.

C.   Conclusion

Misconduct that is not clearly defined leaves members with the impossible task of trying to comply with provisions they do not fully understand. Undefined acts or standards that lack clarity or precision in their wording are more likely to be successfully challenged by a member in court than clearly worded acts. A legal case illustrative of this point is *White* v. *North Carolina St. Bd. of Examiners of Practicing Psychologists.*[13] Although the case involved a psychologist, the court's comments are very apropos. In that case the Board of Examiners voted to revoke White's psychologist's license to practise for violating various ethical principles. White filed a complaint against the Board in state court claiming that various principles under which he was charged were unconstitutionally vague and did not provide him with proper notice of the potential misconduct. He alleged that it was fundamentally unfair for the Board to deprive him of his right to practise on the basis of standards that were not comprehensible to the reasonably intelligent psychologist. Although the court rejected his complaint, the decision could be

---

12.   *Ibid.*, s. 36.
13.   97 N.C. App 144, 388 SE (2d) 148 (1990), review denied, 326 N.C. 601, 393 SE (2d) 891 (1990).

considered a clear message to all professional regulatory bodies and the drafters of professional standards of what was expected from the standards.

> Psychologists . . . have a right and fundamental need to be guided by ethical codes of conduct of sufficient clarity and specificity to meet applicable constitutional standards and to apprise practitioners of the boundaries of conduct.[14]

The difficulty for social workers trying to comply with the regulation is to determine what misconduct means. While some aspects of the regulation are quite specific, others are quite vague. The regulation uses qualifying words like "reasonable," "adequate," "knows or ought reasonably to know," "appropriate," and "inappropriately." Words like this make it difficult for the member to know what is acceptable and even more difficult for a Discipline Committee to enforce. Using qualifying language as stated above raises the question of whether this regulation can be used to enforce anything but the most serious moral and ethical transgressions, behaviour that is so wrong that the misconduct is self-evident.

---

14.   *Ibid.*, at p. 25.

Chapter 9

Confidentiality

A client's right to confidentiality is one of the most important tenets of social work. The client's right to have difficult and sensitive information about his or her life kept confidential is paramount in a therapist-client relationship. There cannot be an appropriate and meaningful relationship between the therapist and the client if the client is not assured that the information disclosed will be kept private. In *Jaffee* v. *Redmond*,[1] a police officer, Mary Redmond, killed a man in the line of duty. Carrie Jaffee, the administrator of the estate of the deceased, alleged that Redmond had used excessive force. Upon discovering that Redmond had received counselling from a social worker after the shooting, Jaffee sought access to the notes of the sessions. Jaffee brought an application for production of the records to court. The court, in hearing the application, observed that "only if confidentiality was assured would clients feel free to disclose their innermost thoughts. And only if their innermost thoughts were disclosed would therapy be successful."[2] This was the first federal case to recognize the importance of confidentiality in a therapeutic relationship. From this and other cases came the principle that it is ethically and professionally wrong for a social worker to disclose to others information supplied in confidence by a client.

Clients clearly have a right to expect that what they disclose in therapy will be held in strict confidence. The social worker has a legal and moral obligation to respect this confidence. Often, however, the client labours under the misconception that everything told to the social worker is absolutely confidential. This is not true, because there are a number of circumstances where the social worker not only can, but must, breach confidentiality.

---

1.   116 S.Ct. 1923 (1996).
2.   V. Lens, "Protecting the Confidentiality of the Therapeutic Relationship: Jaffee v Redmond" (2000) 45 Social Work 273 at 274.

A.   What is Confidentiality?

Principle V of the College's *Standards of Practice Handbook* (reprinted as Appendix II) states:

College members respect the privacy of clients by holding in strict confidence all information about clients. College members disclose such information only when required or allowed by law to do so or when clients have consented to disclosure.

The issue of keeping all information confidential is one that most social workers are familiar with. Do they, however, truly understand what confidentiality means? As Lena Ross and Manisha Roy remark, "Although few practitioners consciously and deliberately violate confidentiality, violations do occur, usually as a result of ignorance or carelessness on the part of the social worker or his agency. The intricacies of privileged communication and formal disclosure of information to others are not fully understood by many helping professionals, and it is easy to understand how one might slip up in these areas."[3] Confidentiality means, among other things, that clients should not be discussed over lunch in public areas such as workplace cafeterias or restaurants. It means that no one should be able to overhear telephone conversations with or about clients, or telephone answering machine messages from clients.

Confidentiality must be considered at all times. A social worker who unexpectedly meets a client outside the office should not approach the client and begin discussing personal information about the client in a way that will compromise the client's privacy. This is of special concern in small communities where there is greater likelihood of chance meetings. A dual (or multiple) relationship can be defined as a situation where one individual functions in more than one professional relationship, or one in which the individual functions in a professional role and another definitive and intended role (as opposed to a limited and inconsequential role growing out of and limited to a chance encounter).[4] Because there are more opportunities for dual relationships in small communities, social workers must take special care to avoid disclosing in non-professional settings knowledge about a client obtained in the course of their professional activities. If a client's situation is used as an anonymous case study for teaching and similar purposes, the social worker must always remain alert to the fact that people acquainted with the client may be able to identify the client if certain details are discussed.

---

3.   L. Ross and M. Roy, *Cast the First Stone: Ethics in Analytical Practice* (Wilmette, IL: Chiron Publications, 1995) at 8.

4.   D. Bersoff, *Ethical Conflicts in Psychology* (Washington, DC: American Psychological Association, 1999) at 227.

It is the responsibility of everyone involved to ensure that confidentiality is respected. If, in conversation, a social worker is given confidential information either that he or she should not have, or in an appropriate setting, it is the social worker's professional and moral obligation to curtail the conversation. Furthermore, if a social worker's supervisor is aware that the social worker is improperly revealing confidential information, the supervisor must "not only stop the improper disclosure of confidential information while it is occurring but must also take action to prevent the offender from continuing his behaviour."[5]

B. Exceptions to the Rules of Confidentiality

Being fully aware of the meaning of confidentiality is necessary before considering situations in which confidentiality cannot be maintained. Communications between a social worker and his or her client are not considered privileged information, unlike, for example, communications between a lawyer and his or her client. It is important for social workers to know when they must or must not invade a client's privacy by disclosing confidential information. On this point, the *Handbook* says the following:

5.1 College members shall not disclose confidential information concerning or received from clients, subject to any exceptions contained in the following interpretation.

This statement is followed by eight exceptions, designated (in accordance with the terminology used throughout the *Handbook*) Interpretation 5.1.1 through Interpretation 5.1.8. These will now be discussed one by one.

I. Conflict between College and Employing Organizations

5.1.1 When College members are employed by an agency, or organization, College standards of confidentiality may conflict with the organization's policies and procedures concerning confidentiality. When there is a conflict, College standards take precedence.

This rule addresses conflicts between an employer's standards of confidentiality and the College's standards of confidentiality. When there is a difference between the two, the member must conform to the standards set by the College. However, the conflict is apparent. As one author has remarked, "The obligations to follow agency rules and regulations go along with one's

---

5.   L. Ross and M. Roy, above note 3, at 15.

employment or placement with that organization. Though it is the responsibility of social workers to raise questions about procedures, they also must . . . obey laws to which they have voluntarily agreed."[6] This advice makes sense in logical terms but can be very difficult to implement in practice. If an agency is not meeting the required standards, it is the member's obligation to point this out to the appropriate person. It is also the member's professional obligation to follow the College's mandate rather than the employing agency's, even if this could jeopardize the member's employment. It is likely that most social service agencies in Ontario already meet College standards. For any that do not, it is to be hoped, for their own sake and that of their clients, that they will adopt the College's standards as they become more aware of the legislation.

II.   Social Worker under Review

5.1.2 When in a review, investigation or proceeding under the Act in which the professional conduct, competency or capacity of a College member is in issue, the member may disclose such confidential information concerning or received from a client as is reasonably required by the member or the College for the purposes of the review, investigation or proceeding, without the client's authorization. College members do not divulge more information than is reasonably required.

A member may be forced to defend his or her actions in response to a client's allegations. In a case where a client has, for example, made a complaint against the member of sexual impropriety, it may be relevant to one's defence to reveal that the client was sexually abused as a child and therefore transference may be a contributing factor to the allegations. It is possible that this client sees all figures of authority as sexual predators and has therefore wrongly interpreted an innocent action. But if the client's complaint is about a breach of confidentiality rather than sexual impropriety by the social worker, it would be inappropriate to reveal that the client was sexually abused as a child. Even in situations where a member is compelled to divulge confidential information, it is still the member's professional obligation to maintain as much confidentiality as possible.

---

6.   C. Bisman, *Social Work Practice: Cases and Principles* (Pacific Grove, CA: Brooks/Cole Publishing Company, 1994) at 52.

III.   Legal Obligation to Disclose

5.1.3 When disclosure is required or allowed by law or by order of a court, College members do not divulge more information than is required or allowed.

This provision, similar to Interpretation 5.1.2, is another example of where disclosure of confidential information may occur. If a social worker is aware of child abuse, for instance, he or she must report it. Confidentiality cannot be maintained if there is reason to believe that a child has been abused or is at risk of being abused. If a mother, for example, tells a social worker that her child has complained that he or she is being inappropriately touched by the father, the social worker is obligated to report the situation to the local children's aid society.

Disclosure may also be court-ordered or a request may be made to produce the social work record or a report based on the record, in divorce actions. When the issue of child custody arises, one parent may want to attempt to prove the other unfit and may attempt to use the information collected by the social worker to do so. If it is court-ordered or the client in question consents the member must disclose only the necessary information. Criminal matters such as cases of domestic violence or sexual assault are other examples of when disclosure may be court-ordered. The records may be required by the accused to discredit the allegation or allegations against him or her. In a case of sexual assault the accused may want the alleged victim's records to show that the victim had a propensity for sexual promiscuity and that the sexual contact was consensual. Again, however, it is the member's responsibility, when disclosure is ordered, to not divulge more information than is required or allowed.

IV.   Collection Agencies

5.1.4 College members wishing to use collection agencies or legal proceedings to collect unpaid fees may release, in the context of legal proceedings, only the client's name, the contract for service, statements of accounts and any records related to billing. This release would not extend to the content of the services provided.

A member who has not been paid for his or her services has the right to use a collection agency if the client is first advised that a collection agency will be contacted if the bill remains unpaid. In such situations, the member is restricted to giving the collection agency only the documentation it needs to collect the unpaid debt, that is, the client's name, contact information, and billing details as well as a copy of the service contract. However, providing information to the collection agency, for example, about what a difficult person the client can be is unethical and a breach of this principle.

V.   Disclosure: Advising the Client

5.1.5 College members inform clients of the parameters of information to be disclosed and make reasonable efforts to advise clients of the possible consequences of such disclosure.

As indicated, there are situations where confidentiality cannot be maintained. There are occasions when client information must be disclosed in order to meet legal criteria or to protect the social worker. In situations where a social worker must disclose information, the client should be forewarned (if at all possible) about what sort of information will be disclosed and what effect this disclosure may have on the client.

When clients mistakenly believe that everything they tell their social worker is privileged information that the social worker is forbidden to disclose, they may tell the social worker things they would not otherwise share. A client, therefore, has the right to be told ahead of time when the social worker will disclose information and what information is subject to possible disclosure. Advising the client on these points only after sensitive information has been disclosed is inappropriate. The client cannot take back what he or she has said and the social worker cannot pretend to have not heard the information.

VI.   Protecting the Client

5.1.6 College members in clinical practice do not disclose the identity of and/or information about a person who has consulted or retained them unless the nature of the matter requires it. Unauthorized disclosure is justified if the disclosure is obligated legally or allowed by law or if the member believes, on reasonable grounds, that the disclosure is essential to the prevention of physical injury to self or others.

The social worker's obligation of confidentiality extends beyond the specific details of a client's case. The social worker may not even acknowledge that an individual has consulted him or her or that the individual is a client. Disclosure can be justified if the nature of the matter requires it to prevent physical harm to someone. Therefore, a client who discloses thoughts of suicide must be told that the social worker cannot maintain confidentiality if the social worker believes the client is likely to act on those thoughts. This, of course, also applies to thoughts of hurting or killing a third party. And even if the duty to disclose this information did not exist, concerns of potentially being indirectly responsible for the harm or death of someone should provide the motivation to disclose the information to the appropriate person.

The issue of suicide gives rise to a dilemma of conflicting values, these being the social worker's right to intervene if a client is a suicide risk versus the client's right of self-determination. Some commentators argue that clients have the right to choose to die, but their arguments do not alter the reporting responsibilities of members of the College. It is important to note that "there are occasions where *the duty to protect life supersedes the ethical principle of self-determination.*"[7] If the limits of confidentiality are clearly outlined in the contract signed by the client before the therapeutic relationship begins, the social worker is protected both morally and legally if he or she later finds that it is necessary to reveal confidential client information.

If the contract has been adequately explained, the client knows that the social worker will report any suicidal or homicidal intentions seriously expressed by the client, and indeed, this may be the response the client is seeking. In cases where a client is engaging in a behaviour that may be detrimental to his or her wellbeing, such as suffering from an eating disorder or engaging in self-mutilation, but is not facing imminent serious harm, it is to some extent a personal decision on the part of the social worker whether to disclose details of the client's behaviour.

Confidentiality in both of the situations above depends, first, on how confident the social worker is that the client will not ultimately kill himself or herself, and second, on the age of the client. If the client is a child (defined as a person less than 18 years old), the social worker should encourage the child to confide in a parent. If the child refuses, the social worker is left with the decision. In making the decision the social worker must consider the effect of disclosure on the child's willingness to continue talking openly to the social worker. The potential consequences of disclosing or not disclosing must be weighed. Of course, if the social worker believes that there is even a remote possibility that the client will suffer genuine harm, confidentiality must not be maintained.

VII. Consent to Disclosure

5.1.7 In clinical practice, College members have clients sign completed consent forms prior to the release of information. A separate consent form is required to cover each authorization for releasing client information. In urgent circumstances, a verbal consent by the client to the disclosure of information may constitute proper authorization. The member should document that this consent was obtained.

On occasion, a client may consent to disclosure of information that is not governed by the mandatory disclosure rules. It may be in the client's best

---

7.   *Ibid.*, at 69.

interest to do so in some situations. A client, for example, may want his or her psychiatrist or family physician to know what has been happening in session, or there may be an insurance claim or legal issue hinging on the outcome of the therapeutic process. In such situations, the social worker may give information to a third party, but before agreeing to release any information, the social worker must obtain the client's written consent. In such situations, the client should, before signing the consent form, know who wants the information, why they want it, what they are going to do with it, who (if anyone) they will be forwarding the information to, and exactly what information is to be disclosed. Once the client has the answers to these questions, he or she should be made aware of the pros and cons of disclosing the information. This is necessary for informed consent. Consent is valid only if it is informed consent, and a consent form signed by a client who does not have the answers to these questions could be challenged in court. In addition, it can be argued that a social worker who releases client information without informed consent is in breach of confidentiality.

The standard form for this purpose is Ministry of Health Form 14, "Consent to the Disclosure, Transmittal or Examination of a Clinical Record under Subsection 35(3) of the Mental Health Act," which is reprinted in chapter 19 of this book.

A separate form must be used in each case where disclosure is required. The social worker may not use a single form as the basis for releasing information to more than one party; using a separate form for each party ensures that the client is clear on who will be receiving the information. Also, using a single form for multiple parties would make each party aware of the names of the other parties to whom information is being disclosed, which would be a breach of confidentiality.

A client who decides to sign a consent form after receiving this information should be told how long the consent remains in effect and how it can be revoked during the time it is valid. It is important for the client to understand that he or she can revoke consent at any time. Information already divulged in accordance with a valid consent is not affected by the client subsequently revoking the consent.

When dealing with a child, the issue of confidentiality can become complicated. It is sometimes difficult for a social worker to maintain the confidentiality of a child because "parents who have legal custody . . . may have a legal right to inspect case records pertaining to their children unless there is compelling evidence that the children would be at risk of serious harm" if the parents accessed the records.[8] In cases of intact families the *Child and*

---

8.   F.G. Reamer, *Ethical Standards in Social Work: A Critical Review of the NASW Code of Ethics* (Washington, DC: NASW Press, 1998) at 68.

Family Services Act,[9] s. 184(1), states that a child of age 12 or over has a right to access his or her own records, but that between the ages of 12 and 16 the parents may veto this right completely or in part. Alternatively, if the child is over 16, the parents need the child's consent to access the records. Although not all social workers fall under the jurisdiction of the *Child and Family Services Act*, this Act provides good guidance to the social worker faced with the dilemma of disclosing a child's records.

In situations where the parents are separated or divorced, the parent or parents with custody have the same rights as parents in intact families. Section 20(5) of the *Children's Law Reform Act*,[10] provides that a person entitled to access also has the right to be given information regarding his or her child. Thus, in cases of joint custody, regardless of where the child resides, either parent has the right to access the records of a child under the age of 16 years. Furthermore, in situations where one parent has custody and the other has access to the child, the parent with access is entitled to information regarding the counselling of a child. It is unclear, however, as to whether this would allow the parent access to the complete file. This information should be discussed with the presenting parent and child at the initial meeting. All of the above remains subject to the premise that to disclose this information will not cause harm to the child. A person age 18 or over is considered an adult and as such, his or her consent is required prior to any disclosure of information.

In any case, the question of children and consent to disclosure of confidential information can be confusing, and social workers would be wise to use extra caution when handling issues of confidentiality and access to files where children are concerned.

As the *Handbook* indicates, in certain circumstances a verbal consent may suffice. Verbal consent is usually restricted to urgent situations, for example, when a client is at risk and unable to attend at the social worker's office to sign a consent form. As the *Handbook* also states, it is important to document the verbal consent.

The member may find that it is beneficial to also accept verbal consent in some situations, such as those involving teenaged clients. Where there is concern that the client is signing the consent form only because he or she has been asked to do so by the social worker, whom he or she may see as an authority figure, or concern that the client does not understand the significance of signing the consent form and therefore is not truly giving informed consent, verbal consent may be more suitable. In such situations a solution may be to agree to talk to the third party, *but only if the third party contacts the social worker first*. In these instances, the third party knows to contact the social worker only because the client has told the third party to do so, and this

---

9.   R.S.O. 1990, c. C.11.
10. R.S.O. 1990, c. C.12.

fact may suffice as implied consent. If a client takes the initiative to ask a third party to call the social worker, the client has indicated more understanding of the interaction than he or she would have by just signing a consent form. In these cases, the social worker should very clearly tell the client what information will be discussed with the third party. It is also important to note that being contacted by a third party does not imply consent to continue communication with the third party after the initial contact.

In any situation where confidential information is released to a third party, neither the client nor the social worker can control how the information will be handled by the third party or prevent the third party from disclosing the information to others. It may be important to inform the client of this state of affairs. The client, in turn, may want to talk to the third party about how the information is to be handled or choose not to release the information at all.

VIII. Limiting Disclosure

5.1.8 College members make reasonable efforts to ensure that the information disclosed is pertinent and relevant to the professional service for which clients have contracted.

When a client agrees to a release of information, it is always, of course, for a reason. The social worker must be sure that the information disclosed relates to this reason. In the event that the client gives the social worker permission to partially disclose, the social worker must keep in mind that the client's right to confidentiality is ongoing, and keep the disclosure focused on the relevant facts.

C.   Confidentiality Amongst Colleagues

5.2 College members inform clients early in their relationship of the limits of confidentiality of information. In clinical practice, for example, when social work service or social service work service is delivered in the context of supervision or multi-disciplinary professional teams, College members explain to clients the need for sharing pertinent information with supervisors, allied professionals and para professionals, administrative co-workers, social work or social service work students, volunteers and appropriate accreditation bodies.

As has already been discussed, clients are entitled to know the limits of confidentiality before disclosing confidential information to a social worker. Clients also have the right to know who will have access to their information. Often there are a number of individuals with a valid reason to access the client's confidential information. As the statement quoted above says, the social worker's service may be delivered in the context of supervision or multi-disciplinary professional teams. For these supports to be useful there is, of course, a need for sharing pertinent information with supervisors, allied professionals and para professionals, administrative co-workers, social work students, volunteers, and appropriate accreditation bodies. In recognition of the client's right to control his or her information, the social worker must explain to the client early in the relationship what will happen to the information and who will have access to it. If the client is uncomfortable with this sharing of information, he or she can choose another setting in which to receive service.

It is imperative, nonetheless, that anyone who has access to a client's confidential information understands the nature and importance of confidentiality and signs a document stating that he or she will respect client confidentiality to the same degree as is expected of a social worker. Such a document entitled Confidentiality Agreement and Notice to Employees/Volunteers, is included in chapter 19.

D.   Public Information

5.3 College members in non-clinical practice distinguish between public and private information related to their clients. Public information, as defined below, may be disclosed in the appropriate circumstances.

5.3.1 "Public information" is any information about clients and/or their activities that is readily available to the general public and the disclosure of which could not harm the client. When in doubt, the College member obtains permission from the client or a duly authorized representative before disclosing or otherwise using such information.

Public information includes, for example, the client's name, address, telephone number (if it is listed in the directory), e-mail address, and employer, as well as information about criminal charges, convictions, and trials that is in the public record. Information in a telephone or e-mail directory, or published in publicly available media such as magazines, catalogues, company brochures, and advertisements, is public information. This information can be passed on to collection agencies or used for research. But the fact that a person is a client, and the client's reasons for seeing the social worker, are not public information. A social worker therefore cannot accede to a request for confirmation that a certain person is a client. Non-identifying information, such as city of residence, age, or gender, may be released without concern. In cases of uncertainty, the social worker should obtain a signed consent.

E.   Community Groups

5.3.2 When working with community groups, government agencies and other organizations, the College member keeps confidential any information about the personal lives, personalities, and personal behaviour of the individuals involved.

If a social worker is working with a community or therapeutic group, it is possible that a group member may, in the group setting, disclose confidential information. Although the issue of confidentiality should be dealt with in this situation just as in other situations — that is, the social worker should discuss the meaning of confidentiality with the members of the group and ask them to commit themselves to the principle of confidentiality — the members of the group must be told that they have no legal recourse if their privacy is violated by another member. Although they may be morally obligated, the group members, in spite of their commitment to confidentiality, are under no legal obligation to maintain confidentiality.

During group work, it is a good idea to have the group discuss what they will do and how they will act if one group member happens to accidentally meet another outside the group. Group members sometimes feel that their privacy has been compromised if another group member approaches them outside the group when they are in the company of others. And even if they are unconcerned about others learning about their participation in the group, they sometimes worry that they may be compromising the privacy of the person who approaches them if they reveal to the people whose company they are in that that person is a member of the group. Discussing privacy issues with the group before the opportunity for an uncomfortable chance public encounter occurs allows the group members to develop a strategy that will satisfy everyone and enhance group dynamics. Group dynamics are also enhanced when the group leader adopts a policy that he or she will not talk individually with one group member about another group member. With these confidentiality safeguards in place, the group becomes a safe therapeutic environment. Group members need to be told, however, that if the social worker believes that a group member poses a threat to another person, confidentiality will not be maintained and the person in danger will be warned of the threat.[11]

F.   Extent of Confidentiality

5.3.3 The College member also keeps confidential any other sensitive information about such clients, including human resources, financial,

---

11.   C. Bisman, *Social Work Practice*, above note 6, at 54.

managerial, strategic and/or politically sensitive material, the disclosure of which could harm the client.

The important thing to note here is that it is not only the client's history or emotional situation that is covered by confidentiality, but also any other information the social worker obtains during professional dealings with the client. If a client, for instance, gives a social worker confidential information about the client's corporation that suggests that its shares are about to go up in price, social work ethics prevent the social worker from acting on that information or passing it on to another person. Nor can a social worker advise someone to not hire the client or vote for the client based on information obtained through the social worker's professional dealings with the client.

G.   Informed Consent for Data Collection

5.4 College members obtain clients' informed consent before photographing, audio or videotaping or permitting third party observation of clients' activities. Where case scenarios are presented for research, educational or publication purposes, client confidentiality is ensured through the alteration and disguise of identifying information.

This standard presents a number of different factors that the social worker must consider. The first is the meaning of "informed consent." Informed consent means, first, that the client consents to a request for photographing or one of the other listed activities because he or she understands the meaning of consent, understands the consequences of giving consent, and freely agrees to give consent (that is, does not give consent because he or she thinks it is mandatory or will please the social worker). In addition, the client must be fully informed about the intended method of data collection. A social worker cannot ask a client to consent to being recorded in a manner to be determined later by the social worker; the activity must be specified. Likewise, it is not informed consent if the social worker asks the client for permission to tape record their sessions but fails to mention that social work students will be present during the recording.

Secondly, for consent to be informed consent, the client must know what the social worker intends to do with the collected material and who will have access to it. Will it, for example, be used only for supervisory or educational purposes, or will it be used during a lecture at a national conference of social workers or as part of an advertising campaign? Obviously, a client may be willing to consent to one sort of use but not another. The social worker must also do whatever is necessary to ensure that the recorded material does not inadvertently reveal the client's identity (except insofar as the client has consented to his or her identity being revealed).

Informed consent requires the client to sign a consent form outlining exactly what has been agreed to, including the type of recording to be used, the audience to whom the data will be made available, and the purpose of the material. A sample consent form is provided in chapter 19.

H.   Information for Research, Educational, and Publication Purposes

5.5 College members may use public information and/or non-identifying information for research, educational and publication purposes.

Interpretation 5.3.1 discusses the meaning of public information. Non-identifying information includes the client's gender, city, or province of residence, age, and marital status. The social worker may use public and/or non-identifying information for any of the above stated purposes without concern of breach of confidentiality.

I.   Consultation versus Supervision

5.6 College members are aware of the distinction between consultation and supervision as it pertains to sharing client information. In consultation, clients are not identified.

Both supervision and consultation involve the discussion of cases with the goal of assisting or advising the social worker. The major difference between the two is that a supervisor is entitled to identifying information, whereas a consultant is not. Supervision is an ongoing relationship between a social worker and a supervisor who is most often also a social worker. The supervisor is an agency representative, or someone hired to perform the role of supervisor. In either case, the supervisor has the right as well as the obligation to know the client record, including any confidential information contained therein. Supervisors are governed by the same confidentiality obligations as the social worker. Under the legal doctrine of *respondeat superior*, which provides that "a supervisor who is in a position of authority or responsibility is responsible for the acts of her or his trainees or assistants,"[12] a supervisor who gives incorrect advice to his or her subordinates may be held legally responsible if the advice is acted on.

---

12.   K. Austin, M. Moline, and G. Williams, *Confronting Malpractice: Legal and Ethical Dilemmas in Psychotherapy* (Newbury Park CA: Sage Publications, 1990) at 230.

Consultation is an *ad hoc* sharing of information between professionals of the same or different professions. In consultation no identifying information is revealed. Cases are discussed in generalities for the purpose of information-sharing regarding things such as techniques, characteristics of an illness, or statistical information. In consultation, a social worker may, for example, ask a lawyer for information on how an abused wife would proceed with charges against her partner and what the repercussions might be if this course of action were followed, or the social worker may consult with a physician regarding the effects an illness might have on a person's ability to parent. Because all situations are discussed in generalities, the consultant cannot be held responsible for any resultant action that the social worker or the client may take. Peer supervision is a form of consultation and so no identifying information is disclosed.

J.   Conclusion

In summary, it is critical for social workers to be aware of confidentiality issues, for confidentiality is an area in which it is very easy for social workers to inadvertently run into legal difficulties. There is further discussion of some of the more unusual aspects of confidentiality in chapter 15, which explores Risky Aspects of Practice. As the profession of social work in Ontario strives to achieve its full potential by capitalizing on its new status as a self-regulating profession, it must adhere to the principles of confidentiality with even greater commitment than before. This is the only way for the profession to demand the respect it deserves.

Chapter 10

Record Keeping

Records are the best way a social worker can document and justify why certain decisions were made. Whereas memory is fallible, complete and accurate records stand the test of time and can be an invaluable asset for the social worker, whose records are legal documents and must be treated as such. Failure to keep records in accordance with the College's standards of practice is a serious breach of the standards and may result in disciplinary proceedings against the errant social worker.

Principle IV of the *Standards of Practice Handbook* reads as follows:

The creation and maintenance of records by social workers and social service workers is an essential component of professional practice. The process of preparation and organization of material for the record provides a means to understanding the client and planning the social work and social service work intervention. The purpose of the social work and social service work record is to document services in a recognizable form in order to ensure the continuity and quality of service, to establish accountability for and evidence of the services rendered, to enable the evaluation of service quality, and to provide information to be used for research and education. College members ensure that records are current, accurate, contain relevant information about clients and are managed in a manner that protects client privacy.

A. Record Content and Format

The *Handbook*'s interpretation section for Principle IV is divided into three parts: record content and format, record maintenance, and access and disclosure.

4.1   Record Content and Format

4.1.1   College members keep systematic, dated, and legible records for each client or client system served.

4.1.2   The record reflects the service provided and the identity of the service provider.

4.1.3   College members document their own actions. College members do not sign records or reports authored by any other person. The exception is the co-signing of records or reports when the College member is acting in a supervisory capacity.

4.1.4   Information is recorded when the event occurs or as soon as possible thereafter.

4.1.5   Recorded information conforms with accepted service or intervention standards and protocols and is in a format that facilitates the monitoring and evaluation of the effects of the service/intervention.

4.1.6   College members may use documentation by exception system provided that the system permits the total record to capture the minimum content as set out in Footnote 3 [of the *Handbook*].

B.   Why Complete Records are Necessary

The importance of good records cannot be overemphasized. It is imperative that the social worker's records provide an accurate and complete picture of his or her interactions with clients. This is critical for the well-being of both social workers and their clients, as the Angie Martin case of 1997 dramatically demonstrated. Martin was the first professional social worker in Canada to be charged with criminal negligence causing death, a charge that carries a maximum sentence of life imprisonment. As an employee of the Catholic Children's Aid Society of Toronto, she was the intake worker for Jordan Heikamp, who died of starvation at five weeks of age despite the intervention of the children's aid society and the fact that he lived with his mother in a government-funded shelter.

After being charged and strip-searched, Martin was required to attend every day of a seven-month preliminary inquiry. At the subsequent coroner's inquest, during which she was on the stand for four days, she was cross-examined by eight lawyers. One of the critical recommendations that came out of this inquest, in spite of the fact that it would have seemed obvious, was that social workers should take good notes. In their commentary on social work accountability and the criminal justice system, Glenn Hainey and Emily Cole, who were part of the legal team representing Martin, highlight the importance of taking good notes:

> This suggestion [to take good notes] arises from the fact that any notes made by a social worker are the best contemporaneous record of what has happened in a particular case. Ms. Martin's notes became a critical piece of evidence during the criminal proceedings and at the coroner's inquest. Social workers should make their notes at the time of the events; document all of the important events carefully, including communications and meetings with their supervisors. A social worker should make sure that his or her notes are clear and unambiguous so they will not be misinterpreted and will record how the social worker handled the case.[1]

Good record keeping is evidence of the adequacy of care a client received. In the words of one author, "Work not written is work not done."[2]

C.   What Is the Social Work Record?

How can social workers meet this obligation? To answer this question, we must first consider the question of what constitutes records. The answer may seem obvious, but it can be more complicated than one might think. Anything that is used to record information about a client is considered part of the record. This includes paper files, computer files, computer diskettes, audiotapes, and videotapes. It also includes anything that the client gives the social worker as part of the work with the client, such as journals and other writings that the client brings to the session at the social worker's request. If the client brings a document of this kind to the session and shows it to the social worker without allowing the social worker to keep it, it remains the client's. If, however, the client transfers possession of it to the social worker, it becomes a part of the file and cannot be returned to the client. If the file is subpoenaed, the document remains with the file and is subject to the same rules of confidentiality as other documents in the file.

D.   What Should Be Included in the Record?

What should be included in the records kept by a social worker? Tim Bond provides the following concise list:

---

1.   G. Hainey and E. Cole, *Professional Vulnerability: Social Work Accountability before the Criminal Justice System* (unpublished), (2001) at 6.

2.   B. Schutz, *Legal Liability in Psychotherapy: A Practitioner's Guide to Risk Management* (San Francisco: Jossey Bass Publishers, 1982) at 51.

- written and signed consents to all treatment
- written and signed consents to all passing of confidential information
- all appointments including non-attendance by client
- treatment contracts (if used)
- up-to-date record of content of sessions with client
- up-to-date record of counsellor's reasoning behind decisions about significant interventions and general strategies
- consultations with anyone else about the client
- copies of any correspondence from the client or relating to work with client
- any instructions given to the client and whether or not the client acted on these[3]

Records are useful only if they are legible, well-organized, and answer the "Five W's" — Who, What, Where, When, and Why. They are of no value if they are illegible or do not contain enough information to support the actions taken. They must be truthful, accurate, and complete.

E.   Record Integrity

Altering or destroying records to avoid their use in a judicial proceeding can result in a charge of obstruction of justice. Falsifying records relating to a member's practice is a breach of the College's standards of practice and may lead to a disciplinary proceeding. If it should happen that a client disputes information in a member's records, the member can allow the client to provide for the file a signed statement explaining the disagreement and indicating what the client believes to be the true information. No one, however, is allowed to eliminate any part of the existing record.

The record should reflect only what was actually said and done, not what the social worker thinks the client really meant or should have done. This may include the reasons justifying the course of action taken or suggested, and the client's response to these, including when the client did not follow through on the agreed-upon plan. The records should also note what is not present, such as lack of affect, absence of suicidal ideation, and/or absence of violent thoughts.

Records are of little use if they can be misinterpreted or if their integrity can be challenged because they include prejudicial or discriminatory comments. They are also of little use if they are full of illegible corrections. For this reason, handwritten records must be written in ink and corrections should be made by striking out passages with a single line. Corrections

---

3.   T. Bond, *Standards and Ethics for Counselling in Action* (London: Sage Publications, 1993) at 175.

should also be initialed to confirm that it was the social worker who made the changes. If, at a later date, the social worker remembers something that should have been entered into the record but was not, it can be added as long as the social worker accurately dates and initials the addition. During sessions with a client, it is often difficult to keep clear, accurate, and complete notes and make corrections in the approved manner, but it is in the social worker's best interest to do so.

It is important to remember that one's notes may at some point be viewed by a client, a client's representative such as a lawyer or insurance agent, or a judge. For this reason, notes should look professional and not have messy scribbles or doodles in the margins. The social worker may, however, find it useful to jot down in the margin questions or reminders about areas that he or she wishes to pursue at a later date.

4.1.7 College members do not make statements in the record, or in reports based on the record, or issue or sign a certificate, report or other document in the course of practising either profession that the member knows or ought reasonably to know are false, misleading, inaccurate or otherwise improper.

This point is self-explanatory and speaks to the honesty and integrity of the member. If a record is inaccurate or incomplete, a member must not imply that it is completely factual by signing it.

F.   Children's Records

Social workers may find that keeping complete and accurate notes when working with children is even more of a challenge than when working with adults. It is difficult to interact with a child and take notes at the same time. Children also tend to want to know what is being written. The more astute children will alter what they report by noting which of their comments motivate the social worker to take notes. It is imperative, however, to keep complete notes of one's sessions with children. There will always be people who will want to know the results of a session with a child, be they parents, judges, lawyers, school representatives, or physicians. The fact that children do not independently make the choice to attend counselling means that someone else always has a vested interest in the information gathered in session.

G.   The Importance of Proper Records

The social worker's records must always be thorough. When making notes of conversations, for example, the social worker must record the name of the speaker and place direct statements within quotation marks. Case notes should include an assessment of the situation and a tentative diagnosis. A diagnosis that is based on a fact, such as child abuse, does not pose a concern, but a social worker must be careful about making statements that suggest a conclusive diagnosis of mental illness in a client, because it would be easy for a lawyer or other opponent to argue that the social worker is unqualified to make the diagnosis — leaving the social worker open to a College proceeding for professional misconduct or a negligence lawsuit. The Ontario Association of Social Workers (OASW) offers the following observations:

> When making, communicating or recording a diagnosis, clinical social workers are reminded that they are restricted to the profession's scope of practice. A clinical social work diagnosis is therefore confined to data gathered in the course of conducting a psycho-social assessment. Social workers are thus prohibited from diagnosing psychiatric conditions based on the American Psychiatric Association's *Diagnostic and Statistical Measurement Manual of Mental Disorders (DSM) IV.*[4]

A note that suggests a possible diagnosis of the client's symptoms, accompanied by a statement that the diagnosis is to be confirmed by a psychiatrist if necessary, may be a more satisfactory approach. The social worker can still formulate and implement a treatment plan based on the tentative diagnosis. Being able to provide reasons for one's actions makes one less susceptible to legal challenge, but good records are still critical.

There is a fine line between having enough information and having too much. The social worker must decide how much information should be included in the record. Frederic Reamer comments that "Too much detail can be problematic, particularly if the practitioner's records are subpoenaed. Sensitive details about the client's life and circumstances may be exposed against the client's wishes."[5] The OASW remarks that "in situations where relationships are known to be very acrimonious, such as cases of family violence, the wording in records again needs to take into consideration the possibility that a defense lawyer may, at some point in time, be interpreting what has been written."[6]

Confidentiality when one is counselling a couple or larger family unit is another consideration that affects record keeping. Sometimes a social worker will see all of the family members at the same time, followed by sessions where the members are seen one at a time (or vice versa). When that happens, what the people being seen individually say to the social worker should be

---

4. Ontario Association of Social Workers (OASW), *Guidelines for Social Work Record-Keeping* (1999) at 5.
5. F.G. Reamer, *Tangled Relationships: Managing Boundary Issues in the Human Services* (New York: Columbia University Press, 2001) at 46.
6. OASW, *Guidelines*, above note 4, at 3.

treated as confidential and not disclosed to the other family members. It may be easiest and most ethical to maintain separate files for each individual and another file for the family unit as a whole. If a request for information on a specific individual is received, the social worker can provide information from that individual's file without risking a breach of confidentiality with regard to the other family members. This approach may be even more relevant for social workers in small communities where there are few social workers and it is more likely that members of a family will be seeing a social worker for a variety of reasons.

In her article entitled "Social Workers and the Law," Joyce Harris poses two questions related to record keeping. The first is "What advice could you give social workers on keeping good notes?" That question is answered as follows:

> The social worker can keep in mind that the record could easily be marked in court as "Exhibit 1." When the social worker is preparing the record, he or she should visualize being sued by a client and having the record become permanent evidence. What would he or she want the record to say if it were being reviewed by a judge and jury?

The second question emphasizes the importance of complete records. It asks, "What do you advise when the social worker is 'caught in the middle' between a client's wishes (e.g., remain in an abusive situation) and his or her own professional judgment?" It is answered as follows:

> We can advise and counsel and go over the pros and cons, but we cannot compel clients to follow our advice. I cannot emphasize enough the importance of documentation — make good notes! A common failing is not to keep good notes. The biggest self-protection device is to record. Social workers cannot afford to be loose on the responsibility of record keeping — otherwise, it is negligent. If, for instance, in my practice, I think that my client should settle the action but he or she wants their day in court, I put it in writing.

> I would like to stress that if the social worker were perceived as careless in keeping notes, the judgment will likely go in favour of the client as the social worker loses professional credibility.

> Of course, child abuse is a completely different situation. It is tied in with obligations to the child. This supersedes obligations to the client and confidentiality issues. If the client were the abuser or protecting the abuser, the client has to be cautioned regarding the professional's obligation to report.[7]

The case of Kim Anne Popen, discussed in chapter 1, should impress upon the reader the importance of keeping comprehensive notes. At the judicial inquiry into Kim Anne's death, the actions taken by the social worker, Mrs.

---

7.   J. Harris, "Social Workers and the Law: Are You Protected?" (Summer 1999) *OASW Newsmagazine*, Vol. 26 No. 2, at 12.

Saul, and everything she wrote, came under intense examination. Dr. Francis J. Turner, a social worker, testified that "Mrs. Saul's report lacked 'an evaluative component' and that 'anyone who carries responsibility to report on a situation,' should provide that component in the report so as to indicate how seriously she viewed the situation."[8] At a later point in the inquiry, Turner described the recording of Kim's case as simply being an exercise in reporting and administratively recording what was seen or done. The Honourable Judge Allen noted that Turner said "it was not what he would expect from a professional in that it essentially lacked the component of diagnostic evaluation and summary."[9] He also commented on the social worker's lack of initiative in the history taking. Had she taken a complete history, the information that surfaced could have alerted her to the potential for child abuse. In Turner's opinion, "If we were talking about a qualified social worker, then he or she should have begun immediately to begin to try and put together an assessment of who these parents were — what were their psychosocial strengths as parents — what were some of the background information."[10]

Because certain things did not appear in the record, it was assumed that Mrs. Saul did not do those things. But what if Mrs. Saul did do at least some of the things she was accused of not doing? Had she recorded her reasons for her course of action, or added a psychosocial history of the parents to the record, she would have been able to defend herself. Had she been able to indicate that she had done her job to the best of her ability given the information she was able to glean, she may not have had to bear the responsibility for the death of an infant. Reamer remarks that "once the decision is made, human service professionals should always be careful to document the steps involved in the decision-making process. Ethical decisions are just as much a part of practice as clinical, community-based, organizational, and policy interventions, and they should become part of the record."[11] Failure to fully document a situation, which some commentators recommend as a way to maintain confidentiality, is obviously not an effective way to avoid potential legal repercussions.

In his report on the Kim Anne Popen case, Judge H. Ward Allen emphasized the importance of keeping proper records. His recommendation 36 reads as follows:

> I recommend that each children's aid society ensure that its social workers are instructed in the art of preparing and recording reports for the files of the soci-

---

8. *Judicial Inquiry into the Care of Kim Anne Popen by the Children's Aid Society of the City of Sarnia and the County of Lambton*, vol. 3 (Toronto: Queen's Printer, 1982) at 1047.
9. *Ibid.*, at 1057.
10. *Ibid.*, at 1054.
11. Reamer, *Tangled Relationships*, above note 5, at 45.

ety and that those workers receive in-service training and instruction therein. Such instruction should emphasize that the recording should be more than mere administrative reporting of what was observed without any expression of opinion, judgement, assessment or evaluation thereof and expression of the perceived significance thereof to the overall plan for management of the case. The recording should contain reference not only to what has been observed, but also to what appears to be missing and what is desired or needed to enable the overall plan to be developed and implemented to successful conclusion.[12]

As members of a self-regulating profession, it is incumbent on social workers to keep accurate, comprehensive notes. One never knows when those records might become the only line of defence against disciplinary or legal proceedings.

H.   Record Maintenance

4.2   Record Maintenance

4.2.1 College members employed by an organization acquire and maintain a thorough understanding of the organization's policies with regard to the retention, storage, preservation and security of records. Self-employed College members establish clear policies relating to record retention, storage, preservation and security.

4.2.2 College members take necessary steps to protect the confidentiality and security of paper records, faxes and electronic records.

4.2.3 College members ensure that each client record is stored and preserved in a secure location for a period of time not less than seven years from the date of the last entry. Longer periods of storage time may be defined by the policies of a member's employing organization or by the policies of a self-employed member. Such policies should be developed with a view to the potential future need for the record.

4.2.4 College members who cease independent practice may (i) maintain their client records in accordance with Interpretation 4.2.3, or (ii) make arrangements to transfer the records to another College member and advise their clients of the future location of their records. The College member to whom such

---

12.   *Judicial Inquiry*, above note 8, at 1512.

records have been transferred complies with the principles regarding retention, storage, preservation and security with respect to the transferred records.

4.2.5 Client records may be destroyed following the time frames outlined in Interpretation 4.2.3. College members dispose of record contents in such a way that ensures that the confidentiality of the information is not compromised.

I.   How Long Should Records Be Kept?

As noted previously, the social work record is the best method of documenting and justifying the social worker's clinical course of action. The client may need this information in the future for a variety of reasons, and the social worker may need it if an allegation is made against him or her. Because the statute of limitations in negligence cases runs for six years and it can take up to a further six months for legal documents to be served on the defendant social worker, records must be kept for a minimum of seven years from the date of the last entry.

Without proper records to refer to, no social worker would want to be in the position of having to defend himself or herself against accusations based on events that occurred seven years ago. As Douglas Bersharov writes:

> Carefully documented records may well mean the difference between a court judgment for you and a court judgment against you. Clear, concise statements summarizing your contacts with the patient are looked upon favorably by judges and juries. Conversely, the professional who comes into court with a confused jumble of notes and who testifies in a like manner (e.g. "On that day we talked about . . . No, wait now. I think it was two weeks before we got into something like that.") will certainly not make a very convincing witness. . . . Good clinical records are the keystone of a defendant's case and in those cases that go to trial, sloppy and incomplete records count heavily against the litigant who relies upon them.[13]

II.   Maintenance of Records

Records must be kept under lock and key in a secure facility and be accessible only to individuals who have a valid reason to access them.

If a social worker is employed by an agency, it is imperative that his or her records be maintained in the agency's required fashion, which of course must meet at least the minimum standards set out in the *Handbook*. When records

---

13.   D. Bersharov, *The Vulnerable Social Worker: Liability for Serving Children & Families* (Washington, DC: National Association of Social Workers, 1985) at 173.

are destroyed, they must be disposed of in such a way that there is no possibility of a breach of confidentiality. This usually means either burning or shredding.

Confidentiality is an issue to consider when maintaining paper records, faxes, and electronic records. The acceptable means for securing the confidentiality of these records are outlined in the footnote to Interpretation 4.2.2 of the *Handbook*. When thinking about record maintenance, it is important to remember that the definition of records includes computer files on diskettes and hard drives. If records are kept on computer, anyone who has access to the computer, including a repair technician, can access the material. There is an added risk, of course, if the computer leaves the office for repairs.

Computerized records must therefore be secured by access codes or passwords if the computers are accessible to people who are not entitled to see those records, and ideally all computerized records should have these security features. All files, no matter what type they are, must be kept under lock and key. A husband waiting in a social work office's waiting area for his wife to complete a therapy session must never, for example, be able to inadvertently see her file or pick up a computer diskette containing the file.

Although the *Handbook* mandates keeping records for seven years, practically speaking they should be kept for as long as possible. Issues can arise at any time that would require the social worker to refer back to his or her records. There is no time limit, for instance, on complaints to the College about a member's behaviour. Barton Bernstein and Thomas Hartsell declare, "The most conservative and safest advice for mental health professionals is: Never destroy client records; maintain them even after death, at least until the deceased therapist's estate is fully probated. One can never know when a claim based on charges of professional negligence or misconduct will rear its ugly head. If the means are available to maintain and store client files permanently, keep them; if not, be sure to maintain them for at least ten years."[14] It is also incumbent on social workers to arrange for proper handling of their records in the event of their death, either by arranging for the records to be transferred to another social worker or destroyed in an acceptable manner.

Social workers should also retain their daily appointment books, which can be cross-referenced with client records to determine when clients attended and how long sessions lasted. Stubs from receipt books provide additional attendance evidence and should also be kept. These additional means of verification are of particular importance to social workers in private practice, who do not have an agency to back them up. Social workers should remember that "a therapist's first, and often best, line of defense against allegations of misconduct is a well-documented client file. Without documenta-

---

14.   B. Bernstein and T. Hartsell, *The Portable Lawyer for Mental Health Professionals* (New York: John Wiley & Sons, 1998) at 50.

tion, even the most resourceful attorney will have a difficult time mounting a spirited and competent defense."[15]

If the social worker does not have the space to keep records indefinitely, the social worker should consider creating a synopsis of client files before the files are disposed of. Synopses should include all identifying information on the client, a note indicating the first and last date the client was seen, summaries of any medical or psychological diagnoses, and any other information considered crucial. The social worker may also want to include a note indicating who terminated the professional relationship and why.

When the client is a child, records should be retained for at least seven years after the client reaches the age of majority, to ensure that they are available if the client decides to lodge a complaint against the social worker. The limitation period for a minor does not begin to run until he or she reaches the age of majority. By the time the child reaches adulthood, the social worker may have forgotten all about him or her, and thus will be very glad to have records to rely on if the need arises.

III.   Records of Telephone Calls

The *Handbook* does not discuss telephone contact with clients. It is a matter of personal preference whether the social worker keeps records of telephone calls or not. The OASW advises social workers to maintain records of all telephone calls, even those from prospective clients formally inquiring about service. On the subject of inquiries about service, the OASW suggests that the records should include the reason for the call, the decision made by the social worker in response to the call, and the reason for the social worker's decision. Of course, if the caller does not provide identifying information, a complete record is impossible.

When one is speaking on the telephone with a client, the best note-taking approach is to enter the notes immediately into the client's file, but that is not always possible when a call is taken in a car, at home, or in another non-office location. Social workers can, if they wish, tell their clients that calls will be accepted outside the office (as far as possible), but notes will usually not be taken and the client will have to repeat during session, in at least an abbreviated form, what was said on the telephone. However, notes should always be made as soon as possible after receiving important information about a client via a telephone call taken outside the office. Examples of such information include the death of a family member or news of a suicide attempt.

Parents will sometimes call in advance of a child's appointment to mention a change in the child's behaviour that the social worker might want to

---

15.   *Ibid.*, at 51.

address in session. These calls should be noted in the record. During any telephone conversation regarding a client, advice should not be given unless it is documented. Nor should telephone conversations be used as interim counselling sessions, unless the client has contracted for counselling by telephone, in which case the conversations must be documented in the usual manner. Joyce Harris has this to say about the professional liability risks of telephone and online counselling: "The law is such that when a professional gives advice for a fee or not, if the circumstances are such that the person at the other end is relying on the advice given, then the professional is liable. To engage in telephone and on-line counselling is widening the net of professional liability a million-fold! If there is a misunderstanding between a client and a professional, the fault is generally with the professional. If a professional is using his or her expertise, he or she can be liable."[16]

I.   Access to and Disclosure of Records

4.3   Access and Disclosure

4.3.1   College members employed by an organization acquire and maintain an understanding of the organization's policies regarding access to confidential client information. Such policies pertain to access requests by the clients themselves as well as by other parties. Self-employed College members establish clear policies regarding access to and disclosure of confidential client information.

4.3.2   College members inform clients, upon request, of their policies regarding access to information. Members furthermore inform clients early in their relationship of any limits of record confidentiality.

4.3.3   College members provide clients or their authorized representatives with reasonable, supervised access to their records or such part or parts of the clients' records as is reasonable in the circumstances. Such access may include providing the client with a copy of a segment of his or her record or of the record in its entirety subsequent to the client's and the member's joint review of the record's contents. The client has the right to receive

---

16.   Harris, "Social Workers and the Law," above note 7, at 16.

appropriate explanations by the College member of the content of the member's reports concerning him or her.

4.3.4   A client's general access to information contained in the record may be restricted for valid reasons. The College member may deem that such access would be extremely detrimental to the client. In such cases, the College member informs the client of the reason for refusal of access and of the recourse available to the client if he or she disagrees. When the work has involved different members of a family, group or community, and access to a record could therefore mean divulging confidential information received from others, or when recorded language could be misunderstood and prejudicial to one of those members, access may also be restricted. In such instances, College members allow individuals to review recorded information that pertains to those individuals only.

4.3.5   When authorized in writing by clients or their authorized representatives, College members release information from the record to third parties within a reasonable time. The authorization must specify, (i) the information that is to be released, for example a partial record, the entire record, or a summary of the member's contact with the client, (ii) the party or parties to whom the information is to be released and (iii) the term of validity of the authorization. Members may release information from the record to third parties without the client's authorization only if disclosure is required or allowed by law or if the member believes, on reasonable grounds, that the disclosure is essential to the prevention of physical injury to self or others. Members may decide not to release information to a third party if, in the member's professional judgment, such a release could result in harm to the client. (See also Interpretation 5.1.6)

4.3.6   Prior to releasing information from a record that pertains to more than one client, for example a couple, family, group, community agency, government department, or other organization/business, College members receive authorization from each individual client.

4.3.7   College members who are served with a formal notice or subpoena to produce client records before a court and

> who are of the opinion that disclosure would be detri-
> mental to the client, should themselves, or through legal
> counsel, advocate for non-disclosure to the court.

4.3.8   College members may permit client records to be used
in a non-identifying manner for the purpose of research,
teaching, or general evaluation of service delivery. (See
also Interpretation 5.4) if [*sic*] the removal of identifying
information does not adequately protect clients'
anonymity, e.g. where clients' roles/activities are highly
specialized and/or publicized, or where confidentiality is
compromised in cases of consultation, research, or policy analysis, the member does not permit access to the
record for these purposes.

4.3.9   College members, to whom another member's client
records have been transferred, comply with the aforementioned standards regarding access and disclosure
with respect to the transferred records.

J.   Releasing Client Records

Client records are not, of course, always totally confidential. People other
than the social worker and his or her colleagues may have a right to see the
records in some circumstances. At this point we therefore need to ask who
these people are and what they must do to exercise this right. As we have
seen, the *Handbook* states that a social worker who works for an agency must
be familiar with the agency's policies on access to client files. Self-employed
social workers must establish their own policies, within the limits set by the
College.

The *Handbook* goes on to say that clients must be informed of these policies if they ask. The social worker must also advise the client on the limits of
confidentiality with regard to records, including the client's right to access
his or her file or portions of it when circumstances allow. The access policies
established by agencies and individual social workers are allowed to contain
a provision that clients must submit a request for access to their files in writing and, if the agency or social worker wishes, only by means of Ministry of
Health Form 14, "Consent to the Disclosure, Transmittal or Examination of
a Clinical Record" (reproduced in chapter 19), will access be granted. The
policy may stipulate that the client is allowed to copy all or part of the file,
and may also allow only supervised access to the file.

Clients must be told that they are not entitled to see a file pertaining to
anyone in their family other than themselves and minor children in their custody. Moreover, if two or more family members have attended sessions

together and there is just one file for the family, individual family members can see the file only if they have a signed permission document — Form 14 is recommended — to do so from everyone else to whom the file pertains. This rule also applies to groups of unrelated people counselled together.

In some cases, the social worker may believe that it is not in the client's best interest to obtain access to his or her file. In these situations the social worker can refuse access to the file but must tell the client the reasons for the refusal. It is advisable to put the reasons in writing and, after discussing them with the client, to have the client sign the document setting out the reasons, which should then go into the file as part of the official record.

If the client wants a third party such as a lawyer, physician, or insurance agent to access the file, the client must sign a Form 14 specifying what portion of the file may be viewed. It is the social worker's professional responsibility to meet this obligation of access in a timely manner after receipt of the Form 14. It is worth remembering that the social worker is entitled to charge a fee and recover any out-of-pocket costs involved in arranging access to a file, no matter what the client's reasons are for wanting access.

After receiving a signed and witnessed Form 14 stating which portion of the file is to be released, the format in which the released information is to be delivered, who is to receive the information, and how long the form is valid for, the social worker can send the information to the intended recipient. The information should never be given to another person to pass on to the intended recipient. If the social worker believes that releasing information to a third party will be detrimental to the client, he or she may choose not to release it. It is advisable, in such cases, for the social worker to record his or her reasons in writing and send a copy to the client and the third party, and also to place a copy in the client's file.

The confidentiality of information in a client's file can be breached by a social worker only when the client's file has been subpoenaed or the social worker believes that the client is in imminent danger of harming himself or herself or someone else. In the former instance, if the social worker believes that releasing the information to the court will be detrimental to the client, he or she, either personally or through legal counsel, should attempt to persuade the court that the client has a right to confidentiality.

To cover all of these confidentiality and record access issues with the client, an intake form that summarizes the issues must be used. This discussion should precede any therapeutic process to ensure informed consent. This form does not grant access to the record; it merely informs the client of his or her rights. The form should be discussed with the client, who then signs the form to acknowledge the discussion. A copy of such a form, entitled Agreement to Provide Services, is included in chapter 19.

Some areas of confusion still exist with regard to file access and disclosure. This is particularly noticeable when dealing with children. Please refer to chapter 9 for a discussion of children and their right to confidentiality.

K.   Conclusion

Although some issues surrounding record keeping have not been completely resolved, it is clear that the social worker must take the initiative to secure the necessary documentation before releasing any information from a file. As two experts on social work and the law remark, "Preventive practice, while not guaranteeing the avoidance of litigation, can reduce its likelihood to the extent possible. To achieve this goal the worker needs to maintain an explicit rationale for every action taken. This rationale should be documented in writing in the client's case record."[17] It also bears repeating that social work agencies and self-employed social workers must establish clear confidentiality policies if they are to avoid becoming embroiled in legal disputes concerning privacy and record access.

It should now be evident that no matter how skilled or experienced social workers are, the work they do is only as good as the records they keep. For this reason, it is incumbent on social workers to maintain proper documentation.

---

17.   R.L. Barker and D.M Branson, *Forensic Social Work: Legal Aspects of Professional Practice* (New York: Haworth Press, 1993) at 30.

Chapter 11

Fees

The charging of fees is a delicate topic for social workers. Because social work is dedicated to helping those in need, social workers are often uncomfortable asking for payment for services rendered. They are, however, frequently required to do just that, whether for the agency for which they work or for themselves if they are in private practice.

Principle VI of the College's *Standards of Practice Handbook* reads as follows:

When setting or administering fee schedules for services performed, College members inform clients fully about fees, charges and collection procedures.

In Ontario, an issue that frequently needs to be discussed with new clients is the fact that the Ontario Health Insurance Plan (OHIP) does not cover social work fees, no matter what service is provided. Indeed, the only time counselling is covered by OHIP is if a psychiatrist or other medical physician is providing it. Ontarians, who have grown accustomed over the past few decades to a wide-ranging, publicly financed social services network (despite recent cutbacks), are frequently astounded to learn that payment is required for a social worker's services. This, of course, can add to the discomfort that social workers feel when discussing or asking for payment.

Kenneth Pope notes that "Establishing safe, reliable, and useful boundaries is one of the most fundamental responsibilities of the therapist . . . One of the first boundary issues that therapist and patient confront concerns fees."[1] Glen Gabbard and Eva Lester observe that "Money is a boundary

---

1. K. Pope, *Sexual Involvement with Therapists* (Washington, DC: American Psychological Association, 1994) at 70.

105

issue in the sense of defining the business nature of the therapeutic relationship. This is not love, it's work." They postulate that unpaid therapy bills may be viewed with suspicion by others who may question whether "the patient could be paying in some other currency," suggesting that the therapist is engaged in questionable behaviour with the client.[2] For these reasons, it is very important to have a clear, precise payment plan to present to the client.

A.   Disclosing Fees and Uncertainties

Before counselling services are provided, the client has a right to know how much each session will cost, how long each session will be, and what supplementary fees, if any, may be charged for additional services. This should all be in writing and included on the intake form. A suitable intake form, entitled Agreement to Provide Services, is included in chapter 19.

Fair and respectful treatment of clients requires the social worker to notify them of anticipated fee increases far enough in advance for them to determine whether they are willing and able to shoulder the increased financial burden and, if not, to give them enough time to find another social worker.

Social workers must also be mindful of the fact that "Counsellors who charge fees for their services are vulnerable to the suspicion that they keep fee-paying clients on longer than is strictly necessary."[3] Some social workers believe that it is the client's responsibility to decide when to terminate the professional relationship; others believe it is the therapist's responsibility. In any event, the topic of who will be responsible for terminating the relationship at the appropriate time should be discussed with the client so that there is no misunderstanding.

The interpretation section for Principle VI in the *Handbook* begins as follows:

6.1 College members do not charge or accept any fee which is not fully disclosed.

6.1.1 College members explain in advance or at the commencement of a service the basis of all charges, giving a reasonable estimate of projected fees and disbursements, pointing out any uncertainties involved, so that clients may make informed decisions with regard to using a member's services.

---

2.   G. Gabbard and E. Lester, *Boundaries and Boundary Violations in Psychoanalysis* (Washington, DC: American Psychiatric Press, 1993) at 192.

3.   T. Bond, *Standards and Ethics for Counselling in Action* (London: Sage Publications, 1993) at 105.

The footnote to Interpretation 6.1.1 adds that "These charges may be based on such factors as the amount of time and effort required and spent, the complexity of the matter and whether a special skill, expertise or service has been required and provided."

B. Limits of Service and Extra Costs

No matter how uncomfortable a social worker may be about discussing monetary issues, Principle VI mandates that fee-related matters must be dealt with right at the beginning of the professional relationship. If the social worker is employed by an agency or confines his or her practice to specific areas of expertise, he or she is obviously required to tell the client about any limits on the services to be provided, such as an agency-determined maximum number of sessions per client. The same considerations apply if the social worker is employed by or under contract to an employee assistance program (EAP). EAPs offer a limited amount of counselling as part of the employee benefit package. Some problems that frequently require counselling or psychotherapy are not acceptable to EAPs because resolving them takes more than the number of sessions the EAP allows for each employee. If the set number of sessions is exceeded, the social worker is unlikely to be paid for the extra time spent with the client.

Whether employed by an agency or in private practice, the social worker must advise the client of the fee for each session, how long each session will last, and how many sessions it is anticipated the client will need. The client also must be alerted to any uncertainties that may have an impact on the fee arrangement, for example, concerning the number of sessions required.

The social worker may want to mention how many sessions will likely be needed to give the client enough of a sense of how the professional relationship is progressing to decide whether the relationship should be continued. Six sessions, the average number of sessions allocated for short-term therapy, is a good benchmark in this regard. After six sessions, the typical client should start to see some alleviation of his or her symptoms. He or she will also have had enough time to establish a relationship with the social worker and evaluate the concept of therapy. By the end of the sixth session, the client may believe that he or she has accomplished enough to be able to use the skills acquired in therapy to make progress without further assistance from the social worker.

The Goods and Services Tax (GST) is a fee-related issue that social workers in private practice need to consider. Private practitioners are obligated to charge GST if their annual income from private practice is $30,000 or more. A social worker who anticipates earning $30,000 or more per annum from private practice must register for a GST number, collect GST from his or her clients, and remit the collected GST to the federal government. He or she must also inform new clients that GST will be collected and explain what the total hourly rate for counselling will be with GST added. The receipts that clients receive to confirm payment of fees should include the social worker's GST number and separately itemize GST.

Social workers in Ontario are allowed to charge not only for counselling services but also for out-of-pocket disbursements such as fax and long-distance telephone charges and for special services such as attending court and preparing written reports for physicians, insurance companies, the Criminal Injuries Compensation Board, and so forth. If the social worker anticipates at the beginning of the relationship with the client (or, for that matter, later in the relationship) that special charges may be necessary, they should immediately be discussed with the client.

Fees may also be charged for specialized services such as hypnosis or eye movement desensitization and reprocessing (EMDR). Services of this kind, which require specialized training and a more intense involvement on the part of the therapist, may justify a higher hourly rate or longer sessions, and clients must be informed of any additional costs before receiving these services.

There are situations, such as matrimonial disputes, insurance claim determinations, and legal battles, where clients may try to influence social workers to act more favourably towards them by offering payment beyond the normal fee schedule (perhaps claiming that the extra payment is simply in recognition of the social worker's exceptional abilities). It contravenes the social work standards of practice to accept such payments, no matter what the justification.

C.   Fee Changes

6.1.2 College members discuss and renegotiate the service contract with clients when changes in the fee schedule are anticipated.

If a social worker raises rates or begins charging for services not previously discussed with the client, the client must be told of the new arrangement in advance. The social worker should notify the client far enough in advance for the client to accommodate the new expense or make alternative arrangements for service. The same approach applies if the social worker begins charging GST.

D.   Billing and Collection Policies

6.1.3 College members ensure that fee schedules clearly describe billing procedures, reasonable penalties for missed and cancelled appointments

or late payment of fees, the use of collection agencies or legal proceedings to collect unpaid fees and third party fee payments.

The *Handbook* notes that interest on late payments should be expressed as an annualized rate. It also points out that members of the College must protect confidentiality when giving information to collection agencies. This point is dealt with in Interpretation 5.1.4 of the *Handbook*.

Most clients eventually pay their bills, but occasionally one does not. To minimize the risk of non-payment, the social worker may find it useful to have clients pay by cash or cheque at each appointment. When a client who owes money terminates the professional relationship without paying the amount owed, the social worker may have to follow up with a telephone call and, if payment is still not made, with an invoice. The social worker, however, needs to be careful about compromising the client's confidentiality. If these collection approaches do not elicit a response, the options of using a collection agency or going to small claims court remain, but these may be neither cost-effective nor encourage good public relations. Accordingly, the social worker in private practice may need to accept the occasional unpaid bill as an operating cost that cannot be avoided.

Clients' cheques that are returned NSF (non-sufficient funds) are another nuisance. Sometimes the social worker's bank will take steps to collect the unpaid amount on an NSF cheque, but at other times the social worker must take the cheque to a branch of the client's bank (possibly even the branch of origin), where the cheque will be held until there are sufficient funds in the account for it to be honoured. Some banks will charge the social worker for this service; others will absorb the cost or pass the cost on to the client. In any case, it is unusual to lose an entire fee because of an NSF cheque.

Missed or cancelled appointments can be an issue where payment is concerned. Agencies frequently have a policy about charges for missed or cancelled appointments, which should be explained to the client during the initial visit if the social worker is working for one of those agencies. Social workers in private practice need to set their own policies, which likewise should be discussed with the client during the initial visit. Private practitioners sometimes hesitate to establish a policy requiring payment for appointments missed or cancelled on short notice, possibly because they believe that enforcement is too difficult or they worry about losing clients. One solution to this dilemma is to tolerate the occasional missed appointment or last-minute cancellation, but to charge the full sessional fee if such events occur too frequently. Whatever policy is adopted, it needs to be discussed with the client during the intake process and noted on the intake form. A copy of such a form, entitled Agreement to Provide Services, is included in chapter 19.

Third-party payments can also present a dilemma. Theoretically, money owed by insurance companies and other third parties for services rendered should be easy to collect. The social worker, however, must ensure that the third party has in fact agreed to pay for the service on behalf of the client and understands that the social worker is a professional entitled to the same consideration as other professionals.

Unfortunately, many third parties are prepared to pay for the services of psychologists but not social workers. It is hoped that the new legislated status of the profession, which guarantees that social workers have met certain educational and training requirements, will convince more third parties to include the services of social workers in their payment plans.

Another problem related to third parties stems from the fact that the social worker must rely on the client to notify the payer and submit the necessary paperwork. If the client has in the meantime terminated his or her relationship with the social worker, the client may no longer be motivated to do what is necessary for the social worker to get his or her money if a dispute over payment arises.

If the third party is an individual such as a lawyer, the social worker has to put a great deal of trust in a person he or she may not know, and hope that the client will take the initiative to help the social worker if there is a dispute over payment. In general, however, third parties who have agreed to pay for a service usually do so in a timely fashion.

E.   Flexible Fee Schedules

6.1.4 College members may reduce, waive or delay collecting fees in situations where there is financial hardship to clients, or they may refer clients to appropriate alternative agencies so that clients are not deprived of professional social work or social service work services.

Many agencies and private practitioners charge for their services on a sliding scale that allows their fees to be adjusted to the client's ability to pay. Agencies frequently base their fees on the client's income as set out in the client's most recent tax return. Private practitioners, on the other hand, may not have the time or knowledge to evaluate tax returns, but instead will ask clients what they believe they can comfortably afford to pay (and hope that the clients do not take advantage of them). Another option is to have a fixed reduced rate (that is, a rate not subject to negotiation) for those who cannot afford the regular rate. Of course, private practitioners must ensure that they do not reduce their rates so often that their ability to continue practising is affected. No one is helped if the social worker cannot sustain his or her practice because of excessive fee reductions.

Waiving rather than merely reducing fees is another issue. Agencies may be able to afford to waive fees, but private practitioners are in a more difficult situation. It is obviously up to the private practitioner to decide whether he or she is willing to see clients at no charge. Many social workers believe that clients should be asked to pay at least some amount unless there are exceptional circumstances. This approach is advantageous for several reasons. First, it allows clients to maintain their dignity. They have chosen to buy a service and they pay for that service accordingly. Second, it explicitly attributes value to the service. Receiving something for nothing often leads people to question whether the thing received has any worth. Third, it forestalls any concerns about the social worker's motives that might arise in a no-fee arrangement. A social worker does not want anyone, especially the client, to believe that the social worker expects some sort of reward in lieu of compensation. A client who is counselled at no charge may out of gratitude try to become the "perfect client" who strives to say and do what he or she believes the social worker wants.

The social worker's attitude towards fee reductions for lower-income clients is an issue that should be discussed with the client before counselling takes place. Clients have a right to know in advance whether they can afford a social worker's services and maintain their dignity while doing so.

The special circumstances where service at no charge may be justified include cases involving teenaged clients in troubled family situations who cannot afford to pay for the service or rely on the financial resources of their parents. Another scenario could involve a paying client who suffers a sudden financial setback and can no longer afford to pay. In that case, the social worker may decide that it is better to continue seeing the client at no charge than to disrupt the client's therapy.

When considering fee reductions, social workers should keep in mind that research suggests about 20% of patients sexually exploited by their therapists are charged no fee at all or a reduced fee.[4] In other words, the social worker should examine his or her own motives before offering a reduced rate and also consider whether a reduced rate might be interpreted as a sign of sexual interest.

Clients who are unable to pay cash will sometimes suggest barter as a substitute. Barter, however, offers an opportunity for the social worker to avoid paying income taxes or charging GST on the value of the bartered goods or services. If the social worker is not prepared to declare the value of the barter as income, accepting barter is illegal. Moreover, the social worker may not want or need what the client is able to offer (which can create an uncomfortable situation for the social worker), or may not be in a position to accept barter because he or she needs cash payments to meet financial obligations. Another uncomfortable situation can arise when the client requires more service than originally anticipated and the value of the service provided exceeds the value of the bartered items that at the start of the professional relationship were expected to cover the full cost of service. In general, it is better to avoid

---

4.   Pope, *Sexual Involvement with Therapists*, above note 1, at 72.

potential conflicts of interest or suggestions of impropriety by avoiding barter altogether. As a footnote to Interpretation 6.1.4 of the *Handbook* states, "College members who accept barter payments are aware of the potential conflict of interest and taxation issues that this style of payment may create. College members avoid this method of payment if it constitutes a conflict of interest."

6.1.5 College members do not charge fees on the basis of material or financial benefits accruing to clients as a result of services rendered or fees which are excessive in relation to the service performed.

If a client seeks counselling to, for instance, prepare for a court case, as an employment requirement, or divorce settlement, the social worker cannot charge an additional fee if his or her efforts contribute to the client's financial success, nor is it acceptable for a social worker to ask for a portion of a monetary settlement on a contingency basis. Furthermore, excessive fees may not be charged simply because the social worker knows that the client has substantial financial resources.

F.   Referral Fees

6.1.6   College members in clinical practice, or in charitable or publicly funded settings, do not accept or give commissions, rebates, fees, other benefits or anything of value for receiving or making a referral of a client to or from another person.

If compensation for referrals were allowed, clients could never be sure that a referral was being made in their best interest rather than for the financial benefit of the professionals involved. For this reason, compensation for referrals is never allowed.

G.   Contracting For Fees

6.1.7 College members seek an agreement, preferably in writing, dealing with the provision [*sic*] of Interpretations 6.1.1 to 6.1.5 inclusive, at the time of contracting for services with a client.

The need for a written agreement that addresses the provisions of Principle VI has already been discussed in this chapter. At this juncture it is worth noting that when a reduced fee has been negotiated, social workers sometimes choose not to commit the reduced amount to writing. Instead, they will prepare an agreement that sets out the full fee, with a proviso that a reduced fee may be considered at the client's request. This is done to facilitate raising or lowering the fee if the client's financial circumstances change. Moreover, clients may feel less inclined to admit that a fee should be raised or lowered if an amount has been committed to writing. Furthermore, noting the reduced fee may suggest that the social worker does not provide the same quality of service to lower-paying clients.

H.   Conclusion

Many of the ethical issues discussed in this chapter are illustrated in the following fictional example:

> Martha recently quit her job at a major medical facility and established a private practice. In the first few months of her practice, Martha treated a client who indicated that he desperately wanted Martha's services but had financial problems and could not pay the $25 copayment required by his insurance plan. In the initial contact, Martha told the client not to worry about the copayment; she had always been uncomfortable in negotiations about money and had no experience in setting client fees. During the next five months, Martha began to have financial problems because of unpaid client bills. She hired a financial adviser, who suggested that she use a collection agency. The collection agency contacted the client regularly at his job and at home, leaving messages about his unpaid bills, and reported his lack of payment to a credit agency. The client sued Martha for violation of his privacy and negligence in meeting the standard of informed consent.[5]

Agency workers and private practitioners alike often fail to realize that fees are an integral part of the social work relationship. Fee negotiations establish boundaries, provide an opportunity for enhancing the client's dignity and self-determination, and create a commitment to the social work process. The task of setting fees and establishing a payment schedule is far more complex than may initially be appreciated by the social worker and as such is worthy of profound consideration.

Private practice is a relatively new development in social work. In the past, the profession frequently perceived the private practitioner as a traitor to the ideals of the profession. In fact, many people questioned whether private practice was social work. Because a private practitioner charges a fee for service does not diminish the value of his or her work and indeed allows for a more efficient delivery of government-funded services to those with fewer financial resources.

---

5.   M.K. Houston-Vega and E.M. Nuehring, *Prudent Practice: A Guide for Managing Malpractice Risk* (Washington, DC: National Association of Social Workers, 1997) at 27.

Chapter 12

Sexual Misconduct

Social work is a helping profession. The social work relationship is meant to enhance the functioning of clients in various walks of life. It is difficult for social workers to acknowledge, therefore, that for the client this relationship can pose as much of a risk of sexual abuse as any other relationship. Although sexual misconduct by social workers is rarely discussed or admitted, it is not as uncommon as we would like to believe. Derek Jehu states, "In malpractice lawsuits against therapists, sexual exploitation of patients is a leading complaint."[1] Robert Barker and Douglas Branson report that "the second most common conduct resulting in malpractice claims occurs when social workers engage in sexual relationships with their clients." As they point out, the problem is not exclusive to social work, but is so widespread that "all mental health professionals' codes of ethical conduct now include specific prohibition against sexual relations with clients."[2] In fact, as Kenneth Pope and Melba Vasquez indicate, "Dual relationships, particularly sexual dual relationships, account for the largest share of formal complaints against psychologists, whether those complaints are filed with the civil courts, licensing boards, or ethics committees."[3] A dual relationship, defined as a relationship where a person fulfills more than one role for another person, was first discussed in chapter 9, Confidentiality, and is discussed more fully later in this chapter.

Principle VIII of the College's *Standards of Practice Handbook* reads as follows:

---

1.   D. Jehu, *Patients as Victims: Sexual Abuse in Psychotherapy and Counselling* (New York: John Wiley & Sons, 1994) at 152.
2.   R.L. Barker and D.M Branson, *Forensic Social Work: Legal Aspects of Professional Practice* (New York: Haworth Press, 1993) at 33.
3.   K. Pope and M. Vasquez, *Ethics in Psychotherapy and Counselling* (San Francisco: Jossey-Bass Publishers, 1998) at 33.

The influence of the helping relationship upon clients is pervasive and may endure long after the relationship has terminated. College members are aware of the potential for conflict of interest and abusive treatment of clients within the helping relationship. Behaviour of a sexual nature by a College member toward a client represents an abuse of power in the helping relationship. College members do not engage in behaviour of a sexual nature with clients.

More than perhaps any other topic covered by the College's standards of practice, the topic of sexual misconduct is fraught with ambiguities and subject to diverse interpretations.

A.   Responsibility of the Social Worker

Principle VIII includes nine interpretive sections, which will now be examined.[4]

8.1   College members are solely responsible for ensuring that sexual misconduct does not occur.

Because of the nature of the social worker–client relationship, no matter how much the social worker believes and tries to assure the client that the client is viewed by the social worker as an equal, there is always an inherent inequality. To a great extent, this inequality exists because of the trust that the client must put in the social worker, whether the relationship is mandatory or voluntary. The social worker–client relationship is always based on client need, which inevitably leads to inequity and client compliance.

As Cynthia Bisman tells us, "fiduciary relationships emanate from the trust that clients must place in professionals. Because professionals have knowledge and use techniques that require special expertise, clients must trust workers to act in their best interest."[5] Simply put, a fiduciary obligation is defined as "a special duty to care for the welfare of one's clients or patients.[6] With this in mind, we can see that sexual contact between client and social worker is much the same as sexual abuse of a child. There is a power differential, with the social worker in the more powerful position — not unlike the relationship between an adult and a child. Because of this

---

4. Interpretation 2.2 ("Integrity") is also relevant to sexual misconduct, but is not discussed in this chapter.

5. C. Bisman, *Social Work Practice: Cases and Principles* (Pacific Grove, CA: Brooks/Cole Publishing Company, 1994) at 6.

6. W. Pryzwansky and R. Wendt, *Professional and Ethical Issues in Psychology* (New York, NY: W.W. Norton & Company, 1999) at 125.

power differential, any sexual activity involving a social worker and a client constitutes sexual misconduct. And no matter what the circumstances, it is the sole responsibility of the social worker to prevent sexual contact. Lena Ross and Manisha Roy observe, "Any kind of sexual acting out during psychotherapy has to be condemned; every acting out during therapy harms the patient psychologically. Sexual acting out during therapy is so harmful because it is a misuse of a power position within transference. It misuses the trust of the patient and is psychologically experienced as incest; therefore, the responsibility for any kind of sexual acting out lies completely with the therapist."[7] The social worker or other therapist has the power in the relationship and therefore consent is no defence.

This point was addressed by the court in the 1975 New York state case of *Roy* v. *Hartogs*.[8] This case involved a patient who sued her psychiatrist for emotional damage allegedly caused by a sexual relationship with the psychiatrist. The psychiatrist had told the patient, who was having issues with her sexual identity, that having sexual relations with him could help her. In examining whether the psychiatrist had breached the standard of care, the court focused its attention on the power imbalance between the parties and noted that sexual activity had occurred because of "coercion by a person in a position of overpowering influence and trust who stood in a fiduciary relationship with [the patient]":

> There is a public policy to protect a patient from the deliberate and malicious abuse of power and breach of trust by a psychiatrist when that patient entrusts to him her body and mind in the hope that he will use his best efforts to affect a cure. That right is best protected by permitting the victim to pursue civil remedies, not only to vindicate a wrong against her but to vindicate the public interest as well.[9]

Whether the client consents to a sexual relationship or even initiates it, the social worker is solely responsible for ensuring that it does not occur.

B.   Defining Behaviour of A Sexual Nature

8.2   College members do not engage in the following actions with clients:

8.2.1   Sexual intercourse or another form of physical sexual relations between the member and the client.

---

7.   L. Ross and M. Roy, *Cast the First Stone: Ethics in Analytical Practice* (Wilmette IL: Chiron Publications, 1995) at 60.

8.   366 N.Y.S. 2d 297 (Civ. Ct., 1975).

9.   *Ibid.*, at 301.

8.2.2   Touching, of a sexual nature, of the client by the member, and

8.2.3   Behaviour or remarks of sexual nature [*sic*] by the member towards the client, other than behaviour or remarks of a clinical nature appropriate to the service provided.

What constitutes behaviour of a sexual nature can be open to wide interpretation. The term behaviour of a sexual nature is not so broadly defined as to encompass all types of touching of a client by a social worker, although one does have to be careful about how the touch is interpreted. Casually touching a client on the shoulder, or patting the client's hand when consoling him or her, does not qualify as sexual misconduct or behaviour of a sexual nature. Studies have indicated that physical contact with patients does not make sexual involvement more likely.[10] In fact, used appropriately, "touch can be exceptionally caring, comforting, reassuring, or healing."[11]

It is essential to understand that the terms sexual misconduct and behaviour of a sexual nature are not limited to sexual intercourse or blatant sexual contact. A footnote to Interpretation 8.2.1 states, "Physical sexual relations . . . include, but are not limited to, kissing of a sexual nature, touching of breasts or genital contact and sexual intercourse." A footnote to Interpretation 8.2.2 defines touching of a sexual nature as "physical contact of a sexual nature," including "hugging, holding, patting, stroking, rubbing and any form of contact which is unnecessary to the helping process." Some of these behaviours are easily recognized as forbidden, but others, such as hugging, holding, and patting, can take on different meanings depending on intent. The same observation applies to remarks of a sexual nature — some remarks are easily recognized as sexual while others are more subtle or suggestive. Some behaviours or words are susceptible to misinterpretation and can cause unanticipated difficulties for the social worker.

So how, then, do we define behaviour of a sexual nature? Tim Bond, the author of a book on ethics in counselling, wrestles with the same question:

> The phrase [sexual activity] implies that it extends beyond sexual intercourse involving penetration to include other behaviours such as masturbation, "heavy petting" etc. But where is the boundary in hugging and kissing which are activities which may or may not have an obvious sexual component? The sexual ambiguity of these activities means that it is impossible to produce a definitive list of what constitutes sexual activity. With some activities, it will depend on the intention of the people involved and, just as importantly, the interpretation to the person on the receiving end. Counselors are wise to be cautious in situations where their actions could be misunderstood.[12]

---

10.   Pope and Vasquez, above note 3, at 170.
11.   *Ibid.*
12.   T. Bond, *Standards and Ethics for Counselling in Action* (London: Sage Publications, 1993) at 111.

Social workers would also be wise to determine at the outset of a professional relationship whether the client is comfortable with any degree of casual touch, because for some clients, any touching, even if it is not perceived as sexual, may be unwelcome.

Jehu offers the following observations on what constitutes sexual abuse:

> [S]exual humour, suggestive looks and remarks, kissing, nudity, fondling, oral sex and intercourse, among other sexual acts with patients, are widely recognized as constituting sexual abuse by therapists. Touching and hugging are not generally regarded as abusive, although there are circumstances in which they are inappropriate and potentially harmful. Finally, sexual attraction and fantasies are commonly viewed as natural reactions which are not in themselves abusive, provided they are not acted out with patients.[13]

Social workers also need to realize that interpretations of some aspects of Principle VIII can vary with differences in culture, locale, and situation. Remarks in a footnote to Interpretation 8.2.3 are particularly problematic in this regard. This footnote states, in part, that behaviour of a sexual nature can include "the wearing of sexually suggestive clothing or adornment" and "displaying pornographic or other offensive material." Although there are some types of, for example, clothing and artwork that most people would likely agree are never appropriate in a professional or public setting, there are many other types of clothing, artwork, and so forth that would be considered proper by some groups or communities but not by others. Again, it is these gray areas that social workers must be aware of if they are to avoid allegations of impropriety. When in doubt about what constitutes appropriate clothing, it may be best to err on the side of caution rather than risk repercussions, even though clothing that most would consider acceptable might not meet with everyone's approval.

A recent Ontario courtroom controversy nicely illustrates the point about appropriate clothing. A headline in the *Toronto Star* on March 27, 2002, asked, "Was lawyer out of order? Outfit gets mixed reviews." The story concerned a female lawyer who appeared in court in a navy pantsuit and a white V-neck T-shirt. Although the shirt, as it appears in the news story photograph, does not look low cut, the judge asked the lawyer to leave the courtroom. The judge later explained that the outfit was inoffensive when the lawyer was standing still but offensive when she moved around because it showed too much cleavage. Of the many commentators who weighed in on the issue, some agreed with the judge but most thought that the outfit was totally appropriate.

As seen, some aspects of behaviour of a sexual nature are difficult to define. Some, however, are less so. The definition of behaviour of a sexual

---

13.   Jehu, above note 1, at 7.

nature also includes sexual assault, sexual abuse, and sexual harassment. These activities are clearly unacceptable in any situation, whether with a client or outside the professional arena. Sexual assault, sexual abuse, and sexual harassment are all activities in which there is a power differential. They all involve unwanted physical or verbal sexual contact in which an aggressor attempts to satisfy his or her needs at a weaker person's expense. Few would disagree that this type of behaviour is inappropriate in any social work relationship. Questions, however, can emerge if the sexual behaviour, whether physical or verbal, is initiated by the client. Some therapists believe that sexual contact initiated by a client cannot be considered abusive. Therapists will sometimes justify sexual contact with a client by stating that the client, whether the initiator or not, was a "consenting adult." Nevertheless, it is important to understand that all sexual contact between a social worker and a client falls under the categories of sexual assault, sexual abuse, or sexual harassment because of the inherent inequality of power.

In the same way that a child cannot consent to sexual contact with an adult because the child insufficiently understands the emotional impact and dynamics of a sexual relationship and therefore cannot comprehend the ramifications of his or her decision, a client is considered unable to make an informed decision about a sexual relationship with his or her therapist. As the author of a legal guide to sexual abuse by professionals declare, "Clients cannot legally consent to sexual relations with their therapists due to the psychological dynamics of the client-clinician relationship. Beyond the sense of the clinician's power and the client's vulnerability, the dynamics of personality and other psychiatric disorders (as well as the transference phenomena) conspire to make clients legally unable to appreciate the facts necessary to make a decision to have sex with a clinician or to appreciate the consequences of such a decision."[14]

As with any other form of sexual abuse, assault, or harassment, the negative effects of social worker–client sexual activity can be catastrophic. It must be emphasized that "the clinician always bears the burden of clinical, ethical, and moral codes and constraints flowing from the professional role; the patient does not. Consequently, in an instance of sexual misconduct, it is the clinician and only the clinician who can be counted culpable, blameworthy, or — in certain circumstances — liable or criminal."[15] Therefore, no matter how the sexual activity originates, the social worker is the party who bears the blame.

14. R.K. Bullis, *Clinical Social Worker Misconduct Law, Ethics and Personal Dynamics* (Chicago, IL: Nelson-Hall Publishers, 1995) at 28.
15. T. Gutheil and P. Applebaum, *Clinical Handbook of Psychiatry and the Law* (New York: McGraw-Hill, 1991) at 661.

An example of this is the well-known Illinois case of *Horak* v. *Biris*.[16] The events that led to the lawsuit against Biris began when the Horaks, a married couple concerned about their relationship, went to Biris, a certified social worker, for marriage counselling. During the time the Horaks were in counselling, Biris began a sexual relationship with Mrs. Horak. When Mr. Horak learned of the relationship, he sued Biris for malpractice. Biris sought to dismiss the husband's suit on the basis that no cause of action existed for social worker malpractice and that as a result, he owed no duty to Mr. Horak. The court disagreed, and in establishing that a cause of action exists for social worker malpractice commented as follows:

> We think that the very nature of the therapist-patient relationship, which was alleged and admitted here, gives rise to a clear duty on the therapist's part to engage only in activity or conduct which is calculated to improve the patient's mental or emotional well-being, and to refrain from any activity or conduct which carries with it a foreseeable and unreasonable risk or mental or emotional harm to the patient.[17]

The court found that Biris had represented himself as a licensed clinician capable of providing marriage counselling, that he did not properly handle the wife's transference during treatment, and that he owed her a fiduciary duty to do nothing that was not in her best interest.

C.   The Issue of Trust

The basic premise of a client-therapist relationship is trust, and this is perhaps the most fundamental reason why sexual relationships between social workers and clients are prohibited. Jehu points out that "As a condition for this trust the therapist enters into a fiduciary relationship with the patient, in which he undertakes always to act in her best interests and to place these above his own. Clearly, a fiduciary relationship is breached if a therapist engages in sexual activity with a patient, because this is likely to be disadvantageous to her."[18] In addition, sexual activity between social worker and client shifts and gradually erodes boundaries and alters the dynamics of the relationship to such an extent that the necessary work component cannot be maintained and any benefits experienced by the client are lost. An example of the importance of the trust issue in relation to prohibited sexual activity is provided by the case of *Roy* v. *Hartogs*, discussed earlier in this chapter.

---

16.   474 N.E. 2d 13 (Ill. Ct. App. 1985).
17.   *Ibid.*, at 17.
18.   Jehu, above note 1, at 7.

D.   When Sexual Attraction Exists

What should a social worker do when he or she is sexually attracted to a client, even when this attraction is not acted on by the social worker or known by the client? Interpretation 8.3 answers this question:

8.3   If a College member develops sexual feelings toward a client that could, in the member's judgment, put the client at risk, the member seeks consultation/supervision and develops an appropriate clinical plan.

Interpretation 8.3 is fraught with difficulties. The onus is on the social worker to decide whether the sexual feelings put the client at risk. Even if the social worker is able to hide his or her feelings from the client, will he or she still be impartial and objective in working with the client? Many of the issues that are relevant to Interpretation 8.2 are also relevant to Interpretation 8.3. As we have seen, the social worker–client relationship is based on trust and on the premise that the social worker will work towards the best interest of the client. It is the social worker's responsibility to establish and maintain the boundaries of the relationship, provide containment, and manage the transference. The social worker who is experiencing sexual attraction to his or her client is unable to make these contributions to the relationship. It is, therefore, imperative for the social worker to deal with these feelings and defuse them appropriately. Pope and Vasquez remark that "sexual attraction to patients seems to be a prevalent experience that evokes negative reactions . . . That sexual attraction causes such discomfort among so many psychologists and social workers may be a significant reason that graduate training programs and internships tend to neglect training in this area."[19] Research suggests that more than four out of five psychologists and social workers experience sexual attraction to at least one client. It also shows that even though the majority of these therapists have no intention of acting on their feelings, most of them feel guilty, anxious, or confused about the situation.[20] Suddenly, the focus of the clinical relationship is on the needs of the therapist and not on the client, which is clearly wrong.

Principle VIII, as was noted above, holds that a social worker who cannot work through sexual feelings towards a client in an appropriate length of time must seek supervision or consultation. There are, however, problems with this approach, namely, that no one wants to talk about the issue of sexual attraction to clients and, in any case, supervisory personnel are not trained to deal with it. As Pope and Vasquez observe, "Most training programs spend

---

19.   Pope and Vasquez, above note 3, at 171.
20.   *Ibid.*

little or no time addressing the prohibition against sexual contact with clients, yet it is the most commonly violated of the ethical principles."[21] To make the supervision process work, we must have non-judgmental, empathetic, and supportive supervisors and consultants whom social workers will not hesitate to approach.

If the supervisor or consultant has the power to affect the social worker's professional future by preventing promotions or terminating his or her employment, the social worker who seeks supervision or consultation is taking a big career risk. Another serious problem is connected with the fact that the College's mandatory reporting rules would require the supervisor or consultant to report the social worker to the College for sexual misconduct if the social worker had determined that his or her sexual feelings constituted a risk to the client. This fear would obviously influence the social worker's judgment on how to deal with his or her sexual feelings for the client.

A footnote to Interpretation 8.3 advises that "it may be appropriate for the College member to seek alternative services for the client and terminate the relationship as soon as possible, in keeping with the client's interests." This advice, however, is problematic. Terminating the relationship disrupts the client's therapy — which most likely has been long-term therapy if it gives rise to problematic sexual attraction on the part of the social worker. In addition, the client will probably not know why the relationship is being terminated and may be confused about what seems to be a violation of his or her trust in the social worker. There may be feelings of abandonment, rejection, self-blame, and victimization. As is the case in sexual abuse, the client may also feel indignant, angry, and violated.

If the social worker tries to reduce the client's confusion by revealing his or her sexual feelings, does this revelation constitute inappropriate sexual behaviour? What if the client treats this revelation as sexual harassment and complains to the social worker's supervisor, the College, or even the police?

Possibly the best advice for social workers in these situations is to take steps to avoid sexual feelings developing in the first place. The following list summarizes the advice of many commentators:

- Be aware of the impact of sexual exploitation on clients.
- Practice in a traditional setting with others present.
- Maintain a businesslike office.
- Dress in an appropriate, professional manner.
- Avoid inappropriate self-disclosure.
- Avoid or minimize non-professional contact with clients.
- Consult or seek supervision if sexually attracted to a client.
- Seek continuing education or training on the topic.
- Monitor and respond to symptoms of burnout.[22]

---

21.   *Ibid.*, at 268.
22.   D.R. Evans, *The Law, Standards of Practice, and Ethics in the Practice of Psychology* (Toronto: Emond Montgomery, 1997) at 63.

It seems, then, that the best defence truly is a good offence, and that the most effective and safest way for a social worker to deal with sexual feelings for a client is to avoid giving the feelings an opportunity to develop in the first place.

E.   Client-Initiated Sexual Behaviour

8.4   If a client initiates behaviour of a sexual nature, the member states clearly that this behaviour is inappropriate by virtue of the professional relationship.

8.4.1   If overtures or provocative sexual behaviour by a client toward a College member become intrusive to the counselling or therapy process, the College member may choose to terminate the relationship and may offer to assist the client to seek alternative services.

At first glance, Interpretation 8.4.1 appears straightforward. Although the *Handbook* gives the social worker permission to terminate the relationship with the client, it fails to address the personal welfare issues affecting the social worker. A client who makes sexual overtures, especially after being cautioned, is a potential threat to the social worker, who would be within his or her rights to file charges for sexual harassment and possibly assault. The lack of respect for the social worker demonstrated by the client raises the possibility that the client is unstable and a potential threat to the social worker's physical safety (not to mention the threat to the social worker's emotional welfare). If the social worker does feel frightened, what is the appropriate response? How does the social worker maintain the client's confidentiality? Indeed, should the social worker even try to maintain confidentiality? Would it be ethical to refer the client to another social worker (or to a professional of a different type), thereby perhaps putting another person at risk?

F.   Dual Relationships and Sexual Misconduct

8.5   College members do not provide clinical services to individuals with whom they have had a prior relationship of a sexual nature.

8.6   Sexual relationships between College members and clients at the time of referral, assessment, counselling, psychotherapy, or other professional services are prohibited.

8.7   Sexual relationships between College members and clients to whom the members have provided psychotherapy and/or counselling services are prohibited at any time following termination of the professional relationship.

8.8   Sexual relationships between College members and clients to whom the members have provided social work or social work [*sic*] services, other than psychotherapy or counselling services, are prohibited for a period of one (1) year following termination of the professional relationship.

8.9   College members do not engage in sexual activities with client's relatives or other individuals with whom clients maintain a close personal relationship when there is a risk of exploitation or potential harm to the client or when such activities would compromise the appropriate professional boundaries between the member and the client.

These five Interpretations lead into a discussion of dual relationships, which social workers are advised by Interpretation 3.7 to avoid. Simply defined, a dual relationship is a relationship where a person fulfills more than one role for another person, for instance a therapist and a friend, or a counsellor and a co-worker. Although dual relationships are not always sexual relationships, this chapter confines its discussion of dual relationships to the context of sexual misconduct.

One problem with dual relationships is that they "can erode and distort the professional nature of the therapeutic relationship, which is secured within a reliable set of boundaries upon which both therapist and patient can depend." In addition, "dual relationships can create conflicts of interest and thus compromise the disinterest (*not* lack of interest) necessary for sound professional judgment."[23] As a therapist, the social worker professes to put the client's interests first, but in dual relationships a set of conflicting interests develops. Rather than acting in the best interest of the client, the social worker in a dual relationship is satisfying his or her own needs at the client's expense. A second concern arises if there is an already established therapist-client relationship because of the fact that the secondary relationship cannot be one of equality. Lastly, it is possible that the social worker could one day be called on to testify about the client in court, in which case the dual relationship could raise concerns about the impartiality of the social worker's testimony. For a variety of reasons, then, dual relationships are not advisable, whether the therapeutic relationship precedes the non-therapeutic relationship or whether they develop in the reverse order.

---

23.   Pope and Vasquez, above note 3, at 193.

The dual relationship problem is even more of a concern for social workers who practise in small towns and rural areas. Frederic Reamer notes that "The likelihood of unanticipated boundary issues increases in geographically small communities, especially in rural areas. Human service professionals in these settings often report how challenging it is when they encounter clients in, for instance, the local supermarket, community center, or house of worship."[24] In smaller communities, where the availability of social work services is limited, it is not unusual for a social worker to discover that he or she is on the same committee, is a member of the same health club, or is a resident of the same neighbourhood as a client or a client's relative. It is also not unusual to get to know someone in a non-professional setting who later asks to become a client.

As has already been explained, sexual relationships with clients, or providing counselling or psychotherapy to those with whom one has had a sexual relationship, is forbidden. Beyond that, it is the social worker's responsibility to manage the dual relationship as best as possible. Maintaining one's privacy and limiting self-disclosure is one difficult aspect of this. Encountering one another in social situations such as parties is potentially very awkward for both the social worker and the client. While accepting that these encounters cannot be avoided, the social worker must try to handle them in the least damaging manner. In discussing the situation of those who practise in small towns, rural communities, and other remote locales, Donald Bersoff reports on a study that notes that many of the dual relationships involved such locales and that many of the subjects interviewed "implicitly or explicitly complained that the principles seem to ignore the special conditions in small, self-contained communities."[25]

Client confidentiality is also an issue when the social worker must refuse to engage in a certain activity to avoid a conflict of interest, but the refusal itself may cause the client's identity to become known. Even quickly greeting a client in a grocery store may compel the social worker or the client to explain to others in the vicinity how he or she knows the person being greeted. Handling dual relationships becomes even more of a challenge when one takes into account the families of both the social worker and the client. One's spouse could be on the same sports team as the client; one's children may want to join a sleepover at the residence of a person one had to report for child abuse; or one's client might complain about treatment received at a local business that is, unbeknownst to the client, run by one's sibling. The list of possibilities is endless. If the social worker is new to a community, avoid-

---

24. F.G. Reamer, *Tangled Relationships: Managing Boundary Issues in the Human Services* (New York: Columbia University Press, 2001) at 173.
25. D. Bersoff, *Ethical Conflicts in Psychology* (Washington, DC: American Psychological Association, 1999) at 70.

ance becomes a more challenging problem as time passes and the social worker and his or her family become more enmeshed in the community.

Obviously, dual relationships can cause a great deal of stress and confusion. A good rule of thumb when questioning the wisdom of a dual relationship may be to "ask yourself if you would be comfortable about having all of your colleagues know exactly what you were doing. If the answer is yes, no need to worry."[26] In any case, increased awareness of the issues may prevent problems for the social worker in the long run.

G.   Who Is a Client?

Although the law clearly holds that social workers and other professionals can be liable for the sexual abuse of their clients and patients within the confines of a professional relationship, what is often not clear is when someone can be considered a client (or patient). How the courts define a client can be seen in the British Columbia Court of Appeal case of *Smith* v. *Kamloops and District Elizabeth Fry Society*.[27] The appellant Smith was employed as a social worker by the Elizabeth Fry Society for 20 years. Her boyfriend, L.I., whom she met in early May 1993, was subsequently convicted of sexual abuse and ordered to undergo counselling by the society. Although Smith was concerned about L.I.'s pending status as a client of the society, her concerns were alleviated by the fact that L.I. would be treated by a therapist on contract to the society and would not be a client of hers. She did not inform her supervisor or the agency about her relationship with L.I. and so the society did not have the opportunity to manage the situation so that it would not constitute a conflict.

Smith's relationship with L.I. eventually came to the attention of the society's executive director, who made it clear that she was in a potential conflict of interest and in breach of the code of ethics governing British Columbia social workers, which provided that a social worker must not permit his or her outside interests to jeopardize professional judgment, independence, or competence. Smith disagreed, was fired, and then brought an action against the society for wrongful dismissal.

At trial, the society conceded that no harm had been done to it, but pointed out there might well have been adverse publicity even though Smith had nothing to do with the sexual offender program and was therefore not involved in counselling L.I. The society took the position that there was certainly the potential for a conflict of interest and that Smith should have been aware of that potential. The trial judge agreed with the society and found that

---

26.   Ross and Roy, above note 7, at 4.
27.   [1996] B.C.J. No. 1214 (C.A.) (QL).

L.I. was indirectly a client of Smith and that Smith's relationship with L.I. could have damaged the society's reputation with the public. The dismissal was justified because her personal relationship jeopardized the trust and confidence of her employment relationship. The appeal court agreed with the trial judge and dismissed Smith's appeal. The court held that Smith's relationship with her boyfriend was incompatible with her duties as a social worker. Her position required a high degree of professionalism, trust, and judgment, which was incompatible with her relationship with L.I.

Interpretation 8.6 states that sexual relationships between clients and members of the College are prohibited "at the time of referral, assessment, counselling, psychotherapy, or other professional services." The meaning of the phrase time of referral is not explained but only makes sense if it is taken to mean the time of initial professional contact between the social worker and the client. In the case of a social work agency, if it means the time of initial contact with the agency, that would imply that the agency would have to refuse services to any partner of a social worker employed by the agency. It would mean, as well, that any social worker considering employment with the agency would first have to check that his or her partner had never received services from that agency. Apart from the obvious logistical nightmare, this checking would compromise the client's confidentiality. Furthermore, in rural settings it would deny many individuals the benefit of services. In private practice, time of referral must necessarily be defined as the time of the actual intake process, because the social worker cannot control the initial referral process or telephone inquiries from potential clients.

That social workers and their clients must never engage in a sexual relationship is clear but, as Barker and Branson ask, "Is there a point in time after which the person is no longer a client and thus eligible for . . . a [sexual] relationship [with the therapist]?" In answer to this question they remark that "Hopefully the benefits of therapy are lifelong; the influence of the therapist exists equally as long. Thus, one never leaves the status of 'client.' Therefore, the defensive practice is this: **Once therapy has begun, a sexual relationship between the therapist and client is permanently inappropriate.**"[28]

H. Consequences Of Sexual Misconduct

An Ontario social worker who has sexual relations with a client will be found guilty of professional misconduct at a College discipline hearing if the College learns of the relationship.

---

28. Barker and Branson, above note 2, at 33.

In sexual misconduct cases, the punishment options open to the Discipline Committee are the same as those for other types of professional misconduct. The committee can suspend or revoke the member's certificate of registration or make it subject to terms, conditions, or limitations, which can include ordering the member to undergo counselling or participate in an educational program. In this regard the Discipline Committee has more leeway than the discipline committees of Ontario's regulated health professions, which must adhere to the provisions of the *Regulated Health Professions Act, 1991*, which specifies a mandatory minimum penalty for sexual misconduct, including a reprimand and revocation of the member's professional license.

The only exception to the prohibition against sexual relations between social workers and clients is contained in Interpretation 8.8, which stipulates that if a social worker provides services *other than* counselling or psychotherapy, a sexual relationship may be commenced after a year has passed since the termination of the professional relationship. If the social worker has provided, for example, community planning or educational services and has not developed a relationship that includes intimate knowledge of the client or the transference phenomenon, the one-year waiting period applies.

I.   Does A Zero Tolerance Policy Go Too Far?

From the professional's point of view, the difficulty with such a zero tolerance policy is that there is no room for discretion or consideration of extenuating circumstances. An extraordinary example of the inflexibility of zero tolerance policies is found in the 2001 case of *A.B.* v. *College of Physicians and Surgeons of Prince Edward Island*.[29] This case involved a medical physician, A.B., who was charged with professional misconduct by the College for having sexual relations with a former patient, Z. A.B. had treated Z. several years earlier, but the physician-patient relationship had ended in 1991. In 1994, A.B. and Z. became reacquainted, and in 1998 they began a sexual relationship. It is important to note that Z. was a mature, educated professional woman and had not complained to the College. There was no evidence that Z. had been taken advantage of or was in any way vulnerable.

The relevant section of the province's *Medical Act* required revocation of A.B.'s medical license for five years on being found guilty of professional misconduct. A.B. and Z. brought an application to have the discipline proceedings quashed on the basis that A.B.'s constitutional rights were being violated. Fortunately, the judge agreed with the applicants and stayed the discipline proceedings. The case, which as of the time of writing is under appeal, is a perfect example of how a policy designed to protect vulnerable

---

29.   [2001] P.E.I.J. No. 89 (S.C.T.D.) (QL).

individuals can be taken too far. A provision in the *Medical Act* states that certain patients will forever remain vulnerable to the treating physician and denies them the right to make their own decisions about personal relationships with their ex-doctors. This flies in the face of the social work concept that clients should be encouraged to exercise self-determination.

J.   Why Sexual Misconduct Occurs

One question this chapter has yet to answer is posed by Ross and Roy: "How does it happen that from time to time analysts have sexual relations with their patients, although they are fully aware of the taboo and the consequences of breaking it?"[30] In reply, we can observe that social workers are at much greater risk of becoming sexually involved with a client if their own lives are chaotic, unsatisfactory, and poorly bounded; if their self-esteem is low or, conversely, they have an inflated sense of their own importance; if they are overworked, overstressed, and experiencing burnout; or if there is no one they can turn to to discuss their concerns. Perhaps in part because they endure secondary trauma from constantly hearing about the ills of the world, social workers run a higher than average risk of attempting to soothe their feelings in destructive ways such as "alcohol and drug misuse, acting out by exploiting patients, manic defenses manifested as overwork and self-neglect, recurrent depressions, and suicide."[31]

As was discussed above, schools of social work rarely address the topic of sexual relations with clients, and it may be that lack of knowledge plays a major role in leading social workers into trouble. Janice Russell points out that "It seems that many therapists do not realize that the problem even exists. This is not helped when the possibilities of either sexual attraction, or of the potential for abuse, are not adequately addressed in training, if at all. There is ignorance about the effect of such exploitation on the clients involved and about how to work reparatively with abused clients."[32] Social workers are generally unaware of the fact that sexual attraction between therapists and clients is not only not unusual but also possibly quite normal. They are frequently embarrassed by their feelings and ashamed to admit them. Because of mandatory reporting and lack of information, they have no one to turn to for help and so they internalize their thoughts, which increases the likelihood of acting-out behaviours, including sexual involvement with clients.

---

30.   Ross and Roy, above note 7, at 59.
31.   *Ibid.*, at 83.
32.   J. Russell, *Out of Bounds: Sexual Exploitation in Counselling and Therapy* (London: Sage Publications, 1993) at 147.

Boundary violations and confusion are generally at the root of sexual abuse cases and have many legal implications. Avoiding sexual misconduct is not as clear-cut an issue as it may initially seem. No matter how it is characterized or explained, the courts will always find that sexual activity with a client is improper and never in the client's best interest. If social workers are going to avoid sexual misconduct they must be able to anticipate potentially dangerous situations, have awareness of the issues, and learn the art of self-care.

Chapter 13

Mandatory Reporting

When the Ontario government drafted the *Social Work and Social Service Work Act, 1998,*[1] it gave the College the authority to pass by-laws governing most aspects of members' conduct. There was a significant exception, however: the obligation of mandatory reports to the College concerning members' conduct. There are two aspects to mandatory reporting. One covers employers of social workers and the other relates directly to the social worker. Conduct by a professional that violates his or her client (or patient) and as such violates the Act, is a subject that in recent years has received a great deal of publicity. The fact that the government refused to give the College the authority to make rules concerning mandatory reporting and instead set out the rules in detail in the Act indicates the seriousness with which both the government and the public view this issue. A fine of up to $25,000.00 is possible for failure to make a mandatory report. Failure to report can also be considered professional misconduct.

Although mandatory reporting is covered in the Act but not in the College's *Standards of Practice Handbook*, it is a topic just as important as any covered in the *Handbook*, and social workers must make the effort to familiarize themselves with their reporting obligations under the Act. These obligations are spelled out in sections 41-45 of the Act, which state as follows:

> 41. (1) A person who, for reasons of professional misconduct, incompetence or incapacity of a member of the College, terminates the employment of the member shall file with the Registrar within 30 days after the termination, a written report setting out the reasons.
>
> (2) If a person intended to terminate the employment of a member for reasons of professional misconduct, incompetence or incapacity but the person did not do so because the member resigned, the person shall file with the Registrar

---

1.   *Social Work and Social Service Work Act, 1998* [*SWSSW Act*], S.O. 1998, c. 31.

within 30 days after the resignation a written report setting out the reasons upon which the person intended to act.

42. (1) A person shall promptly notify the College in writing if the person becomes aware that a member of the College who is or has been employed by the person has been convicted of an offence under the *Criminal Code* (Canada) involving sexual conduct.

(2) A member of the College shall promptly notify the College in writing if he or she is convicted of an offence under the *Criminal Code* (Canada) involving sexual conduct.

43. (1) A member of the College shall file a report to the College in accordance with section 44 if, in the course of his or her practice, the member obtains reasonable grounds to believe that another member has sexually abused a client.

Exception
(2) A member is not required to file a report under subsection (1) if the member does not have information to identify the member who would be the subject of the report.

Information from client
(3) If a member is required to file a report because of reasonable grounds obtained from one of the member's clients, the member shall use his or her best efforts to advise the client of the requirement to file the report before doing so.

Definition
(4) In this section and section 44,
"sexual abuse", with respect to a client by a member of the College means,

   (a)   sexual intercourse or another form of physical sexual relations between the member and the client,

   (b)   touching, of a sexual nature, of the client by the member, or

   (c)   behaviour or remarks of a sexual nature by the member towards the client, other than behaviour or remarks of a clinical nature appropriate to the service provided.

Time for filing report
44. (1) A report under section 43 shall be filed,

   (a)   forthwith, if the person who is required to file the report has reasonable grounds to believe that the member will continue to sexually abuse the client or will sexually abuse other clients, or

   (b)   within 30 days after the obligation to report arose, otherwise.

Contents of report
(2) The report shall include,

   (a)   the name of the person filing the report;

   (b)   the name of the member who is the subject of the report;

   (c)   an explanation of the alleged sexual abuse;

   (d)   if the grounds of the person filing the report are related to a particular client of the member who is the subject of the report, the name of that client, subject to subsection (3).

Consent required re name
(3) The name of a client who may have been sexually abused shall not be included in a report unless the client, or if the client is incapable, the client's representative, consents in writing to the inclusion of the client's name.

No proceeding against person reporting
45. No proceeding shall be instituted against a person for filing a report in good faith under this Part.

A.   Whistleblowing

Although mandatory reporting is also provided for in the *Regulated Health Professions Act, 1991*,[2] and its value is not in question, it does run contrary to what social workers may be comfortable with. The requirement to report a colleague whenever sexual abuse is alleged, even if reporting is opposed by the client who provided the information on which the report rests, flies in the face of the social work values of client confidentiality and self-determination, and requires social workers to do something they commonly oppose, namely whistleblowing, often referred to by some as "snitching." This places a heavy burden on members of the College by requiring them to become "whistleblowers" in cases of suspected sexual abuse.[3] This obligation does not extend to any other aspect of practice.

B.   Mandatory Reporting by Social Workers

There are three distinct ways that a social worker may obtain information suggesting that another social worker has sexually abused a client. He or she may get the information from a client who was the victim of abuse by another social worker; the information may come from a client who tells the social worker of someone else who has been sexually abused by another social worker; or the social worker may be told in a non-professional setting about the sexual abuse of a client by a social worker.

The third of these is the easiest to deal with: the Act states that the social worker must get the information in the course of his or her practice. Hearing about the improprieties of another social worker in a non-professional setting, such as a party or the gym, constitutes gossip, and as such, is not reportable.

In the first scenario, the information about alleged sexual abuse by another social worker comes from a client who claims in session that he or she was the one abused. The client may not believe that he or she has been harmed by the relationship and is disclosing the information only because, for example,

2.   *Regulated Health Professions Act, Procedural Code*, ss. 85.1, 85.2, 85.3, 85.4.
3.   Reporting obligations are also imposed on the employers of social workers. These are set forth in sections 41-42 of the Act and discussed in chapter 13.

he or she wants to discuss relationship patterns. The social worker is, nevertheless, required to report the alleged abuse, even if the social worker believes that the client will be harmed more by the reporting than by the abuse itself. The social worker has no discretion in this regard because the provisions of the Act are not meant to assist the victim but rather to police the profession by punishing the perpetrators and preventing future victimizations. In a sense the client is viewed as a child who lacks the capacity to make an informed decision about whether the abuse should be reported.

The second scenario is the one where a client tells a social worker about another individual who has been sexually abused by another social worker. This does fall under the duty of mandatory reporting and, again, the social worker has no discretion in this matter. In any case, it is not up to the social worker to evaluate or verify the allegations, but merely to file the report.

C.   Mandatory Reporting by Employers of Social Workers

Mandatory reporting by employers of social workers is required in three situations. First, when an employer terminates an employee for professional misconduct, incompetence, or incapacity, the employer must file a report stating the reasons for the termination within 30 days.[4] The second situation to which mandatory reporting applies arises when an employee resigns before the employer can carry out his or her intention to terminate the employee. Lastly, the reporting requirement applies if the employer learns that an employee has been convicted of an offence under the *Criminal Code* involving sexual misconduct. (In addition, any member of the College convicted of such an offence is required to report the conviction to the College.)

D.   Determining When to Report

Mandatory reporting is thus required for, among other things, inappropriate comments of a sexual nature, including sexual innuendo and jokes. Accordingly, a member whose inappropriate behaviour is restricted to comments faces disciplinary proceedings just as severe as those faced by a member who actually has sexual relations with a client.

How does a member know when he or she should report an incident of sexual abuse? Richard Steinecke's guide to the *Regulated Health Professions Act, 1991* provides an excellent checklist of items to consider before report-

---

4.   *SWSSW Act*, above note 1, s. 41(1).

ing sexual abuse. A report should be submitted if one can answer yes to all six of the following questions:

1. Do you know the name of the alleged abuser?
2. Is the alleged abuser registered with the College?
3. Was the other person involved a client of the alleged sexual abuser?
4. Did the conduct involve one or more of the elements of sexual abuse as defined in the Act?
5. Was the information about the alleged sexual abuse obtained in the course of practising your profession?
6. Does the information constitute "reasonable grounds"?[5]

As Steinecke makes clear, a member is required to submit a report only if he or she knows the name of the abuser and the abuser is a member of the College. Also, it is important to consider the circumstances in which the information is obtained. Information obtained in the course of practising one's profession, not information obtained at a party or in some other social setting, is required. The reporting member must also be clear about the veracity of the information; there must be "reasonable grounds" for submitting a report, which means something more than rumour or innuendo.

E. Dilemmas of Mandatory Reporting

In the United States, some states also have laws that require therapists to report suspicions that a client of theirs has been the victim of sexual misconduct by a previous therapist. In Wisconsin, the law states that if a therapist has reasonable cause to suspect a client has been the victim of sexual conduct by another therapist, the therapist must ask the client whether he or she would like the therapist to file a report on the client's behalf. The client need not be identified in the report but does have to give written consent for it to be submitted. Unlike the situation in Ontario, then, final control remains with the client. The client's dignity and right to self-determination are preserved.

There are some inherent dilemmas with the duty to report another social worker. When a social worker files a sexual abuse report without the client's consent, is it not inevitable that the social worker will compromise his or her relationship with the client by failing to recognize the client's right to confidentiality and autonomy? Of course, there is no breach of confidentiality if the client is told about the reporting requirement at the outset of the profes-

---

5. R. Steinecke, *A Complete Guide to the Regulated Health Professions Act* (Aurora, ON: Canada Law Book, 1995) at 10-9 & 10-10.

sional relationship, but this may limit the topics that the client feels able to discuss, thereby weakening the professional relationship and diminishing the psychotherapeutic benefits of counselling.

As we have seen, under the *Social Work and Social Service Work Act, 1998* the allegedly abused client can refuse to allow his or her name to be used in a report. For the client's name to be included in the report, a signed consent form therefore needs to be obtained. If the client refuses to give permission, what action can the College take? Can it pursue the alleged victimizer without being able to name the victim? Does the accused not have a right to face his or her accuser? And what if the allegation is untrue? Transference allows many misguided emotions and beliefs to be acted out. Clients can become confused and misinterpret words or actions.

The probable result if the client's name is withheld will be the same course of action set out in the *Regulated Health Professions Act, 1991*, which provides that the report is to be held for future reference, so that if further allegations against the alleged abuser come to light, the College can ask the social worker who made the original report to revisit the consent issue with the client in the hope that the client, on hearing that others have made similar allegations, will come forward.

There are a number of reasons why a client, even if promised that his or her name will not appear in the report to the College, may not want to disclose that he or she has had a sexual relationship with a social worker. If the social worker in question has had a sexual relationship with just one client, simply making the report will divulge the client's identity to the abuser. If the abuser becomes angry or feels threatened, the client's safety could be endangered. Or the client may not want to report the sexual contact because it was relatively minor and the consequences of reporting the incident will be more harmful to the client than the incident itself. In small communities, for instance, a client may be unable to avoid a dual relationship with an abuser, or the community may be able to easily identify the accuser if the allegation becomes public.

If a social worker is told by another social worker that the latter is or was involved in a sexual relationship with a client, this information must be reported to the College. Although in this case no client is being confronted with the choice of allowing his or her name to be disclosed, the abuser is not only being denied the benefit of confidentiality, but also he or she may be a client of the reporting social worker.

Although the Act is very clear on how a social worker must deal with the issue of mandatory reporting, many pitfalls and moral dilemmas remain. It is very difficult to espouse the inherent social work principles of belief in the intrinsic worth of the client, of the egalitarian relationship, and of the client's right to make his or her own decisions, while at the same time upholding the view of the client as a child unable to give informed consent, make his or her own decisions, or evaluate decisions already made. As Koocher notes, "to violate [the client's] wishes in favor of the more diffuse 'public good' would be tantamount to inflicting a second emotional assault to a specific victim in the hope of preventing harm to persons unknown. I would therefore favor respecting and protecting the vulnerable client even if that meant committing a technical violation of the law."[6] The quandary of the social worker caught between the best interests of the client and the public good is apparent.

Mandatory reporting denies clients the right to discuss issues that may be important to them for reasons other than those mandatory reporting is intended to address. Consider, for example, a client who is in a relationship with her former therapist and wants to terminate the relationship for reasons that have nothing to do with the fact that he is her former therapist. She wants to discuss the situation with her current therapist, but fears that any discussion will divulge the identity of her former therapist. Windy Dryden believes that "in these circumstances the wishes of the client with regard to confidentiality ought to be given priority. It is possible that the harm done to the client personally or professionally by any breach of confidentiality by yourself could be considerable and this needs to be taken into account."[7] Dryden acknowledges the importance of offering the client an opportunity to lodge a complaint against the therapist, but emphasizes that the current therapist's priorities should be the client's well-being, and then the abuser, in that order. This is clearly a different view than now exists in Ontario. Even though social workers in Ontario claim to make the client's best interest their priority, they are nonetheless placed in a paternalistic role of believing that they and the social work profession know what is best for the client.

Another concern relates to mentally unstable clients who have a sense of grandiosity and a need to inflate their own importance by presenting themselves as people constantly at the heart of a crisis. A client of this kind who wants attention can create quite a stir by falsely reporting sexual abuse by a previous therapist. Many other scenarios that would encourage a false report can be imagined, for example, the client who is angry at a previous therapist for reasons unrelated to sexual abuse, and alleges sexual abuse simply to cause trouble for the previous therapist. But even if the current therapist knows the client well enough to realize that the allegations are probably untrue, there is no room for individual discretion, and a report must still be filed.

A British perspective on reporting of allegedly abusive colleagues is provided by Caroline Jones, a member of the British Association for Counselling. Jones acknowledges that it is rare to witness an individual

---

6. G. Koocher, "Ethical & Professional Standards in Psychology," in B.D. Sales, ed., *The Professional Psychologist's Handbook* (New York, NY: Plenum Press, 1983) at 103.

7. W. Dryden, *Questions and Answers on Counselling in Action* (London: Sage Publications, 1993) at 110.

counsellor's work with a client, which means that one is unlikely to have direct evidence of ethical breaches. She also believes that the client has a right to self-determination vis-à-vis reporting and recognizes that the client may be using his or her present counselling arrangement to talk through concerns about previous therapy. Jones discusses the options that must be considered when deciding whether to take action. Her discussion presents a four-step decision-making process. It is clear that British counsellors have some leeway with regard to reporting, while Ontario social workers are denied any input into the decision to report. If abuse by a social worker is alleged, then the Ontario social worker must report it.

A safeguard exists, however, in that a legal action may not be commenced against a social worker who files a report so long as he or she made it in good faith and without malicious intent. In this way the social worker is protected from liability if the report turns out to be erroneous. This, of course, means that the allegations do not have to be verified before the report is made. As in cases of suspected child abuse, it is not the social worker's obligation to substantiate the claim. The fact that the social worker does have to give his or her name can make for some very awkward situations. In a small community or in an agency, for example, the two social workers may frequently and unavoidably come into contact with each other through their employment or community involvements. The problems that can arise are unending: gossip, anger, maliciousness, and lack of mutual cooperation are just some concerns. But what if a member does not report a fellow social worker because he or she just does not want to get involved or is a friend of the alleged abuser? Can an action for failure to report be commenced against a member under these circumstances? How mandatory is mandatory reporting?

In the 1994 Ontario case of *Toms* v. *Foster*,[8] two physicians were sued by the victims of a car accident for failing, before the accident, to report to the Ministry of Transportation that their patient — the driver who caused the accident — was medically unfit to drive. Although both physicians had asked the patient to stop driving, neither reported him to the Ministry, even though legislation made reporting mandatory. The physicians argued that they used their professional judgment not to report the patient in this instance as they both felt he could be trusted not to drive. The Ontario Court of Appeal rejected the physicians' arguments and held that the duty to report was mandatory and must therefore be obeyed. The court found that the duty to report was not just a duty to the patient but also to the public; the legislation, the court held, was designed to protect not only patients but also the people they might harm if permitted to drive. According to the court, failure to report creates civil liability if the failure leads to others being harmed.

---

8.   [1994] O.J. No. 1413 (C.A.) (QL).

There is no reason to believe that the result in *Toms* would not apply to a situation in which a social worker failed to report sexual abuse of a client by a fellow social worker who then went on to sexually abuse another client. The second client could sue the social worker who failed to make the report on the basis that the abuser would not have been in a position to abuse the second client had the social worker reported his or her colleague.

No matter what the setting, the social worker also needs to "consider the possible consequences for his own career if he is earnest about blowing the whistle"[9] and remember that "the danger of retaliation against a social worker who reports irregularities or maltreatment of clients occurring within their own agencies is always present."[10] This in turn forces the social worker to ask, "To what extent is it legitimate for him to factor [career-related considerations] into the equation?"[11]

And what if animosity between the two social workers already exists? It is not hard to imagine that there may be some social workers who would be prepared to submit a false report as a means towards taking a colleague's job or injuring a colleague in some other way. The College begins their investigation presuming that the report was made in good faith, but this presumption can be wrong. In situations where, for example, a social worker makes a report out of vindictiveness or to retaliate against another therapist, the accused social worker can sue the reporting social worker for damages as a result of the false or erroneous report.

Mandatory reporting creates yet another dilemma for social workers: The social worker who is in need of personal counselling may be denied this support. "Mental health professionals are expected by everyone, including themselves, to be paragons. The fact that they may be unable to fill that role makes them a prime target for disillusionment, distress, and burnout. When this reaction occurs, the individual's ability to function as a professional may become impaired . . . Unfortunately, relatively little is known about the extent to which impaired human service professionals, especially those who violate clients' boundaries or engage in unethical dual relationships, voluntarily seek help for their problems."[12] What does an impaired Ontario social worker do when he or she approaches burnout? And will the social worker recognize when he or she is burned out? Burnout can be described as a "kind of emotional exhaustion resulting from excessive demands on energy,

---

9.   E. Gambrill and R. Pruger, *Controversial Issues in Social Work* (Needham Heights, MA: Allyn and Bacon, 1992) at 71.

10.   E. Vayda and M. Satterfield, *Law for Social Workers: A Canadian Guide* (Toronto: Carswell, 1989) at 304.

11.   Gambrill and Pruger, above note 9, at 71.

12.   F.G. Reamer, *Tangled Relationships: Managing Boundary Issues in the Human Services* (New York: Columbia University Press, 2001) at 50.

strength and personal resources in the work setting."[13] The social worker may find himself or herself in a state of depression and not really connecting with clients. The social worker's emotions are blunted and his or her sense of self is lessened. The social worker reacts rather than developing a planned response; his or her sense of personal boundaries as well as the boundaries of others becomes blurred. This is burnout, but it is hard to recognize in one's self.

It is in this state that sexual misconduct is most likely to occur. "Supervisors have an important ethical responsibility to ensure that the supervisory relationship provides a safe and supportive opportunity to learn to recognize and handle such feelings appropriately. Most training programs spend little or no time addressing the prohibition against sexual contact with clients, yet it is the most commonly violated of the ethical principles."[14]

Unlike social workers who arrogantly disregard the ethics of their profession, believing that they are above the law and have the right to put their own needs first, the social workers who burn out are the workaholics, the ones who attempt to give their all to their clients. The crossing of inviolate boundaries is often the shocking event that alerts them to their desperate state. And as they approach burnout or become burned out, where can they look for help? They cannot approach their colleagues or supervisors for support or counselling without running the risk of being reported, even if they have merely contemplated a sexual encounter with a client. Although sexual involvement with one's clients is never acceptable, the requirement to report claims of sexual abuse, even against a client's will, may not always help the client, nor does it allow the social worker who has contemplated or engaged in inappropriate behaviour to get help for the problem or for the burnout.

If the social worker did not fear being reported, supervision or consultation could circumvent much of the burnout and subsequent sexual abuse of patients by social workers. Janice Russell states that "The supervisor's responsibility is to ensure that as far as possible, the supervisee is enabled rather than disabled. If the supervisee feels that he or she is in danger of transgressing boundaries and knows that disclosure of this will result in being immediately reported to a disciplinary body, then no disclosure will take place. Thus this will be counterproductive for the client"[15]

Others echo this view. Although mandatory reporting appears at first glance to be the most responsible approach, there may be more effective

---

13.   G. Koocher and P. Keith-Spiegel, *Ethics in Psychology* (New York, NY: Oxford University Press, 1998) at 69.
14.   K. Pope and M. Vasquez, *Ethics in Psychotherapy and Counselling* (San Francisco: Jossey-Bass Publishers, 1998) at 268.
15.   J. Russell, *Out of Bounds: Sexual Exploitation in Counselling and Therapy* (London: Sage Publications, 1993) at 125.

means to support our colleagues while protecting our clients. According to Derek Jehu,

> Effective clinical supervision of trainees and practitioners can help to prevent the sexual abuse of patients by identifying and responding to the risk characteristics and preconditions including:
>
> 1. Personal distress.
> 2. Misuse of drugs or alcohol.
> 3. Sexual or emotional attraction to patients.
> 4. Distorted perceptions and feelings about sexual abuse of patients.
> 5. Violation of boundaries.
> 6. Personality problems involving narcissism, power or antisocial behaviour.[16]

Through appropriate supervision or consultation, the warning signs of potential difficulty should be detectable. However, "when one undertakes to supervise the work of another therapist, one also assumes a legal liability not only for one's own acts but for those of the supervisee."[17] With this in mind, as well as the thought of the potential fine of up to $25,000 for failure to report, the supervisor or consultant will probably feel the need to report any concerns to the College, no matter how inconsequential. In Great Britain, the extent to which supervisors are legally liable for the actions of the therapists in their charge is as yet mostly untested and probably quite limited. In the United States, on the other hand, their liability is more firmly established.[18] It is unfortunate that supervision or consultation as an initial attempt to cope is unavailable to social workers in Ontario because of fear of repercussions not only to the social worker but also to the supervisor or consultant.

F.   Conclusion

It is possible that the College, its members, and its members' clients would be better served if supervisors and consultants were freed from the burden of reporting. To reiterate: "supervision is a necessity to good practice rather than a luxury, . . . it needs to be enabling rather than constricting, . . . it is a skilled process, and . . . it is *for the client's interests and safety.* Good supervision is one way to pre-empt an overstepping of boundaries."[19] When the

---

16. D. Jehu, *Patients as Victims: Sexual Abuse in Psychotherapy and Counselling* (New York: John Wiley & Sons, 1994) at 198.
17. B. Schutz, *Legal Liability in Psychotherapy: A Practitioner's Guide to Risk Management* (San Francisco: Jossey-Bass Publishers, 1982) at 47.
18. P. Jenkins, *Counselling, Psychotherapy and the Law* (London: Sage Publications, 1997) at 68.
19. Russell, above note 15, at 147.

Social Work and Social Service Work Act, 1998 comes up for review in 2005, it may be a good idea for policymakers to revisit the issue of mandatory reporting as it relates to supervisors and consultants.

Chapter 14

Malpractice and Other Sources of Civil and Criminal Liability

A.   Introduction

In the past, lawsuits against mental health professionals were relatively rare. For social workers, psychologists, and other mental health professionals who did not administer medication, the risk of incurring professional liability was extremely low. In recent years, this relative immunity from litigation has begun to erode in the United States, and it is not impossible that the same will occur in Canada.[1] The largest insurer of social workers in the United States, the National Association of Social Workers Insurance Trust, tracked the number of claims filed against its members and found that 634 claims were filed between 1965 and 1990.[2] Only one claim was filed in 1970, but by 1980 the annual number of claims had climbed to 40. The relatively few claims made against social workers in the 1970s were typical of this period as a whole for all health professions. By 1990 the annual figure was 126, an increase of over 200% in the ten years from 1980 to 1990.[3] This trend has almost certainly continued since 1990. Although Canada has not experienced American levels of litigation against social workers, it would be imprudent for Canadian social workers to believe that they cannot or will not be sued for malpractice.

Every social work setting provides the potential for liability. For example, social workers in a group practice can be held liable for the actions of other members of the group. Social workers employed by social service agencies can find themselves embroiled in a lawsuit if they give in to pressure from cost-conscious superiors to prematurely terminate service or to choose an

---

1.   F.G. Reamer, *Social Work Malpractice and Liability* (New York: Columbia University Press, 1994) at 4.
2.   *Ibid.*, at 5.
3.   *Ibid.*

143

inappropriate but less expensive course of treatment for a client. Children's aid societies and other child protection settings create liability risks of many kinds, for example, for failure to properly investigate or report child abuse or neglect, for wrongful removal of a child (and conversely, for returning a child to dangerous parents), for failure to adequately monitor a case, and for alleged malicious prosecution of parents and guardians. Social workers in private practice face risks associated with sexual impropriety, failure to protect and warn, incorrect treatment, and improper referral. As more and more social workers turn to private practice, the potential for liability will only increase.

It is therefore imperative for every social worker to have some knowledge of the law of malpractice, negligence, and liability. One of the trade-offs for enjoying the privilege of professional self-regulation is the public's expectation of accountability. If a regulated professional holds himself or herself out as possessing certain kinds of professional knowledge or skill, the public will assume that he or she does in fact have that knowledge and skill, and the professional's efforts will be judged against a standard of performance generally expected of other professionals in the field.

A professional who engages in actions that fail to meet this standard may be sued and found liable for damages. One of the leading cases to establish this principle was heard in 1964 by the English House of Lords, which held that

> It should now be regarded as settled that if someone possessed of a special skill undertakes, quite irrespective of contract, to apply that skill for the assistance of another person who relies on such skill, a duty of care will arise. The fact that the service is to be given by means of . . . words can make no difference. Furthermore, if . . . others could reasonably rely on his judgment or his skill or on his ability to make careful inquiry . . . to give information or advice to . . . another person who, as he knows or should know, will place reliance on it, then a duty of care will arise.[4]

The duty of care in negligence cases means that a reasonable person is required to conduct himself or herself in a particular manner so as to not increase the risk of harm to another person.

The greatest areas of risk for social workers are connected with civil liability rather than the criminal arena. Civil liability encompasses malpractice, intentional torts such as assault and battery, and breach of contract.

---

4.   *Hedley Byrne & Co.* v. *Heller & Partners*, [1964] A.C. 465 at 483, [1963] 2 All E.R. 575 at 594 (H.L.).

B. Malpractice

I) Introduction

Malpractice occurs when a professional harms a client through improper performance of his or her professional duties or by failure to perform a duty that ordinarily would be expected of that professional. It does not matter whether the professional's conduct is intentional or the result of carelessness or ignorance.[5] Some examples of improper performance (also called, in legal terminology, acts of commission or misfeasance) are sexual exploitation, breach of confidentiality, improper termination of service, and failure to obtain informed consent. Examples of failure to perform a duty (also called acts of omission or nonfeasance) can include failure to prevent a client's suicide, failure to protect third parties from harm, or failure to diagnose correctly. Most malpractice actions involve negligence or failure to meet a standard of care.

In a malpractice lawsuit, which is a civil rather than a criminal action, the client is the plaintiff and the social worker is the defendant. If the plaintiff wins the case, monetary damages are awarded. Usually these damages are paid by the social worker's insurance company or, if the social worker is uninsured, by the social worker personally.

II) The Elements of Malpractice

Four elements must be proved by anyone alleging malpractice against a social worker. They are

1. *Duty of Care.* That there was a professional relationship between the social worker and the plaintiff, and thus a duty imposed on the social worker to exercise care in dealing with the plaintiff.
2. *Standard of Care.* That the social worker's actions failed to meet an acceptable standard of care.
3. *Causation.* That the social worker's actions were the proximate cause of the plaintiff's injury.
4. *Actual Loss.* That the plaintiff suffered actual injury or harm.

a) Duty of Care

The existence of a professional relationship is the easiest element to prove. Appointment cards, receipts, or invoices from the social worker may be

---

5. R.L. Barker and D.M. Branson, *Forensic Social Work: Legal Aspects of Professional Practice* (New York: Haworth Press, 1993) at 25.

enough. If there is no professional relationship between a social worker and another person, the social worker is not bound by the professional duty of care. Social workers should thus avoid giving casual advice to others, which could be interpreted as creating a professional relationship. Whether a duty of care exists depends on the facts of the case. The courts have declined to find that a duty of care is owed by a professional to another person where there has been minimal contact between the two.

An example of the application of the duty of care principle is found in *Sisson* v. *Seneca Mental Health/Mental Retardation Council Inc.*, a West Virginia case.[6] That case involved two individuals at a mental health centre: Sisson, a female patient, and Malcomb, a male counsellor. Sisson had attended the centre before, but had been counselled by another person. On the occasion in question, however, her regular counsellor was on vacation, and she was seen by Malcomb, the on-call counsellor. During that first session she and the counsellor began a sexual relationship that lasted more than a year. Ultimately, Sisson initiated a malpractice suit against the mental health centre in which she alleged negligence on the part of its employee, Malcomb.

The court held that a relationship of trust must exist between a client and a therapist to sustain a negligence action against the therapist. The court defined a trust relationship as one resulting from an emotional bond that forms between a client and a therapist. To support a finding of a trust relationship, the therapy must take place over a sufficient period of time to warrant the client putting trust in the therapist, and there must be some evidence that therapy actually took place. The court found that Sisson's allegations did not support the longevity requirement for the establishment of a trust relationship and dismissed her action.

b)   *Standard of Care*

Establishing that a social worker's actions failed to meet an acceptable standard of care can be somewhat more difficult to prove. First it is necessary to establish what the standard of care in the given circumstances should be. Some standards are relatively easy to determine — for example, that a social worker must not have sexual relations with a client. Other standards, however, can be more difficult to determine. For example, although Ontario's *Standards of Practice Handbook* establishes standards with respect to termination of service, those standards are open to interpretation because of their imprecise wording.

Once the plaintiff has established that a particular standard applies, he or she must prove that the social worker did not exercise

---

6.   404 S.E.2d 425 (W. Va. 1991).

1.   the minimally accepted degree of knowledge or skill possessed by other practitioners, or
2.   the minimally acceptable degree of care, attention, diligence, or vigilance exercised in the application of those skills.[7]

It is important to keep in mind that a social worker who presents himself or herself as a specialist in a particular area of social work will be held to the standards expected of other specialists in that area. For example, if a social worker claims special expertise in treating substance abuse, post-traumatic stress disorders, or eating disorders, then his or her actions will be judged against the actions of other social workers with similar expertise in those same areas.

In court cases, existence of a standard of care is established by the testimony of experts, who can also testify on the question of the defendant's adherence or lack of adherence to the standard. The majority of malpractice cases rise or fall on expert testimony. If the expert or experts can establish that the social worker's actions met the standard of care expected of a reasonable social worker with similar experience acting in similar circumstances, the lawsuit will fail.

The courts, however, recognize that social work counselling and therapy are influenced by various (and sometimes competing) schools of thought. Since it can be difficult for the courts to ascertain which school is the appropriate one in the circumstances, judges often rely on the concept of "a respectable minority of the profession." If a "responsible and competent body of professional opinion, even a minority one," endorses a particular course of action, a social worker who follows that course of action will usually be found to have met the expected standard of care.[8]

It is important for social workers to be familiar with the codes of ethics, practice standards, and regulations that set out the minimum standards by which a social worker's conduct will be judged. Liability in a malpractice case can be established simply on the basis of the social worker's failure to adhere to an ethical or practice standard or an applicable regulation. For example, if the standard is clear, such as the prohibition against sexual relationships with a client, the social worker's failure to adhere to this standard will result in him or her being held liable in a malpractice case. Failure to adhere to an applicable law, rule, administrative procedure, or professional standard can create liability even if the defendant was unaware of the law or other legal requirement. Good faith is rarely a defence against failure to adhere to a law, rule, administrative procedure, or well-established professional standard of skill or conduct.

---

7.   B. Schutz, *Legal Liability in Psychotherapy: A Practitioner's Guide to Risk Management* (San Francisco: Jossey-Bass Publishers, 1982) at 5-6.
8.   *Brett* v. *Ontario (Board of Directors of Physiotherapy)* (1993), 104 D.L.R. (4th) 421 (Ont. C.A.), aff'g 77 D.L.R. (4th) 144 (Ont. Div. Ct.).

c)   Causation

The next step after establishing that a breach of a standard of care has occurred is to establish that the breach was the proximate or immediate cause of the damage or injury. The breach must be the direct cause of the injury. Establishing a causal link between the breach and the injury is easier in cases where the social worker directs or assists the client to do something concrete, such as confronting an abusive parent. Therapists have been sued in the United States for recommending that a client get a divorce or change jobs when that advice has had a detrimental effect on the client.

It can be difficult to establish a causal link in traditional forms of therapy such as "talk therapy." The test usually applied is the "but for" test, under which the client must prove that the loss or injury would not have occurred "but for" the social worker's negligence. Causation in malpractice cases was considered by the Supreme Court of Canada in *Snell* v. *Farrell*.[9] In that case the appellant, an ophthalmologist, had performed surgery on the respondent to remove a cataract from her right eye. The respondent subsequently lost the sight in her eye because of bleeding during the surgery, which resulted in optic nerve atrophy. At trial, the ophthalmologist was found to have been negligent. He then appealed the finding of negligence on the basis that neither of the two experts called at trial was able to state with certainty what had caused the nerve to atrophy. The Supreme Court, however, held that causation did not need to be determined with scientific precision. Although the court reinforced the principle that the legal burden of proof remains with the plaintiff, in the absence of evidence to the contrary introduced by the defendant, the courts may draw an inference of causation.

Causation is usually proved by experts who can provide documentary evidence and specialist opinion tying the plaintiff's injury or loss to the defendant's actions. The British Columbia case of *Madalena v. Kuhn* shows, however, how difficult it can be for a plaintiff to prove that the injury or loss he or she suffered was linked to a social worker's actions.[10] In that case, the plaintiff was a woman who had engaged in sexual intercourse with her foster father at age 15. The foster father was subsequently found guilty of having sexual relations with a minor and sentenced to nine months' imprisonment and two years' probation. When the plaintiff reached the age of majority she brought an action for damages against the foster father as well as the province's Superintendent of Family and Child Services. Her action against the latter defendant was founded on a claim that the Superintendent had breached a duty to the plaintiff to ensure that she would not suffer neglect or physical or sexual abuse while in the foster home. The plaintiff

---

9.   [1990] 2 S.C.R. 311.
10.   (1987), 35 D.L.R. (4th) 222 (B.C.S.C.).

claimed that the Superintendent was negligent in placing her in this particular foster home and in failing to adequately monitor the home.

At trial, evidence was introduced concerning the Superintendent's foster care policies, which included regular visits to the foster home, annual reviews, monitoring the activities of the child, and the development of a life plan outlining goals for each foster child. In the context of these polices the court looked at the conduct of the social service worker assigned to the case. The court found that the social service worker had not regularly visited the foster home and that other policies of the Superintendent's office had not been followed. However, the social service worker's actions, though found by the court to have been inadequate, were also found to have fallen short of being negligent.

The court also held that even if the social service worker had been so careless as to be negligent, the plaintiff would still not have succeeded because she had not proved that the harm she had suffered was a result of the social service worker's actions. There was no evidence to suggest that the plaintiff would have avoided sexual relations with the foster father if the quality of the social service work had been impeccable. The harm suffered by the plaintiff was a result of her having encouraged and freely consented to sexual intercourse with her foster father. Although in this instance the plaintiff's case was dismissed, it can be argued that the result might have been very different had the plaintiff not encouraged or freely consented to sexual relations.

d) Actual Loss

For a negligence case to succeed there must be evidence that the plaintiff has suffered an actual loss of a legally recognized kind. A variety of physical and psychological injuries can be claimed, including these negative effects on a plaintiff:

1. Exacerbation of the presenting symptoms;
2. Appearance of new symptoms;
3. Client misuse or abuse of therapy resulting in a dependent relationship with the therapist;
4. Client taking on tasks before he or she can adequately complete them, possibly to please the therapist or due to inappropriate directives by the therapist. The inability to complete these tasks can lead to failure, guilt, or self-contempt;
5. Disillusionment with therapy, leading to feelings of hopelessness in getting help from any relationship.[11]

---

11. Schutz, above note 7, at 8-9.

In addition, claims can be based on economic loss, emotional harm, relationship breakdown, or suicide.

An early case involving a claim based on emotional harm was the American case of *Rowe* v. *Bennett* in 1986.[12] In that case, the client sued her social worker therapist after the social worker became romantically involved with the client's companion. The client, who had originally come to the social worker for help with her relationship with her companion, and continued to be counselled by the social worker during the social worker's relationship with her companion, alleged that she had suffered mental and emotional distress as a result of the social worker's actions. An expert called by the plaintiff at trial testified that the social worker had failed to adhere to applicable psychotherapeutic standards when she continued to treat her client after becoming involved with her client's primary companion. On appeal, the Judicial Court of Maine found that the social worker had undertaken to counsel the plaintiff and as her therapist was "under a duty to provide care in accordance with the standards of practice applicable to similar professionals engaged in counselling and psychotherapy."

The court in *Rowe* looked at whether the claimed emotional distress was sufficient to meet the actual loss requirement in a malpractice action. Normally, emotional injury must be accompanied by physical injury for a case to succeed, but the court held that because of the nature of the psychotherapist-patient relationship, a client can sue a social worker for professional negligence causing serious mental distress.

Rowe was significant for three reasons: it was one of the first cases that litigated sexual misconduct by social workers; the court called on experts to provide opinions on what was the appropriate standard of care and whether the defendant had breached it; and it set a precedent for future cases.

Before a court reaches a decision in a malpractice case, it will ask itself whether there was any "contributory negligence" on the plaintiff's part — that is, behaviour by the plaintiff that contributed to the plaintiff's loss. If a court finds that there was contributory negligence, it will determine what percentage of the loss was attributable to the plaintiff's actions and reduce the damage award by that percentage.

If the necessary elements of malpractice are proved, damages are awarded to the plaintiff. The standard of proof in a civil lawsuit is "proof on a balance of probabilities," which is less stringent than the "proof beyond a reasonable doubt" standard in criminal matters. Proof on a balance of probabilities is simply that evidence which is of a greater weight or more convincing than the evidence that is offered in opposition to it. It is evidence which best accords with reason and probability.

---

12.   514 A.2d 802 (Me. 1986).

The damages that can be awarded fall into two basic categories, compensatory and punitive. Compensatory damages are, as the name implies, damages awarded to compensate the plaintiff for the harm he or she suffered. They can include general damages for pain and suffering and special damages for economic losses, including loss of income and out-of-pocket payments for past and future medical care and so forth. Punitive damage awards are usually in addition to compensatory damages and are viewed more as punishing the wrongdoer for outrageous conduct than as compensating the plaintiff. Punitive damage awards are based on "setting an example" for similar wrongdoers. In social worker malpractice cases, punitive damages are usually awarded when the social worker's conduct has been particularly reckless, malicious, or willful. Punitive damages are rarely awarded in Canada, and so far there have been no reported cases involving therapists or social workers.

Decisions in malpractice cases are based on common law — case law that draws on previous judicial decisions known as precedents. Relying on the doctrine of *stare decisis* (Latin for "to stand by that which was decided"), a judge will attempt to determine whether the case he or she is hearing falls within the rationale of a previously decided case. If it does, the judge will follow the reasoning in that earlier decision and reach a decision along similar lines. Sometimes, however, the facts of earlier cases may not apply to the case being heard by the judge, so he or she will be unable to decline to follow the precedent and will instead make new law. There is thus an element of uncertainty in the law, and it is not always possible to know whether a civil action against an alleged wrongdoer will be successful. For that reason, most cases are settled outside the courtroom.

C. Common Malpractice Claims

Although any failure of a social worker to meet the standard of care required in his or her professional relationship with a client can give rise to a malpractice claim, some claims are more commonly seen than others. This is likely because of two factors: the potential for harm to the client resulting in injury, and the ease with which these types of claims can be proved. Some of the more common claims are briefly discussed below.

I. Failure to Obtain Informed Consent

Obtaining informed consent from one's client before therapy begins is the legal obligation of every social worker. The precedent for what constitutes informed consent was set by the Supreme Court of Canada in the 1980 case of *Reibl* v. *Hughes*.[13] In that case, the court held that for a negligence action to succeed against a health professional, the plaintiff must prove that a reasonable patient would not have consented to the treatment in question had he or she been informed of the possible consequences.

Four elements are necessary for informed consent: the client must be competent, the social worker must disclose material information concerning risks associated with the treatment, the client must understand the information, and the client must voluntarily consent. Obtaining proper informed consent is a critical component of a prudent social worker's practice. Chapter 16 will introduce the reader to a more detailed explanation of informed consent and the guidelines to use to ensure that informed consent is being given by his or her client.

II.   Negligent or Improper Diagnosis

Although mental health diagnosis is not a routine part of what most social workers do, a social worker can be held liable for an incorrect diagnosis if proper care is not taken in arriving at that diagnosis, particularly if treatment is based on the incorrect diagnosis. However, because psychology is an imprecise science and it is often difficult to judge with certainty what a correct diagnosis might be, lawsuits brought on the basis of an allegedly negligent or improper diagnosis are difficult to win. Nevertheless, the fear of lawsuits prompts many social workers to refrain from making diagnoses; instead, their reports will refer to a client's mental health problems in vague or undefined terms.

III.   Negligent or Inappropriate Treatment

A lawsuit based on an allegation of negligent treatment arising out of a typical therapy or counselling setting is extremely difficult to prove. Because therapy and counselling are usually one-on-one processes involving just the professional and his or her client, and rely on talk rather than other forms of intervention, it is very difficult to prove that the treatment in question fell below the standard of care. A common complaint is that the social worker overstepped the limits of his or her professional training or expertise, for example, by using a controversial method of treatment, or by using a specialized form of therapy without adequate training.

---

13.   114 D.L.R. (3d) 1 (S.C.C.).

IV. Physical or Sexual Contact with a Client

A lawsuit based on an allegation of clearly prohibited physical or sexual contact with a client is probably the easiest type of lawsuit for a client to win. The standards of professional conduct with respect to sexual relationships with clients are clear. They are quite simply not permitted. It is easy to see that once the allegations of sexual contact are proven in court the social worker will be found to have breached the standard. Judges will have no difficulty finding that the client has suffered an injury as a result of the contact, because such contact with a client is so clearly frowned upon by the courts, the public, and the profession.

V. Breach of Confidentiality

As we have seen, a social worker has a duty not to disclose information received from a client in the context of a professional relationship. A breach of confidentiality can have serious repercussions for a social worker, not only in the form of a client lawsuit but also in the form of professional sanctions by the social worker's provincial regulatory body. As far as possible, a social worker should not disclose any information about a client without his or her written permission. A social worker should also be careful about placing derogatory comments about the client in the record.

VI. Undue Influence

A social worker must not attempt to influence a client to obtain a personal benefit. Convincing a client to make the social worker a beneficiary of the client's will, or to leave his or her spouse for the social worker, are the most common examples of undue influence by social workers to secure a personal benefit. Suggesting certain courses of action to a minor that contravene the wishes of the minor's parents can also constitute undue influence. Although not every piece of advice that contravenes parental wishes automatically constitutes undue influence, the onus is on the social worker to prove that he or she did not exert undue influence on the client. The particular facts of the case will determine the presence of undue influence.

Social workers should try to dissuade clients from giving them gifts. Sometimes, however, refusing a gift can seriously harm the professional relationship, particularly if the client offering the gift is a child. Therefore, a decision to accept a gift or not must balance the impact on the relationship of a refusal against the potential for an allegation of undue influence. As the authors of a book on ethics in psychotherapy remark, "Influence gained by kindness and affection is not likely to be regarded by the court as undue. However, when a psychotherapist utilizes the power of the therapeutic relationship for the purpose of personal financial gain, the court is likely to find that undue influence was exercised."[14]

VII. Termination

This area of potential liability can include everything from failing to terminate service appropriately, to failing to continue a needed service, to being unavailable to a client in need. Once a social worker begins to provide service to a client, he or she has both an ethical obligation and a legal responsibility to continue providing the service as long as necessary or, if the social worker is unable to continue providing service, to refer the client to another service provider. A social worker wishing to terminate service must ensure that he or she adheres to the professional standards for termination of service set by his or her provincial regulatory body.

Termination can occur for one of three reasons: the social worker and the client mutually agree to terminate the relationship, the client unilaterally decides to terminate the relationship, or the social worker determines that he or she is no longer in a position to effectively assist the client. If the client unilaterally decides to terminate the relationship, and the social worker believes the client's decision is unwise, the social worker is obliged to explain to the client why he or she thinks termination is premature. If the social worker is no longer able to effectively assist the client, he or she must tell the client why and refer the client to another professional with appropriate qualifications.

A social worker has a fiduciary duty, once therapy has begun, not to "abandon" the client. If the social worker is going to be unavailable to the client for a long period of time, as a result of illness or an extended holiday, then he or she has an obligation to arrange for alternative service for the client.

A social worker cannot abruptly terminate service to a client because the client can no longer pay for the service. Once again the social worker must arrange alternative service for the client that the client can afford.

VIII. Supervision/Consultation

When a client is no longer making progress in therapy, it may be considered negligent if the social worker does not attempt to resolve the situation by consulting or referring the client to another therapist. Lengthy treatment without results may be the grounds for a lawsuit by an unhappy client. Con-

---

14.   K. Austin, M. Moline, and G. Williams, *Confronting Malpractice: Legal and Ethical Dilemmas in Psychotherapy* (Newbury Park, CA: Sage Publications, 1990) at 227.

sulting another therapist when it appears that the client is no longer making progress can serve as support for what the social worker is doing in the event of a lawsuit or it can help the social worker consider another approach to treatment.

Often, social workers seek out supervision or are required to be supervised as part of their conditions of employment. A social worker who undertakes to supervise another social worker can be held liable for the actions of the person he or she is supervising under the legal doctrine of *respondeat superior*, which translates as "let the master answer" and makes people in authority potentially liable for the actions of their subordinates.

From a legal standpoint, the most difficult aspect of supervision is the quality of the information available to the supervisor, who must to some extent rely on the information provided by the individual being supervised (unless, of course, the supervisor actually observes the activities being supervised). If the person being supervised fails to disclose all relevant details about his or her activities, the supervisor is not truly in control but still can be held liable for that person's activities. A social work supervisor can face legal exposure for, among other things, failing to review client records prepared by the supervised social worker; failing to review proposed treatment plans to ensure that they are free of errors; failing to meet with the supervised social worker on a regular basis; failing to follow up with the supervised social worker to ensure that approved plans of action are actually carried out; and failing to be extra diligent when supervising a social worker who is treating a suicidal or dangerous client.

D.   Intentional Torts

Intentional torts (acts that one person intends to do that the law has declared wrong) in the social work context can include assault and battery, defamation of character, invasion of privacy, and fraudulent misrepresentation. Actions alleging an intentional tort can be more attractive to a potential claimant than negligence actions because intentional torts are generally easier to prove in court (although also easier for social workers to prevent in the first place). Although actions based on an intentional tort are easier to win where the facts to support the claim actually exist, such as in an assault and battery case, lawsuits for malpractice outnumber lawsuits for intentional torts. As we have seen, the elements that must be proved in a malpractice action are imprecise and open to many different interpretations. This vagueness leaves many fact situations open to interpretation, which makes malpractice actions riskier for defendants and thus makes settlements more attractive to insurance companies.

I.   Assault and Battery

In the context of intentional torts, an action for assault and battery is one of the more likely lawsuits a social worker may face. Assault and battery in a civil context is far different from what we normally know in a criminal setting. In civil law, assault does not mean actual touching, but the intentional creation by one person of an apprehension of immediate harm in another. Battery refers to an actual act of harmful or offensive touching. A social worker can commit a battery on a client if he or she, in the course of a specific treatment, causes physical pain to the client. To prove assault and battery, a client only needs to prove a lack of informed consent, proximate cause for the injury, and an actual loss. It is not necessary to address the standard of care in proving assault and battery — the critical element is the presence or absence of informed consent. This is one of the primary reasons why it is imperative for a social worker to always obtain informed consent. Proof of informed consent will defeat any claim by a client that the social worker touched him or her inappropriately.

II.   Defamation of Character and Invasion of Privacy

Defamation can be expressed in writing (libel) or speech (slander). To prove this tort, a client must prove that the written or spoken words were published (that is, made public) and that the client's reputation was injured as a result. A true statement cannot be defamatory, even if it embarrasses a person or harms his or her reputation.

A social worker who purposely, or even inadvertently, releases true but confidential information about a client risks a lawsuit for invasion of privacy. It does not even matter if the information enhances rather than harms the client's reputation — the mere fact that confidential information has been disclosed can be enough to support an action. Calling a client's place of work and identifying oneself as a therapist, or sending the client correspondence in an envelope with a return address indicating that the sender is a therapist, are both examples of disclosure of confidential information (that is, of the existence of a patient-therapist relationship).

III.   Fraud

Black's Law Dictionary defines fraud as "the intentional or negligent perversion of truth for the purpose of inducing another in reliance upon it to part with some valuable thing."[15] Therapists may be sued for fraudulent misrep-

---

15.   *Black's Law Dictionary* (St. Paul, MN: West Publishing Company, 1979) at 594.

resentation if, for example, for monetary gain, they misrepresent the risks or benefits of therapy to induce a potential client to undergo therapy. Another obvious example of fraudulent misrepresentation is telling a client that sexual intercourse with the therapist is a necessary and beneficial part of therapy.

E. Breach of Contract

It is also possible for a client to bring an action against a social worker on the basis of breach of contract. A lawsuit is possible even if there is no written contract, because a professional relationship in which a client is paying for a service can create an implied contract between social worker and client. Breach of contract lawsuits are rarer than lawsuits based on allegations of negligence, however.

Because the therapeutic relationship is unequal, social workers who are sued by their clients are faced with the burden of demonstrating to the court that every effort was made to fully inform the client of his or her rights and of what could be expected in therapy. In this regard, the existence of a written contract can be very helpful to one's defence. When there is a written contract, it becomes difficult for a client to claim lack of informed consent. The provisions of the contract remove the vagueness that is found in negligence actions. The determination of a standard of care by one's peers in a field where hundreds of schools of psychotherapy exist is replaced by the narrower question of whether the therapist did what he or she promised to do.[16] A written contract can also help answer the questions of a College investigator in the event of a complaint against a social worker. Conversely, the existence of a written contract increases the likelihood of success in court against a social worker who violates the terms of the professional relationship.

Social workers should be careful not to suggest to clients that a particular course of treatment will end in success, for that may provide the basis for a lawsuit for breach of contractual warranty if the treatment is not as successful as the client expects.

A written contract will usually address some or all of the following points:

1. The focus of the therapy (issues to be addressed).
2. Therapeutic techniques to be used (for example, guided imagery, touching, or meditating).
3. The client's desired outcome and the likely outcome.

---

16. Schutz, above note 7, at 41.

4. Fees for specific services and the social worker's policy on appointment cancellations.

5. A statement that the contract can be renegotiated or terminated at any time without penalty.[17]

F.   Criminal Liability

Although it is rare in Canada for social workers to face criminal charges in connection with their duties, such charges are becoming more common, particularly in cases where children are involved. One of the earliest cases involved a social worker employed by the Brockville Children's Aid Society, who along with her supervisor and the Society's director was charged with unlawful exposure of a child under the age of ten, which exposure was likely to endanger the child's life or health.[18] They were all subsequently acquitted, but not until after they had suffered the indignity and embarrassment of being arrested. In the 1990s, a few well-publicized cases in Ontario such as the Olsen case provided the impetus for social work legislation designed to regulate the profession. This brought the issue of accountability front and centre and the public began looking at social workers and child welfare workers in particular with a critical eye.

In 1997, the unthought-of finally happened — for the first time in Canada, a social worker was criminally charged for the way she performed her duties. Angie Martin, a professional social worker with the Toronto Catholic Children's Aid Society, was charged with criminal negligence causing death in the case of Jordan Heikamp. The details of the case were previously noted in chapter 10. Martin was subjected to a preliminary criminal inquiry that required her to attend court every day during the seven months it took the Crown attorney to call more than 100 witnesses. At the end of the preliminary inquiry the trial judge "found no evidence whatsoever on each of the essential elements of the charge" and discharged Martin.[19]

In her decision, the judge outlined the three essential elements that would have had to have been present in this case to support a charge of criminal negligence causing death:

1)   a marked and substantial departure by the accused from the standard of a reasonable Catholic Children's Aid Society intake worker in the circumstances;

---

17.   *Ibid.*, at 41.

18.   *R.* v. *Leslie* (29 April, 1982) United Counties of Leeds & Grenville (Ont. Co. Ct.).

19.   *R.* v. *Heikamp and Martin* (December 3, 1999) (O.C.J.) at 20 [unreported]. (Judgment on Committal.)

2) a wanton or reckless disregard for the life and safety of Jordan in the manner in which the accused handled the case; and,

3) evidence that the accused's act or omissions were a contributing cause of Jordan's death by chronic starvation.[20]

Although the judge noted that there were mistakes and errors in judgment on Martin's part, they did not meet the test for criminal responsibility. On this point, the judge commented as follows:

> I should emphasize here that having found that mistakes or errors in judgment were made does not, therefore, mean that there is evidence on any of the essential elements of criminal negligence. People make mistakes all the time, professionals make errors in judgment but this doesn't mean that these mistakes or errors constitute criminal negligence unless it can be proved that they were of such a nature as to satisfy the essential elements of the charge. In this case, I have found that they did not.[21]

The Crown's inability to secure a conviction in the Martin case does not mean that social workers are immune from criminal prosecution, particularly after incidents involving the death of children, when there is public pressure on the Crown to bring charges. One of the essential elements in this case that the Crown did not prove was "a marked and substantial departure from the standard of a reasonable CCAS intake worker in the circumstances." In the future, Crown attorneys will no doubt obtain experts' opinions as to the standard of care expected from a professional social worker in the particular circumstances before proceeding against a social worker. This will give the Crown a greater chance of obtaining a conviction than it had in the Martin case.

Although the Crown's efforts did not meet with success in the Martin case, the preliminary investigation's emotional and financial toll on Martin and other participants cannot be underestimated. Martin's family and career both suffered greatly as a result of the criminal charge against her and the lengthy coroner's inquest — nearly thirteen weeks — that followed the preliminary inquiry.

G.   Conclusion

The increased exposure of social workers to legal liability is, ironically, an indication of the profession's greater status, visibility, and sphere of responsibility. That the public expects social workers to behave in a particular way

---

20.   *Ibid.*, at 4.
21.   *Ibid.*, at 20.

and to be accountable for their behaviour is one hallmark of a recognized profession.[22] Social workers who ignore the issue of malpractice increase the risk that they will incur legal liability by failing to meet the public's expectations. As one author has observed,

> Examination of malpractice is important both because of potential usefulness in saving the skin (or pocketbook) of the social work educator, student, or practitioner and because of the seemingly obvious relationship of malpractice to questions related to competent social work practice. Because they are opposite sides of the same coin, to learn about malpractice is to learn about competent practice as well.[23]

22.   M.K. Houston-Vega and E.M. Nuehring, *Prudent Practice: A Guide for Managing Malpractice Risk* (Washington, DC: National Association of Social Workers, 1997) at 1.
23.   G.R. Sharwell, "Learn'em Good: The Threat of Malpractice" (1979) 6 *Journal of Social Welfare* 39 at 40.

Chapter 15

Risky Aspects of Practice

This chapter looks at some of the aspects of practice where social workers most often run into difficulty in terms of lawsuits and complaints to regulatory bodies.

A.   Confidentiality

Issues surrounding confidentiality (which are also discussed in chapter 9) are some of the most difficult a social worker will face in his or her professional life. While chapter 9 discusses the legal mandate of confidentiality, this section will focus on the murky areas of confidentiality, where the course of action is not as clear and where the social worker is most likely to run into unexpected difficulty. In the context of professional activity, confidentiality is "the obligation of a social worker or other professional not to reveal records of or communications from or about a client obtained in the course of practice."[1] The duty of confidentiality was first established in the American case of *MacDonald* v. *Clinger*, where the court held that a patient could sue a psychiatrist for disclosing to a third party personal information acquired during therapy.[2]

It has often been said that the duty to keep matters confidential is governed by ethics, whereas the right to disclose information is governed by law.[3] As we have seen, in some circumstances, mandatory reporting, for example, the social worker is legally bound to disclose information obtained

---

1.   A. Saltzman and K. Proch, *Law and Social Work Practice* (Chicago: Nelson-Hall, 1994) at 392.
2.   446 N.Y.S.2d. 801 (App. Div. 1982).
3.   C. Bisman, *Social Work Practice: Cases and Principles* (Pacific Grove, CA: Brooks/Cole Publishing Company, 1994) at 47.

during therapy. Herein lies the contradiction inherent in the concept of confidentiality. How does the social worker navigate between his or her ethical obligations to keep matters confidential and the obligations to disclose under certain circumstances, when those circumstances are very often not clearly articulated?

I.   Duty to Warn

Although clients have a right to confidentiality, there are exceptions to this right, particularly in cases where the rights of others are in danger of being infringed. The most common exception is the professional's "duty to warn" when a client threatens to commit a criminal act or harm a third party. The best-known legal precedent establishing a duty to warn is the 1976 California Supreme Court decision in *Tarasoff* v. *Board of Regents of the University of California*.[4] In this case, Prosenjit Poddar, a client of the student health service at the University of California at Berkeley, confided to his psychologist that he was going to kill a young woman, Tatiana Tarasoff, when she returned to university after the summer break. The psychologist then telephoned the campus police to warn them that they should consider Poddar a candidate for possible hospitalization because he might be a danger to himself or others. The telephone call was followed by a letter to the campus police chief advising him of the situation. The campus police responded by temporarily taking Poddar into custody, but released him when they determined that he was rational and not a danger to himself or others. They also warned him to stay away from Tarasoff. Sometime later, the chief of the university's psychiatry department contacted the campus police and asked them to return the psychologist's letter. He then ordered the destruction of the letter and the psychologist's notes, and directed the psychologist to take no further action against Poddar. Poddar, who never returned to therapy, murdered Tarasoff two months later. Tarasoff's parents sued the university, the campus police, and employees of the student health service for negligence in not notifying their daughter about the threat. A lower court dismissed the parents' action, but on appeal the Supreme Court of California reversed that judgment and found the defendants negligent for failing to warn Tarasoff. The court held that a therapist has, under certain circumstances, a duty to protect an intended victim:

> When a therapist determines, or pursuant to the standards of his profession should determine that his patient presents a serious danger of violence to another, he incurs an obligation to use reasonable care to protect the intended victim against such danger. The discharge of this duty may require the thera-

---

4.   529 P.2d 553 (1974), vac. reheard in bank and aff'd 551 P.2d 334 (1976).

pist to take one or more of various steps depending upon the nature of the case. Thus it may call for him to warn the intended victim or others likely to apprise the victim of the danger, to notify the police, or to take whatever other steps are reasonably necessary under the circumstances.[5]

The court added that "Public Policy favoring protection of the confidential character of the patient-psychotherapist relationship must yield in instances in which disclosure is essential to avert danger to others; the protective privilege ends where the public peril begins."[6]

Since *Tarasoff*, many health professions have included limits on confidentiality in their ethical codes. There have been, as well, numerous U.S. judicial decisions on the duty to warn. Although the law is far from settled on this issue, a review of the U.S. cases establishes four conditions that must be met to permit disclosure of confidential information by social workers and other therapists.

First, the therapist must know or have a reasonable and honest belief that the client poses a risk to the safety of another person. The therapist is generally in the best position to assess the risk of violence not only because of the special training he or she receives but also because of the special relationship that exists between therapist and client.

Second, the therapist should have evidence that the client has a discernable plan and a means of carrying out that plan. The plan would include details such as the method to be used. Furthermore, the client's plan must be viable for the client. If, for example, the client is known to have a violent temper, carry a knife and act impulsively, and he states that he is going to stab the victim, then the likelihood that he will commit a violent act against the intended victim is foreseeable. A violent act is foreseeable if, for example, a client names an intended victim and describes a specific plan for committing the violent act, or expressly and clearly provides a reason for wanting to harm a specific person.

Third, the therapist must reasonably believe that violence is imminent. The problem with this criterion, however, is that the meaning of "imminent" has not been defined. Does it mean minutes, days, weeks? Whatever period of time the therapist decides qualifies as "imminent," he or she must be able to provide evidence for his or her conclusion that violence may occur within that period.

Finally, the therapist must be able to identify the potential victim.[7] At first glance this point seems straightforward, but there are situations that cloud the issue. What if, for example, the patient does not disclose the name of the

---

5.   *Ibid.*, 529 P.2d 553 at 559.

6.   *Ibid.*, at 560.

7.   B. Schutz, *Legal Liability in Psychotherapy: A Practitioner's Guide to Risk Management* (San Francisco: Jossey-Bass Publishers, 1982) at 61.

intended victim, but it is within the therapist's power to learn the person's identity by reviewing the case notes or taking some other investigative step? Are therapists required to actively take steps to determine the intended victim's identity so that they can then warn the intended victim? Does the social worker's obligation to disclose confidential information extend so far as to take these additional steps in order to satisfy the criterion for disclosure? Unfortunately, there are no clear answers to these questions.

Another potential confidentiality-related problem arises when a therapist is treating a suicidal patient. In a case of this kind a number of options are available, including keeping the fact that the patient is suicidal confidential while attempting to help the patient overcome his or her suicidal feelings; arranging for the patient's involuntary commitment to a mental institution; referring the patient to a psychiatrist for assessment; or trying, with the patient's consent, to involve the patient's family in an attempt to resolve the problem. A prudent approach is to obtain, at the outset of therapy, the patient's consent to notifying a designated person if the patient poses a serious threat to himself or herself.[8] Breaching confidentiality can put social workers in a difficult position both legally and ethically. One way to avoid ethical problems is to make it perfectly clear to clients that confidentiality cannot be protected if they disclose that they intend to harm themselves or a third party.

The dilemma that therapists face in the United States — how to balance a client's right to confidentiality with a society's right to protection — also exists, of course, in Canada. But whereas in many American states a failure to warn can result in criminal charges being laid against a social worker, in Canada the *Criminal Code* imposes no such duty on social workers (or other professionals, for that matter). Moreover, there has never been a case in Canada like *Tarasoff* that clearly sets out a test for deciding whether a duty to warn exists. Although Canada has not had a definitive case like Tarasoff, the duty to warn issue has been touched on in some cases.

In Canada, the duty to warn arose in the 1991 Alberta case of *Wenden* v. *Trikha*.[9] The plaintiff, Wenden, brought an action for injuries suffered in a motor vehicle accident caused by Trikha, a university student who suffered from a mental disorder and had voluntarily admitted himself to hospital on several occasions, including the day before the accident. On the day of the accident, Trikha left the hospital without permission, got into his car, and drove off at a high rate of speed — behaviour that ultimately caused the accident, in which Wenden was seriously injured. Wenden sued Trikha, the hospital, and the hospital psychiatrist who had treated Trikha, claiming that the

---

8.   *Ibid.*, at 125.
9.   [1991] A.J. No. 612 (QL).

hospital and the psychiatrist owed her a duty of care and had breached that duty by reason of the way in which they had cared for Trikha.

At trial, the case against the hospital and the psychiatrist was dismissed. The trial judge held that a hospital that treats mentally ill patients owes a duty of care to a person other than a patient or a member of its staff only if it can be said that it is foreseeable that the person will suffer harm as a result of a patient's behaviour. To determine whether the hospital or the psychiatrist had been negligent, the judge asked whether a reasonable man could have anticipated the accident as a natural result of a particular act or omission. In dismissing the action, the judge found that the duty of care owed to a third party, in this case the plaintiff, had been discharged. Neither the psychiatrist nor the hospital staff could reasonably have known that Trikha had driven his car to the hospital. The psychiatrist had warned Trikha that his mental state made it dangerous for him to drive. Moreover, Trikha's behaviour before the day of the accident had never been such that any reasonably competent psychiatrist or hospital employee working in a psychiatric ward could have anticipated that he posed a danger. There had been nothing in Trikha's behaviour to suggest that he would leave the hospital.

Although the judge did not rule on the issue of whether the psychiatrist was bound by a duty to warn or protect third parties such as the plaintiff, he did refer to the concept in his judgment. Because the case did not turn on the duty to warn issue, the judge's comments on this issue are not binding on other courts, but they are worth noting. The judge wrote that

> both a hospital and psychiatrist who becomes aware that a patient presents a serious danger to the well-being of a third party or parties owe a duty of care to take reasonable steps to protect such a person or persons if the requisite proximity of relationship exists between them . . . . whether or not a person or persons fall within the necessary category will depend upon the particular nature of the risk posed by the patient, the predictability of future behaviour giving rise to the risk, and the ability to identify the person or class of persons at risk. The standard of care in determining whether or not action should be taken by a psychiatrist to protect the person or class of persons and, if so, what should be done, is . . . "that reasonable degree of skill, knowledge, and care ordinarily possessed and exercised by members of that professional specialty under similar circumstances."[10]

It can be argued from this that if a psychiatrist or mental hospital knew that a patient intended to harm an identifiable third party, and did not intervene to protect the third party by at the very least warning him or her, either might be found liable for any damage resulting from their failure.

The judge noted that for a therapist to be bound by a duty to warn, he or she must be under an obligation to control the patient, and there must also be

---

10. *Ibid.*, at 50-51.

a specific intended victim who is in danger of being hurt if the patient is not controlled. His comments seem to suggest that, for social workers, something more than a therapist-client relationship is necessary, because it is unusual for a social worker therapist to have the degree of control over a client that a psychiatrist can have over a patient (a psychiatrist, of course, can order a patient committed, whereas a social worker does not have that power).

The duty to warn issue was revisited a few years after *Wenden* by the Manitoba Court of Queen's Bench in *Kings Estate* v. *Lychuk Estate.*[11] This action, brought by the widow and children of Del Brian Kines, was for damages arising from the alleged wrongful death of Kines at the hands of the defendant Lychuk, who was found not criminally responsible for the death on account of a mental disorder. The plaintiffs sued four of Lychuk's psychiatrists, alleging that the death occurred as a result of the psychiatrists' negligence in failing to order an involuntary psychiatric assessment or committal for Lychuk. Although the psychiatrists had provided psychiatric treatment to Lychuk for 18 years, in the 3 years preceding the shooting Lychuk had shown no discernable signs of mental illness. The court held that where a physician is unaware of a specific threat posed by a patient, there is no liability in negligence vis-à-vis a third party who has neither been treated by the physician nor received medical advice from him or her. This is true even if the patient becomes violent while in the physician's care and has a history of violence. It can therefore be argued that a duty to warn or protect third parties exists when a patient has a history of violence, makes a specific threat that is deemed by the physician to be serious, and has an opportunity to carry out the threat.

Unlike the United States, Canada has no legislation (provincial or federal) requiring therapists to report clients who threaten to seriously harm a third party. Because the case law on this issue is also unclear, social workers are placed in the difficult position of having to maintain the ethical obligation of client confidentiality while worrying about liability for breaching a poorly defined duty to warn. The problem is compounded by the failure of regulatory bodies to set standards for deciding when confidentiality should be breached. The Ontario College's code of ethics, for example, allows social workers to disclose confidential client information only when required or allowed by law to do so — leaving the social worker no further ahead in solving the dilemma of determining precisely what it is that the law requires or allows.

The other difficulty for social workers is determining how serious the risk of violence by their client to a third party is. If a person under a social worker's care threatens to seriously harm another person and expresses the

---

11.   [1996] M.J. No. 423 (Q.B.) (QL).

threat in the form of a clear, detailed, and realizable plan against a person whom the client can gain access to, it would be prudent practice for the social worker to notify the police and the intended victim if it appears likely that the threat will be carried out.[12]

Better guidance is needed from courts, legislatures, and regulatory bodies so that social workers can know when the duty to warn arises. But until such time as that guidance is provided, social workers should include, as part of the process of obtaining informed consent from their clients, an agreement by the client that confidential information can be released if the social worker believes releasing the information is necessary to protect a third party.

One of the most difficult situations facing social workers concerns the duty to warn third parties in HIV or AIDS cases. Breaching an infected person's right to confidentiality can be devastating for that person. Yet the failure to warn that person's sexual partners can also be devastating. So how does the social worker choose which course of action to take?

In the United States, *Tarasoff* has become the leading case with regard to AIDS-related confidentiality issues, despite being decided five years before the first case of AIDS was discovered in the United States. An infected individual is obviously a great risk to any uninformed sexual partner he or she may have. This risk would certainly fulfil the "imminent, foreseeable, and serious danger of harm" test in *Tarasoff*. On the other hand, it can be argued that *Tarasoff* is not a clear enough precedent to be used in AIDS cases. Most HIV-positive individuals in a sexual relationship who fail to disclose their medical status to their partners do not explicitly or implicitly threaten their partners with an act of harm. Most are concerned about their partners and practise safe sex, but are unwilling or unable to disclose their condition. The social policy reasons for protecting HIV-positive individuals cannot be minimized. Confidentiality is paramount if we, as a society, are serious about stopping the spread of AIDS.

> Maintenance of confidentiality is central to and of paramount importance for the control of AIDS. Information regarding infection with a deadly virus, sexual activity, sexual contacts and the illegal use of IV drugs and diagnostic information regarding AIDS-related disease are sensitive issues that, if released by the patient or someone in health care, could adversely affect a patient's personal and professional life.[13]

The balancing of an individual's right to confidentiality with a social worker's duty to warn a third party at risk can be very difficult. The law on confidentiality as it relates to disclosure of a patient's HIV status is settled in

---

12.　D.R. Evans, *The Law, Standards of Practice, and Ethics in the Practice of Psychology* (Toronto: Emond Montgomery, 1997) at 125.

13.　F.G. Reamer, *Social Work Malpractice and Liability* (New York: Columbia University Press, 1994) at 43.

Canada. Before 1994, health care providers in Ontario were prohibited from disclosing the HIV status of a patient under their care without the patient's consent. The 1994 Ontario case of *Pittman Estate* v. *Bain* changed all that.[14] Pittman, a married man who died of AIDS-related pneumonia, had contracted HIV from blood transfusions during surgery. Although his physician, Bain, knew that the blood products Pittman had received were probably tainted, and that Pittman, if infected, could transmit the disease to Mrs. Pittman, he elected not to warn Pittman, based on his belief that the couple was not having sex. Mrs. Pittman, however, did contract HIV from her husband, and brought an action against Bain, who was found negligent for failing to protect a third party, namely Mrs. Pittman. This case would suggest that health care professionals are now bound by a duty to protect the sexual partners of sexually active HIV-positive patients.

Social workers (and other therapists) employed by agencies sometimes encounter confidentiality-related problems arising from the nature of their employment. They may come into conflict with a superior who believes that he or she needs and has a right to information about a particular client. A social worker, under these circumstances, must tell the client that confidentiality cannot be maintained. A similar problem can occur when a client is seeing a social worker under an Employment Assistance Program (EAP), and the EAP provider stipulates that payments to the social worker are contingent on the provider being given certain confidential information about the social worker's clients. Under such circumstances, clients should be advised that confidential information will be given to the provider. The social worker should, of course, protect client confidentiality to the greatest extent possible by ensuring that no more information than is strictly necessary to meet the provider's requests is disclosed.

In addition to these breaches, made necessary for the most part by circumstances and the law, there are, of course, also breaches resulting from accidents or carelessness. The most common accidental breaches of client confidentiality are caused by modern technology such as computers, fax machines, and cell phones. For a further discussion on this area please refer back to chapter 9 on confidentiality.

B.   Privileged Communications

It is important to understand the difference between privilege and confidentiality. Confidentiality is a professional obligation to keep private all information received from a client in the context of a professional relationship.

---

14.   112 D.L.R. (4th) 257 (Ont. Ct. Gen. Div.).

Confidentiality protects the client from having the information disclosed to other people without the client's permission. The right belongs to the client. Privilege is a legal concept and an exception to the rule that information passing between two individuals may be subject to disclosure in a court of law or other legal forum:

> Where persons occupy toward each other certain confidential relations, the law, on the ground of public policy, will not compel, or even allow one of them to violate the confidence reposed in him by the other, by testifying without the consent of the other, as to communications made to him by such other in the confidence which the relation has inspired . . . . Courts may not compel disclosure of confidential communications thus privileged.[15]

The test for privilege was created by Dean Wigmore, one of the most influential American legal scholars in the field of evidence. According to the Wigmore test a communication is considered privileged if four conditions are met:

1. The communication must originate in confidence that it will not be disclosed.
2. The element of confidentiality must be essential to the full and satisfactory maintenance of the relationship between the parties.
3. The relationship must be one which, in the opinion of the community, ought to be sedulously fostered.
4. The injury that would inure to the relationship by the disclosure of the communication must be greater than the benefit thereby gained for the correct disposal of litigation.[16]

Psychotherapist-patient privilege — the focus of this section of the chapter — is a relatively new type of privilege. The laws of most U.S. states establish some type of psychotherapist-patient privilege, although the nature of the privilege varies widely from state to state. Moreover, the privilege is not absolute, as most states provide for disclosure in cases of murder and other criminal or harmful acts.

In its landmark 1996 decision in *Jaffee* v. *Redmond*, the U.S. Supreme Court was required to rule for the first time on whether the psychotherapist-patient privilege governs communications between social workers and their clients.[17] The issue in *Jaffee* was whether a conversation between a social worker and her client was privileged and therefore protected from disclosure in a civil action. The facts of the *Jaffee* case were set out in chapter 9.

The court first considered two questions: whether a psychotherapist-patient privilege should exist at all and, if so, whether it should apply to

---

15. R. Albert, *Law and Social Work Practice* (New York: Springer Publishing Company, 1986) at 173.
16. 5 *Wigmore on Evidence 3rd ed.*, s. 2285.
17. 116 S.Ct. 1923.

social workers. In answering the first question, the court considered the value of psychotherapy to individuals and to society as a whole. The court remarked that therapy can work only if the patient has confidence in and trusts the therapist. Therapy cannot succeed unless the patient's need for confidentiality is considered paramount. Patients must feel free to disclose their innermost thoughts and feelings without fear of public disclosure, which could lead to embarrassment or disgrace. There is also the issue of the public good. The court wrote that "the public interest is also served by protecting therapist-patient communication because doing so facilitates treatment and the 'mental health of our citizenry, no less than its physical health, is a public good of transcendent importance'."[18] The court held that the privilege's usefulness in protecting the mental health of citizens gives it an importance that outweighs the need of a court to hear all relevant evidence.

The court then considered the question whether the privilege should extend beyond psychiatrists and psychologists to social workers. On this point the court was divided. The majority decided to extend the privilege on the basis that social workers are the providers of a large proportion of mental health services. In their decision, the majority observed that "Today, social workers provide a significant amount of mental health treatment . . . . Their clients often include the poor and those of modest means who could not afford the assistance of a psychiatrist or psychologist . . . . But whose counseling sessions serve the same public goals."[19] The minority, who did not want to extend the privilege, condemned therapy in general and social workers in particular. In their view, therapy is not useful or important enough to be protected by privilege, and the work done by social workers is not to be valued by society. Nevertheless, *Jaffee* was a victory for social workers in the United States, whose therapeutic relationships were now covered by the same degree of privilege existing in marital and lawyer-client relationships. The court, however, gave little guidance on when the privilege should be applied and under what circumstances it will be considered to have been waived, other than to state that a therapist must be licensed for the privilege to apply, and that the confidential communication must take place "in the course of diagnosis or treatment."

Although the Jaffee decision created the concept of privileged communications between therapist and client, that privileged communication has not been considered absolute in Canada. The Supreme Court of Canada in 1997 examined this issue in *A.M.* v. *Ryan*.[20] In that case the appellant sought psychiatric treatment from a psychiatrist, Dr. P., for sexual abuse suffered at the hands of another physician. The appellant had sued this physician for dam-

---

18.   *Ibid.*, at 1929.
19.   *Ibid.*, at 1931.
20.   A.M. v. *Ryan*, [1997] 1 S.C.R. 157, [1997] S.C.J. No. 13 (QL).

ages and in the course of the lawsuit the physician sought production of the counselling records from Dr. P. Both Dr. P. and the appellant opposed production of the records on the grounds that the records were privileged. The Supreme Court first looked at the four conditions that must be met for a communication to be privileged (the Wigmore test). The court held that the first three conditions were met, since the communications between the appellant and Dr. P. were confidential, their confidence was essential to the psychiatrist-patient relationship, and the relationship itself and the treatment it makes possible were of public importance. The case primarily dealt with whether or not the fourth condition of the test had also been met. The fourth requirement is that the interests served by protecting the communications from disclosure outweigh the interest of pursuing the truth and disposing correctly of the litigation.

The court held that the issue of privilege in circumstances such as this should be left open for a judge to determine. Once the first three requirements are met and a compelling case for protection is established, the focus will then be on balancing the fourth condition. If a judge determines that a particular document must be produced to get at the truth and prevent an unjust verdict, it must permit production to the extent required to avoid that result. On the other hand the need to get at the truth and avoid injustice does not automatically negate the possibility of protection from full disclosure.[21] In examining the balancing required in respect of the fourth condition the court had this to say about the therapeutic privilege:

> It must be conceded that a test for privilege which permits the court to occasionally reject an otherwise well-founded claim for privilege in the interests of getting at the truth may not offer patients a guarantee that communications with their psychiatrists will never be disclosed. On the other hand, the assurance that disclosure will be ordered only where clearly necessary and then only to the extent necessary is likely to permit many to avail themselves of psychiatric counselling when certain disclosure might make them hesitate or decline.[22]

It is clear from this case that the privilege does not attach in all circumstances and there are many areas where exceptions are made to the privilege and social workers' records producible. The client must have an expectation of privacy for privilege to attach. If the client does not expect that the information he or she provides will be kept confidential, or agrees to disclosure of the information, there is no privilege. As we have seen, for example, if a client commences a lawsuit that deals in part with his or her mental or emotional condition, privilege will not necessarily attach and the therapist's records might be producible at the request of any defendant. In addition there

---

21. *Ibid.*, para. 33.
22. *Ibid.*, para. 35.

have been many decisions by Canadian courts where the client is viewed under these circumstances as having waived the privilege and implicitly consented to disclosure of the confidential information.[23] This can be an important consideration for anyone who has been the victim of abuse and wishes to sue the abuser. In such circumstances, the social worker is obligated to inform the client that the treatment records will, in all likelihood, be producible.

Treatment records can also be producible in family court proceedings, particularly child custody hearings. In *Gibbs* v. *Gibbs*, an often-quoted child custody decision of the Supreme Court of Ontario,[24] Mr. Gibbs sought production of his wife's psychiatric records to show that she should not be awarded custody of the children. Mrs. Gibbs had a long history of mental illness and was experiencing a recurrence of her symptoms at the time of the custody battle. Her physician resisted production of the records on the basis that disclosure would be harmful to the wife's mental health. The judge, however, ordered the records produced on the basis that the potential harm to the children was greater than the harm to Mrs. Gibbs, thereby setting a precedent for disclosure of therapy records in family court proceedings.

A request by parents for access to the records of their child's therapy is another situation in which records will be producible. In Ontario, both the *Children's Law Reform Act*[25] and the *Child and Family Services Act*[26] state that custodial parents, and noncustodial parents who have access to their children, have the right to review the clinical records of their children without their consent if the children are under the age of 16.

For adult patients, it used to be thought, until the introduction of legislative and judicial reforms in the 1990s, that counselling records were the sole property of the health care professional or institution providing the counselling and that the professional or institution had complete control over disclosure of those records. In 1990, however, Ontario passed the *Mental Health Act*, which gave patients the right to request and review their clinical records.[27] This was followed by the 1992 decision of the Supreme Court of Canada in *McInerney* v. *MacDonald*.[28] In that case the Supreme Court confirmed the right of access by holding that it was beneficial to the patient to have access to his or her records. The Supreme Court, moreover, extended the right to include all clinical records in the treatment professional's possession, even if those records included information received from third parties such as other treatment professionals and family members.

---

23.   *P. (L.M.)* v. *F. (D.)*, [1994] 22 C.C.L.T. (2d) 312 (Ont. Ct. Gen. Div.).
24.   [1985] 1 W.D.C.P. 6 (Ont. S.C.).
25.   R.S.O. 1990, c. C.12, s. 20(5).
26.   R.S.O. 1990, c. C.11, s. 184.
27.   R.S.O. 1990, c. M.7.
28.   [1992] 2 S.C.R. 138.

If a treatment professional involved in legal proceedings believes that the disclosure of information contained in his or her treatment records could harm a patient or a third party who provided the information, he or she may apply to the court hearing the case for an order denying the request for access. This is in keeping with Interpretation 4.3.4 of the Ontario *Standards of Practice Handbook*, which provides that access that may be "extremely detrimental" to the client can be restricted. It is interesting that the drafters of this interpretation used the words "extremely detrimental," given that the Supreme Court of Canada used the word "harmful," which suggests a lower standard for refusing access.

If an Ontario social worker believes that disclosure would be extremely detrimental to a client, he or she is obligated to inform the client of the reason for denying disclosure and to advise the client of the options available to him or her to contest the denial. If the social worker is then served with a subpoena to produce the client's records, but still believes that disclosure would be detrimental, he or she is obligated to appear before the court to argue for nondisclosure. This can place a significant burden on the social worker not only in terms of time but also in terms of cost, if the social worker is required or believes it is necessary to retain counsel.

Obviously, no disclosure to a client should be made without the appropriate consent form being signed by the client. In Ontario, this is Form 14 under the *Mental Health Act*.

Criminal law, and in particular sexual assault cases, provides perhaps the most contentious area for the disclosure of social workers' records. It is now established law in Canada that the treatment records of a client who is charged with a criminal offence may be obtained by the police or produced in open court. If ordered to be produced by law, this should not be a cause for concern for social workers unless the records contain inappropriate comments. Social workers should therefore keep in mind that any client-related notes they make may end up in court and be read by strangers.

The foremost area of controversy involving the disclosure of client records occurs in sexual assault cases where the accused wants to obtain records prepared by a therapist who counselled the victim. In 1995, the Supreme Court of Canada in *R. v. O'Connor* tried to set out guidelines for breaching the confidentiality of records in sexual assault cases.[29] The accused, Bishop O'Connor of the Catholic Church, was charged with sexually assaulting four women at a residential school for Native children in the 1960s. O'Connor's lawyer obtained a court order requiring disclosure of all of the victims' medical, counselling, and school records, including the clinical record from a sexual assault centre where one of the victims had gone for

---

29. [1995] 4 S.C.R. 411.

counselling to cope with the psychological aftermath of O'Connor's actions. The bishop's lawyer argued that disclosure was necessary to test the victims' credibility and to determine whether any of the records contained evidence to corroborate the victims' testimony. In a unanimous decision, the Supreme Court ruled that the request could be made, and depending on the circumstances of the case, third parties in general may be required to produce the records. The court held that the concern for fairness outweighed the victims' right to privacy, and thus the records in this case were disclosed.

This decision and subsequent decisions that relied on it caused a great deal of concern among therapists who worked with sexual abuse victims. In reaction to this concern, the federal government attempted to balance the wishes of therapists and victims against the rights of accused individuals by amending the *Criminal Code* to ensure that the lawyer for a person accused of sexual assault has access to the plaintiff's counselling records, but only under certain conditions. One of those conditions was the obligation of the accused to establish that the records were necessary in order for the accused to fully defend him- or herself against the charges. The amendments, contained in Bill C-46,[30] were immediately subjected to legal challenges, and within four months of its passage the bill had been overturned by courts in Ontario and Alberta on the grounds that it infringed the constitutional rights of accused persons under the *Canadian Charter of Rights and Freedoms*. The difficulty with the amendments, these courts determined, was that an accused could not satisfy the requirements of the amended section of the Code that disclosure was necessary without having access to the contents of the records in the first place. Other courts in Canada declined to follow the Ontario and Alberta decisions, so the state of the law remains unclear.

Many social workers and other health care professionals working at sexual assault centers responded to O'Connor by refusing to record information about a client's sexual history. *O'Connor* and the amendments to the *Criminal Code* did give the creators of such records standing in court to challenge production of the records.

The procedure for obtaining records from third parties in sexual assault cases is laid out in sections 278.2 to 278.9 of the Code. These sections start from the premise that the complainant's health records are producible only if the accused applies to the judge hearing the case. In the application the accused must clearly identify the records he or she wants, who has them, and the grounds on which the accused intends to establish that the records are relevant to an issue at trial or to the competence of a witness to testify. At least seven days before the hearing, the accused is required to serve the application on the prosecutor, the person who has possession or control of the

---

30.   *An Act to Amend the Criminal Code*, S.C. 1997, c. 30.

records, and the complainant. The accused must also subpoena the person who has possession or control of the records. The judge then holds a private hearing at which the complainant and the creator of the records can argue against production. In determining whether to grant the application and order production, the judge must take into account the accused's right to make a full answer and defence, the complainant's right to privacy and personal dignity, society's interest in ensuring that sexual offences are reported and victims can obtain treatment, and the effect of the judge's decision on the integrity of the trial process.[31] The judge can order production if he or she believes that it is necessary in the interests of justice. The judge is also entitled to impose conditions to ensure the greatest possible privacy for the complainant.

A recent Ontario Court of Appeal case, *R.* v. *R.C*,[32] provides further guidance on when a counsellor's records will be producible. This appeal concerned the scope of the protection offered by the *Criminal Code* provisions discussed above.

The facts are straightforward: the accused, the respondent in the appeal, sexually assaulted his girlfriend, the complainant. After the assault the two of them attended several counselling sessions together. Just prior to trial, the accused brought an application for production of all of the records kept by the therapist, including records from the sessions he did not attend. The accused argued that because he had been present for some of the sessions, he was entitled at a minimum to the records of the sessions he attended.

The principal question was whether the provisions apply to so-called joint records relating to counselling sessions in which both the accused and the complainant participated. The trial judge had held that the provisions did apply, but concluded the accused had not met the threshold test for production. The accused appealed and the summary conviction judge who heard the appeal held that the test had been met and ordered the records produced.

The Crown then appealed to the Court of Appeal, which confirmed the trial judge's decision with respect to the records. In its decision, the court considered the complainant's reasonable expectation of privacy with respect to her therapeutic records and discussed how an expectation of privacy protects therapeutic relationships. The court noted that privacy concerns are at their strongest where aspects of one's individual identity are at stake, such as in the context of information "about one's lifestyle, intimate relations or political or religious opinions." As the Supreme Court of Canada had made clear, however, there are limits on the right to privacy, and if an accused can meet the test set out in the *Criminal Code*, counselling records are producible. The Ontario Court of Appeal had no difficulty finding that the

---

31. *Ibid.*, s. 278.5(2).
32. [2002] O.J. No. 865 (C.A.) (QL).

records concerned the complainant's "lifestyle, intimate relations or political or religious opinions." The fact that the accused was present at some of the sessions and may have been privy to some of the complainant's disclosures did not undermine her reasonable expectation òf privacy. The court added that disclosures made during group therapy do not lose the protection of the *Criminal Code* simply because other persons are present. *R.* v. *R.C.*, therefore, stands for the proposition that the records of a counselling session involving a criminal complainant may remain private even if the complainant's partner participates in the sessions or the counselling takes place in a group setting. Production of records in these circumstances will still have to meet the test set out in sections 278.2 to 278.9 of the *Criminal Code.*

C.   Subpoenas and Search Warrants

A social worker whose client records are subpoenaed should first determine whether the client has provided written consent for release of the records. No information should be released until one is sure that written authorization has been provided. This is the easiest way to deal with a subpoena. If the client has no objection then the social worker is not faced with the dilemma of how to respond to the subpoena. If there is no written authorization from the client, however, then the records should be copied and the copies placed in a sealed envelope pending a determination of the accused's application for production. Only a copy of the records should be removed by the individual who is executing the subpoena. The social worker should never release his or her original file, unless required to do so by law.

When faced with a search warrant relating to client records, a social worker should claim psychotherapist-client privilege to protect the client's confidentiality and immediately contact a lawyer.

D.   Duty to Report Abuse

Specialized training and public awareness campaigns have improved the ability of social workers and other professionals to recognize signs of child abuse. At the same time, the public have come to expect that social workers and other helping professionals will be able to recognize abuse and will report all suspicions of abuse. For this reason, it is likely that social workers who are obligated by law to report abuse and fail to do so will be deemed negligent for their failure to report.

All of Canada's provinces have legislation making reporting of child abuse mandatory. These statutes usually include a presumption of good faith; in other words, a social worker will not be held liable if he or she mistakenly reports abuse, as long as the report is made in good faith. The presumption of good faith is rebutted by evidence that the report was made maliciously, because of prejudice or personal bias, or as a result of reckless or grossly negligent decision making.

At present, only three provinces — Nova Scotia, Prince Edward Island, and New Brunswick — have a statute that imposes a mandatory reporting requirement with regard to abuse or neglect of adults. The Prince Edward Island and New Brunswick statutes, however, make reporting mandatory only if the person consents. Mandatory reporting of abuse or neglect of adults is intended as a deterrent and to relieve victims of the burden of reporting their victimization. But it can create a dilemma for social workers, namely that a victim may hesitate to seek a therapist's help if he or she believes that the perpetrator of the abuse or neglect will be reported to the authorities.

E. Duties Owed to Patients and Clients

I. Introduction

Once a therapist begins counselling a patient, a professional relationship is created. With this relationship come a number of rights and obligations, the most important of which is the duty of care owed to the patient. These rights and obligations are created under the general principles of tort law and are discussed in greater detail in chapter 14.

II. Sexual Relationships

Professional colleges and the courts have consistently condemned therapists who enter into sexual relationships with their patients. Courts and juries will continue — and quite properly so — to treat therapist-patient sexual relationships as *prima facie* or presumptive evidence of negligence because of the potential for exploitation in a relationship in which there is an imbalance of power that favours the therapist.[33] Proof of sexual relations or certain kinds of social contact with a patient, or manipulation of a patient's life outside the bounds of therapy, may be sufficient to create a *prima facie* case for a patient in a lawsuit against his or her therapist, without the need for expert testimony.[34]

---

33. B. Furrow, *Malpractice in Psychotherapy* (Toronto: Lexington Books, 1982) at 34.
34. *Ibid.*, at 36.

III.   Duty of Nonabandonment

A therapist-patient relationship can be terminated by mutual agreement or by the client without the therapist's agreement. If the therapist agrees to termination, he or she must be careful about how termination occurs. The therapist has a duty to discuss the termination with the client and to help the client find a new therapist. Abandonment of a client without sufficient notice or adequate excuse amounts to a dereliction of duty. If the therapist refers the client to another therapist he or she must follow up with the client to ensure that the client contacts the new therapist. In addition, when a therapist believes that his or her treatment is no longer benefiting the client, he or she is bound by a good faith duty to tell the client.

IV.   Duty to the Suicidal Client

> While the law generally does not hold anyone responsible for the acts of another, there are exceptions. One of these is the responsibility of therapists to prevent suicide and other self-destructive behavior by their clients. The duty of therapists to exercise adequate care and skill in diagnosing suicidality is well established . . . When the risk of self-injurious behaviour is identified an additional duty to take adequate precautions arises . . . . When psychologists fail to meet these responsibilities, they may be held liable for injuries that result.[35]

Social workers have an absolute duty to take reasonable steps (including disclosure of confidential information) to prevent a client from committing suicide if they become aware that the potential for suicide exists. Social workers with suicidal clients should be familiar with the methods for assessing the potential for suicide. They must also keep current with the clinical literature on counselling suicidal clients. The support and guidance of other mental health professionals should be sought when necessary.

There are two ways in which a therapist can incur liability for failing to prevent a patient's suicide: by failing to recognize the signs of suicidal intent in the first place, or by abandoning a patient in the middle of a personal crisis. Specifically, a therapist will be held liable if his or her negligence creates in the patient an uncontrollable impulse that leads to suicide, or if his or her negligence is a substantial factor in creating a mental illness that leads to suicide.[36] If a therapist is sued in the wake of a client's suicide, the plaintiff must, to satisfy the legal requirement of proximate cause, demonstrate that the therapist's actions were sufficient to cause the suicide, that the suicide would not have otherwise occurred, and that there were no intervening

---

35.   F.G. Reamer, *Ethical Standards in Social Work: A Critical Review of the NASW Code of Ethics* (Washington, DC: NASW Press, 1998) at 61.
36.   Schutz, above note 7, at 77.

actions by others to break the chain of causation. Liability will rarely be imposed on a social worker in the absence of some prior observable acts or verbal threats by the client. In one case a college student at a state college saw a guidance counsellor for personal problems. After five months of sessions the counselor suggested that the sessions be terminated. Six weeks later the student committed suicide. His parents sued the counsellor. In finding the counselor not liable the court noted that there had been no clear indications of suicide and no behaviours that would have prompted the counsellor to initiate civil commitment procedures.[37]

Suicidal statements by clients can create a lot of stress for therapists. Every therapist must have a plan of action in place for dealing with clients who express suicidal thoughts. Overreacting can be as harmful as underreacting to a threat of suicide.

F.   Conclusion

Social workers frequently confront situations where they must choose between their duties to warn or protect and their ethical obligation of confidentiality. Situations involving spousal violence, child abuse, elder abuse, suicidal clients, and sexual relations between HIV-infected and uninfected individuals are some of the situations in which this dilemma can arise. Obtaining the client's consent to disclosure at the outset of therapy is the best way for social workers to protect themselves against unforeseen conflicts between the duty to warn and the requirement of confidentiality.

It is important to note that health care professionals are held responsible for their failures to follow appropriate procedures, not for errors in judgment. Health care professionals can be wrong as long as they follow the appropriate process to arrive at their decisions. It would be prudent, therefore, for a social worker to document his or her decision-making process at all times.

Social workers are responsible for ensuring that they are always in compliance with the obligations of their profession. Ignorance of the laws and rules that bind social workers is no defence against a lawsuit or a disciplinary proceeding if a client or a third party suffers harm because of a social worker's failure to recognize and have a plan for dealing with any of the situations discussed in this chapter.

---

37.   *Bogust* v. *Iverson*, 102 N.W. (2d) 228 (Wisc.,1960).

Chapter 16

Malpractice Avoidance and Insurance

A. Introduction

No social worker is immune from legal or disciplinary action, and therefore it is important to learn how to prevent both. The key to avoiding malpractice is having the appropriate policies and procedures in place *before* one is in the difficult position of having to respond to an ethical dilemma that may have no clear-cut solution. The best way to avoid such dilemmas is to uphold the standards of practice and ethics established by the body that regulates social work in one's province. Adherence to professional standards greatly reduces the potential for complaints and lawsuits.

This chapter provides concrete suggestions, tips, and guidelines to help social workers avoid the pitfalls that can result in career-breaking lawsuits and disciplinary proceedings. It should be noted, however, that the advice offered in this chapter is by no means exhaustive, nor is it offered as the only way to approach a problem.

The following are a few pieces of general advice that should be followed by every social worker:

1. Become familiar with the legislation and the policies and procedures that provide the legal framework for the province's social work profession.

2. Read the code of ethics and standards of practice publications issued by the provincial governing body for social workers, and use both in day-to-day practice.

3. Keep skills and knowledge of changes in the profession up to date by taking courses, attending seminars and lectures, and reading professional journals and newsletters.

4. Listen to clients and respond promptly to their concerns; this is the best way to head off problems before they become potential

lawsuits. A social worker's skill at handling a client's hostility and disappointment is critical for avoiding lawsuits.

5. Do not guarantee the results of treatment or make other promises that possibly cannot be fulfilled.

6. Document, document, document! Keep detailed and complete records of all transactions with clients. The best way to lose a lawsuit is to keep incomplete and inaccurate records.

7. Keep the roles clear in the therapist-client relationship. Be on the lookout for potential blurring of boundaries and other role confusion.

8. If in doubt about a professional situation, do not be afraid to seek assistance, whether it is supervision, consultation, or legal advice. It is always better to ask a question in anticipation of a problem than after the problem has arisen.

As was discussed in previous chapters, suicidal or dangerous clients can create potential liability problems for social workers. The importance of planning ahead when one has dealings with such clients cannot be overemphasized. A social worker who has a well-thought-out procedure for handling these challenging clients is much less at risk for a lawsuit than a social worker who does not.

When dealing with suicidal clients, social workers should heed the following suggestions:

1. Social workers employed by an agency should become familiar with the agency's policies for dealing with suicidal clients. Social workers in private practice should seek regular peer supervision.

2. Ask the client for information on who should be contacted in case of emergency.

3. Have the client sign an authorization form giving one permission to contact the client's emergency contacts if it appears that suicide is imminent.

4. Conduct a formal assessment to determine the probability of suicide. This should include gathering information on the client's past treatment and history of suicidal thoughts or attempts.

5. Document all observations, impressions, and courses of action related to the client's suicidal thoughts or behaviour.

6. When the risk of suicide is high, social workers are obligated to seek emergency treatment or hospitalization for their clients. Be sure to document all such efforts.

7. Establish a procedure for ensuring that a suicidal client's needs are being looked after when one is on holiday or otherwise unavailable.

8. Increase the frequency of counselling sessions if the client's situation warrants more intensive counselling.

9.   Be sure to refer the client to a psychiatrist or other physician if it appears that medication is required.
10. Know the law as it relates to a social worker's duty to warn and protect third parties.
11. If the client commits suicide or seriously harms another person, consult one's malpractice insurer immediately.

A social worker with a client who may pose a threat to others faces a difficult dilemma, namely balancing the client's right to confidentiality against the social worker's obligation to protect innocent third parties. As we have seen, the Ontario College's *Standards of Practice Handbook* allows a social worker to disclose confidential information if he or she "believes, on reasonable grounds, that disclosure is essential to the prevention of physical injury to self or others" (although the *Handbook*, regrettably, fails to define "reasonable" and "essential").

Social workers with a client who presents a potential danger to a third party should consider the following pieces of advice:

1.   Attempt to ascertain the seriousness of the perceived threat.
2.   When warning the third party, disclose only the minimal amount of information necessary to convey the warning.
3.   Refer the client to a psychiatrist or other physician for appropriate medication.
4.   Increase the frequency of monitoring and counselling sessions.
5.   Document all efforts to defuse the situation.
6.   Seek a lawyer's advice regarding the duty to warn and protect under provincial law.

B.   Informed Consent

It cannot be stressed enough that where suicidal or dangerous clients are concerned, a social worker's best defence against allegations of misconduct or a lawsuit is a well-documented file that includes a signed consent form from the client. When conflicting evidence is admitted in court or before a licensing board in our consumer-oriented society, the word of the consumer is often given greater weight than that of the professional.[1] A well-documented file and a signed consent form will, most of the time, tilt the scales of justice in the social worker's favour.

---

1.   B.E. Bernstein and T. Hartsell, *The Portable Lawyer for Mental Health Professionals* (New York: John Wiley & Sons, 1998) at 51.

Consent must, of course, be informed consent.[2] The concept of informed consent hinges on two factors, capacity to consent and consent itself. The latter is defined as "the voluntary and continuing permission of the patient to receive a particular treatment, based on an adequate knowledge of the purpose, nature, likely effects and risks of that treatment including the likelihood of its successes and any alternative to it. Permission given under any unfair or undue pressure is not 'consent.'"[3]

For consent to be legally valid, six standards must be met:

1. There must be no coercion or undue influence.
2. The client must be capable of providing consent.
3. The client must consent to specific procedures.
4. The form of consent either written or verbal must be valid.
5. The client must have the right to refuse or withdraw consent.
6. The client's decision must be based on adequate information.[4]

Validity therefore requires that the client is able to make choices, comprehend the issues, and appreciate the nature of his or her circumstances. Consent forms should refer to specific details or specific activities whenever possible. And although an oral consent can be legally valid, it is prudent to obtain written consent.

For informed consent, information must be presented to clients in understandable language, without coercion or undue influence, and in a manner that encourages clients to ask questions.[5] Common areas of disclosure include the nature and purpose of the recommended service, treatment, or activity; its advantages and disadvantages, including any significant risks to the client and possible effects on the client's family, job, social activities, or other aspects of his or her life; possible alternative interventions; and the anticipated cost to be borne by the client.

Providing information in written form can be vital for ensuring that clients have the information they need. A printed document, however, cannot be a substitute for an adequate process of informed consent. The social worker must discuss the information contained in the form with the client to ensure that the client has a basic understanding of it. Naturally, if the client's first language is not English, the social worker must ensure that the client understands English and can read well enough to know what he or she is signing.

---

2. Readers should also consult the guidelines on informed consent prepared by the Canadian Association of Social Workers, available at http://casw-acts.ca.
3. P. Jenkins, *Counselling, Psychotherapy and the Law* (London: Sage Publications, 1997) at 95.
4. F.G. Reamer, *Ethical Dilemmas in Social Service* (New York: Columbia University Press, 1990) at 115.
5. *Ibid.*, at 118-19.

A better approach if possible would be to provide the consent form in the client's language. A sample consent form is provided in chapter 19.

Sometimes social workers find it difficult to know how much information to give a client. If a large amount of information is supplied, it may be more than the client can handle, particularly if the client is in crisis. Yet too little information will not satisfy the requirements for informed consent. And how does a social worker handle the client who is unconcerned about the consent process and simply says, "I trust you, do what you think is right"? In that case, the social worker should at least review with the client the problem being addressed by the proposed intervention, the nature of the proposed intervention, its potential or anticipated risks and benefits, and the likely results.

A client's capacity to provide informed consent can be judged by questioning him or her on the following points:

1.   Does the client understand the social worker's qualifications and that the social worker is the person who will be providing the service?

2.   If the client has been referred by another professional, does he or she understand the reason for the initial session?

3.   Does the client understand the nature, extent, and possible consequences of the service the social worker is offering?

4.   Does the client understand any potential financial limitations on the service being offered?

5.   Does the client understand the social worker's fee policies and procedures, including the policy on missed or cancelled appointments?

6.   Does the client understand the policies and procedures concerning access to the social worker?

7.   Does the client understand the exceptions to confidentiality, privilege, and privacy?[6]

If the social worker is satisfied that the client has considered and properly answered the above questions, the social worker can assume that he or she has obtained a legally valid consent.

The consent form must provide that the client can stop or refuse treatment, or withdraw his or her consent, at any time. The consent must be given freely and signed without duress for it to be valid. It is also important to note that informed consent is an ongoing process. The social worker must continually take steps to ensure that there have been no changes in the nature of the client's consent. The social worker should periodically review the consent

---

6.   *Ibid.*, at 133.

form with the client and recheck the client's understanding of it. If changes have occurred the consent form should be amended to reflect the changes.

Informed consent is also an issue when dealing with requests for information about a client. Even if the client orally consents to releasing the information, it should not be released without a signed authorization. For the signed authorization to be valid, the client must not only agree to the social worker releasing the information but also know what information is to be released, who wants the information, why the information is wanted, how the person requesting the information intends to use it, whether the information will be passed on to others by the person requesting it, the repercussions of giving or refusing consent, the expiration date of the consent, and how consent can be revoked.[7]

C.   How to Respond to a Lawsuit

Being sued affects a social worker both emotionally and professionally. If one is sued, one must first and foremost try to keep the lawsuit in perspective. Even good social workers get sued, and a lawsuit may simply be the result of a disgruntled client's incorrect belief that negligent or improper conduct has occurred. It is also important to remember that a lawsuit is (usually) an action by just one former client, and does not necessarily reflect how other clients perceive a social worker's abilities or behaviour.

A successful, well-publicized lawsuit can be very detrimental to a social worker's practice because clients may be reluctant to see a social worker who has been found professionally negligent. Whether a social worker has insurance coverage or not, it is professional suicide to not vigorously defend a lawsuit.

A social worker who has the misfortune to be sued should consider the following advice:

1.   Treat the lawsuit seriously even if it appears completely groundless.
2.   Contact the insurance company immediately (failure to report a claim can jeopardize a social worker's insurance coverage).
3.   Do not attempt to personally resolve the lawsuit, for this can also jeopardize insurance coverage. Do not make promises, offers, or payments to the client, or admit responsibility.

---

7.   N. Linzer, *Resolving Ethical Dilemmas in Social Work Practice* (New York: Allyn & Bacon, 1999) at 51.

4.   Terminate all contact with the client and do not talk to members of his or her family.

5.   Cooperate with the lawyer appointed by the insurance company, and remember that the lawyer's mandate is not only to provide a proper defence, but also to minimize what the insurance company may be required to pay at the end of the lawsuit.

6.   Do not discuss the case with anyone other than the lawyer. What a person tells his or her lawyer is protected by solicitor-client privilege and cannot be disclosed, but what a person tells friends or relatives can become public knowledge and used against him or her in a court of law.

7.   Refer all questions and correspondence concerning the lawsuit to the lawyer.

8.   Do not destroy or alter the client's file. Give the lawyer a complete copy of the file.

9.   Prepare a summary of the events leading up to the lawsuit. This will assist the lawyer and be a useful memory aid when one's evidence is taken.

10.   Realize that the lawsuit may take years to resolve, particularly if it goes to trial. It should not be allowed to take control of one's personal and professional life.

D.   Insurance

I.   Introduction

Malpractice claims cannot always be prevented, but their impact can be reduced if one carries insurance. Every social worker should obtain comprehensive liability insurance. Those who choose not to be insured because they believe that lack of coverage reduces their attractiveness as targets for a lawsuit may find themselves sadly mistaken, because lack of coverage will not deter most lawyers.

A social worker without insurance is bound to incur substantial legal fees if sued, and may ultimately be faced with having to satisfy a sizeable judgment. Many social workers operate their businesses without the protection of incorporation, and where that is the case a successful plaintiff may try to collect on a judgment by seizing the social worker's personal assets, including houses, cars, and savings accounts. It is also possible to seize a portion of a social worker's income to satisfy a judgment.

Social workers who are agency employees may believe that they do not need personal liability insurance because they are covered by their agency's policy. In a lawsuit against a social worker employed by an agency, however, the agency's insurance company may attempt to show that the social worker's behaviour fell outside the scope of his or her employment and therefore was not covered by the policy. In such cases, a personal liability insurance policy will ensure that the social worker has a lawyer who will strongly defend the social worker's interests.

II.   Questions to Ask about Insurance

If one is thinking of working for an agency or other employer, one should ask whether the employer has a liability insurance policy and, if so, whether it provides personal coverage for the individual social worker. One should also ask about restrictions to coverage, the policy's definition of "scope of employment," and whether it is expected that the social worker will be required in certain circumstances to reimburse the agency for what it or its insurer had to pay to settle the lawsuit.

If one is purchasing an individual policy, one should ask what amount of coverage is provided and also inquire about the deductible (the amount that the social worker will be expected to pay in the event of a successful claim).

Questions to ask about any insurance policy include the following:

1.   What types of claims are included or excluded?
2.   What risks are covered?
3.   What are the exclusions? (The risks covered and the exclusions are usually clearly spelled out in the policy.)
4.   Are punitive damages covered? (Most policies do not cover punitive damages.)
5.   Is the policy a claims-made or an occurrence policy? (These terms are discussed below.)
6.   Are legal fees covered and, if so, what are the limits?
7.   Can the social worker choose the lawyer he or she wants or is he or she required to work with a lawyer chosen by the insurance company?

III.   Types of Policies

There are two main types of liability insurance for social workers: claims-made policies and occurrence policies. Under a claims-made policy, the social worker is covered only for claims reported while the insurance is in force. Under an occurrence policy, the social worker is covered for any claim relating to events that occurred during the period that the insurance was in force, regardless of when the claim is reported. Both types of policy typically place limits on the amounts payable for each wrongful act or series of wrongful acts, as well as a limit on the aggregate amount payable under the policy.

IV.   Types of Coverage

A prudent social worker should have the following types of insurance coverage: professional liability (malpractice), public liability, and libel and slander. Public liability coverage relates to the death or injury of persons other than employees, such as a passerby who slips and falls on property owned by the social worker, and also covers damage to the property of others. Social workers who work from home and are relying on their homeowner's insurance to protect them from personal injury claims may be in for a big shock in the event of a claim. Most homeowner's policies do not cover business-related activities in the home. Libel and slander coverage relates to harmful comments about clients or third parties in, for example, reports to agencies and courts.

V.   Legal Costs

A major feature of professional liability insurance is coverage of legal costs. Most claims against social workers fail, but not before substantial legal costs have been incurred. Social workers purchasing insurance should check whether the policy covers the cost of legal representation for disciplinary hearings. It is also important to check what sort of coverage applies in cases of alleged sexual impropriety with a client. Insurance companies have begun to exclude or limit coverage in sexual misconduct cases.

Some insurers will reimburse social workers accused of sexual impropriety only if the defence is successful, and even in those cases the social worker may be required to cover the legal costs out of his or her own pocket until the disciplinary or legal proceedings are over.

E.   Conclusion

In conclusion, here are six steps to reduce legal vulnerability:

1. Become familiar with the concept of professional liability and its legal ramifications for social workers.
2. Adhere to applicable legal and administrative requirements.
3. Maintain professional standards of conduct and performance (including, where applicable, agency standards).
4. Keep complete records.
5. Ensure financial protection by having appropriate insurance.
6. Be sensitive to high-risk situations.[8]

---

8.   D. Bersharov, *The Vulnerable Social Worker: Liability for Serving Children & Families* (Washington: National Association of Social Workers, Inc., 1985) at 167.

Chapter 17

A Look at the Other Provinces

A.   Introduction

The practice of social work is separately regulated by each province, although the substance of the provincial Acts is strikingly similar from province to province. Each province, for example, restricts the use of titles such as social worker and registered social worker to individuals who meet certain requirements, and it is an offence in all of the provinces to use the restricted titles without authorization. The practice of social work itself, however, is not always as tightly restricted. Some provinces, such as Prince Edward Island, make it an offence to practise social work unless registered, while others, such as New Brunswick, exempt certain social work practitioners (such as nurses) from registration.

Some provinces, such as Alberta, Nova Scotia, and New Brunswick, have bestowed regulatory authority on an existing provincial association of social workers, while other provinces, such as Manitoba, British Columbia, and Prince Edward Island, have established new regulatory bodies. As we have seen, Ontario's legislation created a college with regulatory authority separate from the provincial social work association.

The criteria for registration differ somewhat among the provinces. Some provinces, such as Nova Scotia, require work experience in addition to post-secondary education before one is entitled to full membership in the regulatory body. Ontario and Alberta, the only provinces to regulate social service workers, require community college training before one can become a social service worker.

Most of the remainder of this chapter is devoted to a province-by-province examination of the legislation governing Canadian social workers outside Ontario. It does not, however, fully examine every provision of the provincial Acts, nor does it include Quebec, whose social workers are governed by

189

the province's *Code des Professions*.[1] At the end of this chapter is a list of the provincial regulatory bodies accompanied by information on how they can be contacted.

B.   The Provincial Legislation

I.   Newfoundland and Labrador

With the enactment of the *Social Workers Association Act* in 1992,[2] the Newfoundland Association of Social Workers was continued as a corporation under a new name, the Newfoundland and Labrador Association of Social Workers. The objects of the Association are very similar to those listed in the Ontario legislation. They include the establishment and maintenance of standards of professional conduct, knowledge and skill, regulation of the practice of social work, promotion of public awareness of the profession, and service to and protection of the public.[3]

The Association is given broad powers to carry out a variety of functions, including the functions necessary to run the Association and regulate the profession. Two of the more important functions of the Association's are the evaluation of the competence of potential members and disciplining members. In addition, the Association can assess and define areas of specialization, evaluate continuing education programs, and develop or approve new programs.[4]

The Association is run by a board of directors. The Act enables the Association to make regulations and by-laws to assist the directors in carrying out the Association's objects.

Unlike the Ontario legislation, the Newfoundland Act establishes a Committee of Examiners. This committee examines and reports to the board on the qualifications of every candidate for registration.[5] The committee also sets the examinations given to candidates seeking admittance to the Association.

To be registered as a social worker and practise social work in the province, a person must have a bachelor's degree or higher degree in social work, or an equivalent education in social work obtained at an educational institution approved by the Committee of Examiners; have passed examina-

---

1.   R.S.Q., c. C-.26.
2.   S.N. 1992, c. S –18.1.
3.   *Ibid.*, s. 6.
4.   *Ibid.*, s. 7.
5.   *Ibid.*, s. 15.

tions in subjects prescribed by the committee; and have paid the prescribed fee.[6]

A person must be a member of the Association to use the titles social worker or registered social worker, and the designation RSW. Only those individuals who are members of the Association can engage in the practice of social work. Any person denied registration may appeal the decision to the board.

The Act also contains a clause prohibiting anyone from suing the Association for actions taken by the Association in good faith.

Complaints about members' conduct are received by the registrar and then referred to the Discipline Committee for investigation. Although the Act does not require a separate Complaints Committee to investigate complaints, similar to the Ontario Act, it does provide that the Discipline Committee must appoint an investigator who is not a committee member. This ensures that some degree of impartiality exists.[7]

In the course of his or her investigation, the investigator can compel the member being investigated to produce copies of all pertinent documents. The investigator also has the power to report on all matters of professional conduct that arise in the course of the investigation. This provision means that an investigator investigating a complaint on one matter may report to the Association on any other matter he or she discovers in the course of the investigation.

Once the investigation has been completed, the investigator makes a report to the members of the discipline committee, who then decide whether to hold a hearing into the complaint. If a hearing is warranted, the member is served with a notice of hearing and the particulars of the conduct or complaint that has led to the hearing. The member may appear before the committee and be represented by counsel. If the member chooses not to appear, the hearing will go on without him or her and a determination based solely on the results of the investigation will be made. A hearing is held in private unless the member requests that it be held in public.[8]

If the Discipline Committee finds that the member's conduct was unprofessional or lacking in skill, the board of directors has the power to do a number of things, including revoking the member's registration, suspending the member, imposing conditions on the member's registration, requiring a further course of study, and imposing a fine.[9] In addition, the member may be ordered to pay the Association's expenses connected with the hearing, which

6.   *Ibid.*, s. 17.
7.   *Ibid.*, s. 35.
8.   *Ibid.*, ss. 40 and 43.
9.   *Ibid.*, s. 46.

are likely to be in the thousands of dollars. A member who fails to pay can have his or her license suspended and be sued for the unpaid amount.

All members have the right to appeal a Discipline Committee decision to the Trial Division of the Newfoundland Supreme Court. Any orders made by the board suspending or revoking a member's registration are stayed pending the outcome of the appeal.

A striking feature of the Act is found in Part V, the penalties section, which contemplates incarceration for an offence committed under the Act. Pursuant to section 54, any person convicted of an offence under the Act, the regulations, or by-laws is liable on summary conviction to a fine or three to six months' imprisonment (the length of the sentence depends on whether this is the member's first or second offence). The notion of jailing social workers for unprofessional conduct is somewhat radical in Canada but not unusual in the United States, where some state legislation makes certain forms of unprofessional conduct, such as sexual relations with a client, felonies. The Ontario legislation provides for larger fines than the New-foundland legislation, but does not contemplate imprisonment.

II.   Prince Edward Island

Prince Edward Island's social workers are governed by the province's *Social Work Act*, which incorporated the Prince Edward Island Association of Social Workers.[10] The Association's purpose is to promote the professional interests of its members as well as activities that will strengthen and foster public awareness of the profession.[11]

The Act also established the Prince Edward Island Social Work Registration Board. The board, which has five members, four of whom are social workers and the fifth a member of the public, is responsible for the regulation of social work in the province. Its mandate is to promote established standards and safeguard the welfare of the public.[12] The board's functions include prescribing educational and other qualifications for registration, examining applicants, issuing certificates of registration, prescribing standards of practice, upholding ethical standards, investigating complaints, and exercising discipline.[13]

Once a person is issued a certificate of registration, he or she is entitled to use the title registered social worker and the initials RSW after his or her name. It is an offence to practise social work or use the title without a valid certificate of registration. Interestingly, it is also an offence to employ some-

---

10.   R.S.P.E.I. 1988, c. S-5.
11.   *Ibid.*, ss. 2 and 3.
12.   *Ibid.*, s. 7.1.
13.   *Ibid.*, s. 7.2.

one as a social work practitioner who does not have a valid certificate of registration. The penalty for this is a fine of not more than $500.

If the board receives information in writing that a registered social worker is allegedly guilty of professional misconduct, gross negligence, or incompetence, it is obliged to investigate the complaint and either dismiss it or impose a penalty. When a social worker is found guilty of professional misconduct, gross negligence, or incompetence, the board may suspend or revoke the social worker's registration, impose conditions on the certificate of registration, impose a retraining requirement, issue a reprimand, or require the social worker to pay costs.[14]

One of the significant differences between the Prince Edward Island and Ontario legislation is the absence in the former of a provision for a separate Complaints Committee to investigate complaints and decide whether to refer them to the Discipline Committee. Under the Prince Edward Island Act the Discipline Committee is the body charged with carrying out an investigation in the first instance. It is difficult to see how the committee can remain impartial in a disciplinary hearing when it refers the complaint to itself.

The Act also contains a clause prohibiting anyone from suing a member of the board for an action taken by the member in good faith.

III. New Brunswick

The practice of social work in New Brunswick is regulated by *The Act to Incorporate the New Brunswick Association of Social Workers*.[15] The Act limits the use of the titles social worker and registered social worker, and the abbreviations for each, to persons who are members of the New Brunswick Association of Social Workers. In connection with its duty to regulate the profession and govern its members, the Association determines standards of professional conduct and appoints members to the Committee of Examiners, who examine and approve applications for membership.

The Act provides for a Complaints Committee separate from the Discipline Committee. As we have seen in the case of Ontario, placing discipline in the hands of two committees with separate memberships adds to the certainty that investigations will be impartial. The Complaints Committee investigates complaints of professional misconduct, incompetence, or breach of the Association's Code of Ethics.[16] Once the investigation is completed, the committee has the authority to dismiss the complaint, refer it to the Discipline Committee, or take some other action that it considers appropriate and is not inconsistent with the Act.

---

14.   *Ibid.*, s. 13.
15.   S.N.B. 1988, c. 78.
16.   *Ibid.*, s. 21.

If a matter is referred to the Discipline Committee, the committee will convene a discipline hearing, at which the member may be represented by counsel. If the Discipline Committee finds that the member has committed an act of professional misconduct or incompetence, it has broad powers to impose a penalty. It can revoke or suspend the member's registration, impose terms, conditions, or restrictions on the certificate of registration, or impose a fine. It also has the authority to publish its decisions.[17]

The provision that the committee can publish its decisions suggests that the committee has the discretion to publish or withhold their decisions from the public. This is contrary to the practice of other provincial bodies that regulate social workers and health professionals, which routinely publish their disciplinary decisions in their professional publications. Many disciplinary decisions are also made available through legal databases that can be accessed by the public.

Another unusual feature of the New Brunswick Act is that it defines the term professional misconduct, whereas other Acts leave that term to be defined in the regulations, thereby allowing the regulatory body itself to decide what constitutes professional misconduct. Section 23 of the Act states that professional misconduct occurs where a member has, in the opinion of the Disciplinary Committee, departed from recognized professional standards or the profession's rules of practice. This definition is so broad that the Discipline Committee is given the power to decide what professional misconduct is. The definition gives rise to two concerns. First, the meaning of "professional standards" is not clarified, and second, professional standards are often capable of many different interpretations. This leaves the social worker unsure as to what conduct departs from standards set by the committee.

IV.   Nova Scotia

The practice of social work in Nova Scotia, including the use of the titles social worker and registered social worker, is regulated by the *Social Workers Act*.[18] The Nova Scotia Association of Social Workers administers the Act and is charged with governing the profession and ensuring that the public receives the services of proficient and competent social workers.[19] The actual responsibility for governing the profession and protecting the public from incompetent or unprofessional social workers rests, however, with the Association's Board of Examiners. This body operates separately from the

---

17.   *Ibid.*, s. 23.
18.   R.S.N.S. 1993, c. 12.
19.   *Ibid.*, s. 5.

rest of the Association, which is primarily concerned with providing continuing education programs for its members.

The Board of Examiners reviews all applications for registration. Nova Scotia has stringent qualification requirements, which demand both post-secondary education and social work experience. To be allowed to use the title social worker or the abbreviation RSW, a potential applicant must have at least a bachelor's degree in social work and three years' experience as a social worker. Applicants without sufficient experience are allowed to use only the designation SWC, which stands for social work candidate. During the three-year qualifying period they must be supervised by a registered social worker. Social workers in other provinces, by contrast, are not required to complete a candidacy period.

Members who are refused registration may apply to the board for a review of its decision. The Act does not appear to allow social workers to appeal a board decision to a court of law.[20]

The Act provides for both a Complaints Committee and a Discipline Committee. Members of the one cannot also be members of the other. The Complaints Committee investigates all written complaints from the public where it is alleged that a member is guilty of professional misconduct, conduct unbecoming, incompetence, or a breach of the code of ethics.[21] If an investigation is commenced, the member in question receives a copy of the complaint so that he or she can respond to the allegations.

The Complaints Committee has several options available to it once an investigation is completed. It can dismiss a complaint, attempt to resolve it informally, refer it to mediation (with the consent of both parties), counsel the member, reprimand the member (with the member's consent) and require the member to undergo treatment or re-education, or refer the matter to the Discipline Committee.[22] A complainant who is not satisfied with a decision of the Complaints Committee can apply to the Board of Examiners to have the decision reviewed.

The Act was amended in 2001 to add a new approach to the disposal of complaints against members. Section 29A permits a member, before the commencement of a disciplinary hearing, to submit a proposed settlement of the complaint to the Complaints Committee. The proposal must contain an admission of guilt and specify how the complaint is to be disposed of. If it is rejected by the committee, the disciplinary hearing proceeds as if the settlement had never been proposed. If it is accepted, the Complaints Committee forwards a recommendation in support of the proposal to the Discipline Committee, which makes the final decision on acceptance or rejection. If it

---

20.   *Ibid.*, s. 25.
21.   *Ibid.*, s. 28.
22.   *Ibid.*, s. 29.

rejects the recommendation, the registrar is advised of this outcome and a new Discipline Committee is appointed. The process set forth in section 29A is very similar to a plea bargain in a criminal matter.

If a disciplinary hearing is convened, the member is entitled to be represented by counsel. The hearing is similar to a trial in that witnesses are called, give evidence under oath, and are cross-examined. Any relevant document can be introduced into evidence at the hearing, and experts may be called to testify. At the end of the hearing the Discipline Committee can find a member guilty of professional misconduct, conduct unbecoming, or incompetence. The penalties that the committee can impose are similar to those of other provinces.

What sort of conduct constitutes professional misconduct is left to the committee to decide. Conduct unbecoming is defined in the Code of Ethics and also in the Act. The latter defines conduct unbecoming as misbehaviour outside the ambit of a social worker–client relationship that reflects on the member's integrity or competence and could bring discredit to the profession.[23] A recent amendment to the Act allows the Discipline Committee to find a member incompetent if, in its opinion, the member has displayed a lack of knowledge, skill, or judgment, or disregard for the welfare of the public, of such nature or extent to demonstrate that the member is unfit to carry out the responsibilities of a person engaged in the practice of social work.[24]

V.   Manitoba

Manitoba's social workers are governed by *The Manitoba Institute of Registered Social Workers Incorporation Act*,[25] which limits the designation registered social worker to persons registered under the Act. It appears, however, that one does not have to be registered to simply call oneself a social worker. This is in contrast to the Ontario Act, which protects both titles. The Manitoba Institute of Registered Social Workers (MIRSW) is the regulatory arm of the profession, but it only regulates those individuals who voluntarily apply for registration.

The MIRSW issues certificates of registration to qualified applicants, who must be committed to following prescribed ethical standards. In addition to its registration duties, the MIRSW also ensures that members participate in continuing education programs and investigates public complaints. Only individuals with Bachelor's or Master's degrees in Social Work are eligible to apply for membership in the MIRSW. Individuals with lesser educational qualifications or work experience are only eligible to join the Manitoba

---

23.   *Ibid.*, s. 33(3A).
24.   *Ibid.*, s. 33(4).
25.   S.M. 1966, c. 104.

Association of Social Workers, which is the professional association for social workers in the province. The Association provides peer support, advocacy, and member services to the profession. It has no regulatory powers. The two associations work together to set policies and respond to issues. They are run by a volunteer board of directors elected by the members.

Complaints are investigated by the Discipline Committee, whose task is to determine whether further action is required. There is both an informal process, in which the committee members attempt to resolve the complaint without a hearing, and a formal process where disciplinary proceedings are commenced. The formal process is open to public scrutiny.

Unprofessional conduct — one of the types of member conduct over which the committee has authority — is conduct that is detrimental to the best interests of the public, in that it contravenes the Canadian Association of Social Workers' code of ethics and/or it displays a lack of knowledge or skill that would be expected from a social worker in the practice of social work. The committee has powers similar to those of its counterparts in other provinces to suspend, revoke, or otherwise cancel a member's registration if there is a finding of unprofessional conduct.

VI.   Saskatchewan

The Social Workers Act, which was passed in 1993,[26] replaced Saskatchewan's *Registered Social Workers Act*. Like the old Act, the new Act recognized the Saskatchewan Association of Social Workers as the provincial regulatory body.

The Association's objects are very similar to the objects set out in Ontario's legislation. In fact, the Saskatchewan statute as a whole is remarkably similar to the Ontario statute.

The Association's objects include, but are not limited to, first, establishing, maintaining, and developing standards of knowledge, skill, and competence among its members for the purpose of serving and protecting the public interest, and second, establishing, maintaining, and developing standards of professional conduct.[27] A council, the majority of whose members are elected members of the Association, manages the Association's affairs. The council has the power to establish committees and make by-laws necessary for carrying out the objects of the Association.[28]

Section 24 of the Act prohibits any person, unless he or she is a member of the Association, from engaging in the practice of social work and using the

---

26.   R.S.S. 1993, c. S-52.
27.   *Ibid.*, s. 4.
28.   *Ibid.*, ss. 14 and 16.

title social worker.[29] Persons who have met the qualifications for membership, paid the requisite fee, and complied with the registration by-laws are issued an annual licence.[30] Whereas in other provinces the registrar of the applicable regulatory body maintains a public register of the membership, under the Saskatchewan Act the Association is required to file once a year with the minister of justice and attorney-general a list of all Association members, including their addresses and dates of admission to membership.

Complaints about members are referred to the Professional Conduct Committee for investigation. The Act clearly states that no one who is a member of the Discipline Committee can sit on the Professional Conduct Committee; this helps ensure that investigations remain impartial.[31] Once an investigation is completed, the Professional Conduct Committee submits a written report to the Discipline Committee, recommending either that a formal disciplinary hearing take place or that no further action be taken.[32]

If a complaint is referred for a formal hearing, the Discipline Committee issues a notice of hearing to the member along with a copy of the complaint. Under the Saskatchewan Act, the Professional Conduct Committee shall prosecute the complaint, but its members shall not participate in any other manner in the hearing of the complaint except as witnesses.[33] The Discipline Committee has the power to hire legal counsel if it so desires to assist it during the hearing phase. Although the disciplinary hearing itself is very similar to a judicial proceeding, in that witnesses testify under oath, are subject to cross-examination, and can be subpoenaed to testify, the committee is not bound by the rules of evidence, but has the power to accept any evidence it considers appropriate. This, of course, weakens the evidentiary safeguards expected by an accused in a normal judicial setting.

If the Discipline Committee finds a member guilty of professional misconduct or professional incompetence, it has the powers typically found in the legislation of other provinces to suspend or revoke the member's registration, impose conditions or restrictions on the registration, or order the member to undergo additional training or receive medical treatment.[34] In addition, the committee can levy a fine of not more than $2,000 or order the member to pay the costs of the investigation and the hearing.

An unusual feature of the Saskatchewan legislation is its distinction between professional misconduct and professional incompetence. In other provinces, professional incompetence is considered an element of professional misconduct rather than a distinct form of conduct by a social worker.

---

29.   *Ibid.*, s. 24.
30.   *Ibid.*, s. 21.
31.   *Ibid.*, s. 25.
32.   *Ibid.*, s. 26.
33.   *Ibid.*, s. 28.
34.   *Ibid.*, s. 29.

In Saskatchewan, professional incompetence is a separate type of conduct and is defined as a lack of knowledge, skill, or judgment, or a disregard for the welfare of members of the public served by the profession of a nature or to an extent that demonstrates that the member is unfit to continue in the practice of the profession.[35] The definition of professional misconduct is the definition typically seen in other legislation without reference to the element of professional incompetence.

Members found guilty of an offence by the Discipline Committee may appeal their conviction to a judge of the Saskatchewan Supreme Court. The appeal does not automatically stay the committee's decision. To prevent a suspension or a revocation of his or her licence while waiting for the appeal to be heard, a member would have to apply to the court for a stay of the proceedings pending disposal of the appeal.

This legislation also provides that a member who has had his or her licence revoked can apply to the council for reinstatement.[36]

The council and the committees enjoy immunity against lawsuits for their actions as long as those actions are taken in good faith.

The limitation period for bringing an action against a member for professional negligence or malpractice is 24 months after a cause of action arises. It can be difficult, however, to determine exactly when a cause of action arises. The courts have consistently held that a cause of action does not arise until the injured person knows or ought to know that he or she has a claim against a member. When a person knows or ought to know that he or she has a claim against a member will turn on the particular circumstances of the case.

VII. Alberta

Alberta's *Social Work Professions Act*[37] provides that only persons registered under the Act can refer to themselves as registered social workers and use the initials RSW. The Act is administered by the Alberta College of Social Workers through its Council. Applications for membership are submitted to the registrar, who is responsible for deciding whether to approve, deny, or defer an application.[38] Any applicant whose application is refused by the registrar may apply to the council to have the registrar's decision reviewed.

A unique feature of this Act (in the Canadian context at least) is its mandatory registration requirement. If, in the registrar's opinion, an individual who has the requisite educational qualifications is providing a service that falls

---

35.   *Ibid.*, s. 30(2).
36.   *Ibid.*, s. 39.
37.   R.S.A. 2000, c. S-13.
38.   *Ibid.*, s. 9(1).

within the definition of social work to any member of the public, or is supervising someone who is providing such a service, the registrar may direct that individual to apply for registration as a registered social worker.[39] The mandatory wording of the registration provision suggests that anyone practising social work can be required to register with the College whether he or she wants to or not. This is very different from the Ontario legislation, which .prevents non-members from using the titles social worker and registered social worker but does not prevent people who do not use those titles from engaging in social work.

Another unique feature of the Act is its establishment of a Practice Review Board empowered to conduct a review of a member's practice without the need for a complaint from the public. This feature is similar to the provisions found in Canadian legislation governing regulated health professions such as medicine, dentistry, and physiotherapy. If, in the course of a review of a member's practice, the investigator appointed by the College finds evidence of unskilled practice or professional misconduct, he or she is required to immediately notify the registrar so that a further investigation under the discipline provisions of the Act can be undertaken.[40]

Complaints about the conduct of a social worker are made in writing to the registrar, who then appoints a person to conduct a preliminary investigation into the complaint. The investigator has the power to compel any person to answer questions and produce documentation.[41] Once the investigation has been completed, the investigator must submit a written report to the registrar. The registrar may then dismiss the complaint or refer it to the Discipline Committee for a hearing. Depending on the severity of the alleged conduct, the member's certificate of registration may be immediately suspended pending the outcome of the hearing. Although the member is subject to a penalty before he or she has been convicted of professional misconduct, this is viewed as a necessary safeguard for the public.

The disciplinary process is a legal process in which the member has the right to be represented, call witnesses, present evidence, and receive disclosure from the College as to the case the member has to meet. Although the disciplinary hearing is very much like a trial, the Discipline Committee is not bound by the rules of evidence applicable to judicial proceedings.[42] If the committee finds a member guilty, it may reprimand the member or suspend, revoke, or impose conditions on the member's certification. In addition, the committee may order the member to pay a fine of not more than $5,000 as well as the costs of the hearing. An appeal to a court of law does not automatically stay a committee decision.

---

39.   *Ibid.*, s. 9.1(1).
40.   *Ibid.*, s. 24.
41.   *Ibid.*, s. 30.
42.   *Ibid.*, s. 38.

Complaints about members are not confined to complaints received from the public. The province's code of ethics and standards of practice for social workers provide that all registered social workers must notify the College if they have reason to believe that a colleague is guilty of malpractice or professional misconduct. This requirement is more expansive than the reporting requirement imposed on Ontario social workers, which is limited to cases of suspected sexual abuse of a client. In other respects, however, the province's standards of practice for social workers are very similar to those of Ontario.

In addition to having a right of appeal to a court of law, a member who has been disciplined can also appeal to the College council.[43]

The Act also contains the usual no-action clause protecting the College and its council and committee members against lawsuits for any actions directed at a member of the College, provided the actions are taken in good faith.

The Alberta Social Work Standards of Practice forms an integral part of the Alberta legislation and is very similar in wording to the Ontario Standards of Practice. The Standards of Practice covers everything from practice requirements, protecting confidentiality of clients, preventing impaired functioning and relationships, to the reporting of violations. As is present in all social work legislation across Canada, a violation of the standards of practice can invariably lead to the commencement of discipline proceedings.

VIII. British Columbia

British Columbia's *Social Workers Act*[44] limits the titles of social worker and registered social worker to persons registered as social workers in accordance with the provisions of the Act. Persons employed by certain designated employers are also entitled to call themselves social workers.[45] The Act goes one step further than most of the other provincial legislation in that it also regulates who can engage in the private practice of social work. In addition to being registered, a social worker must have a master's degree in social work and have been approved by the board for private practice.

The Act is administered by a body called the Board of Registration for Social Workers in B.C., which has the authority to apply to the province's Supreme Court for an injunction restraining a person from using the title social worker or registered social worker. The board is responsible for making rules concerning the registration, education, and training of social workers; professional misconduct and incompetence; and disciplinary hearings.

---

43. *Ibid.*, s. 51.
44. R.S.B.C. 1996, c. 432.
45. *Ibid.*, s. 8.

The board comprises 10 to 12 members, two of whom are not social workers by profession.

Complaints against social workers are reviewed by a Practice Review Committee, which submits its recommendations to the board. The board has the power to issue a warning or reprimand, impose limitations on a member's right to practise, or suspend or cancel a member's registration. A person whose registration is limited, suspended, or cancelled has a right of appeal to the province's Supreme Court. If the member disagrees with the Practice Review Committee's recommendation he or she can ask for a full hearing of the board.

Alternatively the Practice Review Committee has the discretion to enter into an agreement with the social worker instead of referring the matter to a full hearing. The social worker can agree to participate in a plan which might involve supervision or taking educational courses with a view to improving his or her practice skills. These agreements are kept confidential.

The British Columbia Association of Social Workers is a voluntary association that provides support and professional development services to its members. The Association is a distinct and separate organization from the Board of Registration for Social Workers.

C.   The Provincial Regulatory Bodies

Newfoundland and Labrador
Newfoundland and Labrador Association of Social Workers
P.O. Box CP 5244, East End Post Office
St. John's, NL. A1C 5W1
Phone: (709) 753-0200
Fax: (709) 753-0120
E-mail: nlasw@nf.sympatico.ca
Web site: http://www3.nf.sympatico.ca/nlasw

Prince Edward Island
Prince Edward Island Association of Social Workers
81 rue Prince St.
Charlottetown, PE. C1A 4R3
Phone: (902) 368-7337
Fax: (902) 368-7180
E-mail: fsbureau@isn.net

New Brunswick
New Brunswick Association of Social Workers
P.O. Box 1533, Station "A"
Fredericton, NB. E3B 5G2
Phone: (506) 459-5595

Fax: (506) 457-1421
E-mail: nbasw.atsnb@nbasw-atsnb.ca
Web site: http://www.nbasw-atsnb.ca

Nova Scotia
Nova Scotia Association of Social Workers
1891 Brunswick Street, Suite 106
Halifax, NS. B3J 2G8
Phone: (902) 429-7799
Fax: (902) 429-7650
E-mail: nsasw@fox.nstn.ca
Web site: http://www.nsasw.org

Quebec
Ordre professionnel des travailleurs sociaux du Québec
5757 avenue Decelles, bureau 335
Montréal, PQ. H3S 2C3
Phone: (514) 731-3925
Fax: (514) 731-6785
E-mail: info.general@optsq.org
Web site: http://www.optsq.org

Ontario
Ontario College of Social Workers and Social Service Workers
80 Bloor Street W., Suite 401
Toronto, ON. M5S 2V1
Phone: (416) 972-9882
Fax: (416) 972-1512
E-mail: info@ocswssw.org
Web site: http://www.ocswssw.org

Manitoba
Manitoba Institute of Registered Social Workers and
Manitoba Association of Social Workers
2015 Portage Ave., Unit 4
Winnipeg, MB. R3J 0K3
Phone: (204) 888-9477
Fax: (204) 889-0021
E-mail: masw@mts.net
Web site: http://www.geocities.com/masw_mirsw

Saskatchewan
Saskatchewan Association of Social Workers
2110 Lorne Street
Regina, SK. S4P 2M5
Phone: (306) 545-1922
Fax: (306) 545-1895

Alberta
Alberta College of Social Workers
10707–100 Avenue, Suite 550
Edmonton, Alberta T5J 3M1
Phone: (780) 421-1167
Fax: (780) 421-1168
E-mail: acsw@acsw.ab.ca
Web site: http://www.acsw.ab.ca

British Columbia
Board of Registration for Social Workers of British Columbia
1755 West Broadway, Suite 407
Vancouver, BC. V6J 4S5
Phone: (604) 737-4916
Fax: (604) 737-6809
E-mail: brsw@telus.net
Web site: http://www.brsw.bc.ca

Northern Canada
The Association of Social Workers of Northern Canada
Fort Smith, NT. X0E 0P0
Phone: (867) 872-7578
Fax: (867) 872-3175

Chapter 18

Final Thoughts

A.   Introduction

The long-awaited time has finally arrived: social work and social service work are now legislatively recognized professions in Ontario. Legislation has given the Ontario College of Social Workers and Social Service Workers extensive powers for governing the profession, and the titles "social worker" and "social service worker" are now confined by law to members of the College.

To the social worker, it may appear that little has changed, but in fact, every aspect of his or her professional life has been affected. It is now incumbent on every member of the College to comport himself or herself in a manner that both enhances the profession and protects the public. Whereas this was once largely a moral rather than a legal responsibility, today the legal element is much stronger. Members of the College who want to safeguard their careers are now obligated to understand how the legislation affects their everyday practice.

Although the legislation and the Ontario College's code of ethics and *Standards of Practice Handbook* provide extensive guidance on the values and behaviour expected of social workers, many areas of uncertainty remain, and there are many legal minefields that can trap the unwary professional. This book has attempted to show Ontario social workers how to navigate around many of these minefields, but there will always be some minefields that cannot be detected and others that unexpectedly appear because of changes in technology or social work theory. Social workers who want to maximize their chances of avoiding these legal minefields — and the costly, time-consuming, and emotionally as well as professionally damaging consequences of a legal attack on their professional status — must always be alert to the legal issues that confront them.

Once armed with the knowledge provided by this book, the prudent social worker should examine his or her daily practice with a critical eye, watching for behaviour that is likely to be questioned by others. Social workers must be sensitive to how others may perceive their actions and how those actions can be misconstrued. It is not enough simply to read this book and the *Standards of Practice Handbook* without thinking about how they apply to one's day-to-day practice. Social workers must develop the habit of anticipating ethically problematic situations and circumventing them.

B.   Minefields

I.   Introduction

As we have seen in this book, many ethical minefields await the unwary social worker. They include the following:

- Defining and maintaining professional boundaries with a client so that the service relationship is clearly separated from the business, personal, social, and especially the sexual domains.
- Fully informing a client about the counselling-related policies of one's employer, the responsibilities placed on the social worker and the client by the counselling relationship, and the risks inherent in the counselling relationship, even when such information could discourage the client from undergoing counselling.
- Conflicts between a social worker's professional values and the policies of his or her employer.
- The limits on confidentiality, such as the duty to warn the potential victim of a dangerous client and the question whether a client's HIV-positive status should be disclosed to an unsuspecting sexual partner.
- The competing rights of a client and his or her parents or other relatives.
- Having to rely on resources that are insufficient to meet a client's needs.
- The conflict between a clients's need for access to the social worker versus the social worker's legitimate need for privacy.
- Conflicts between one's personal values and the duty to aid a client in cases involving sensitive issues such as abortion, cocaine use by expectant mothers, child abuse, and end-of-life decisions.
- Withholding of potentially traumatic information from some family members at the request of others.
- Concerns surrounding a client's right of access to his or her clinical records.

- The question whether it is ethical to terminate a service relationship with a client who fails to pay one's fees or comply with the requirements of therapy.[1]

Possibly the most difficult challenge for social workers is maintaining their sense of ethics in the face of what they perceive as unethical behaviour by another professional or a client. In pursuing what we view is right, might we not be imposing our values on others while at the same time violating their rights? Or adopting a supercilious attitude that allows us to delve into private lives while distrusting the motivations and actions of others? This is not to suggest that social workers should disregard standards of practice, but merely that they must never follow policies blindly without regard for the implications of their actions. The remainder of this chapter discusses some of the areas of conflict in more detail and expands on topics covered in previous chapters by drawing the reader's attention to ongoing dilemmas and concerns.

II.   Sexual Abuse of Clients

The conflict in values is nowhere more evident than in the act of reporting a colleague for the alleged sexual abuse of a client. First of all, implicit in the act of reporting is the assumption that the client is not competent to decide for himself or herself about the desirability of a sexual relationship with the therapist. Second, by making reporting mandatory, the legislation (in Ontario at least) fails to respect the fact that the client might legitimately view reporting as creating undesirable consequences for himself or herself.

Consider, for example, a situation in which a social worker in a small town treats a client for stress and anxiety over a number of months. The treatment is successful and counselling is terminated. A year later, the social worker and the client meet again when they separately join a charity committee. They become friendly and would like to begin a more serious relationship, which would undoubtedly become sexual. As the law stands, they would not be able to do so under any circumstances. In a small community, is this social isolation fair to the social worker? Would a relationship really be detrimental to the client? These are only a few of the questions that arise.

III.   Remaining Ethical in the Face of Unethical Behaviour

As representatives of a profession that wants to live up to its newly enhanced legislative status, is it not possible that members of the Ontario College will

---

1.   M.K. Houston-Vega and E.M. Nuehring, *Prudent Practice: A Guide for Managing Malpractice Risk* (Washington, DC: National Association of Social Workers, 1997) at 11.

act overzealously toward other members who have allegedly breached professional ethics? Social workers in Ontario must be careful not to overreact when one of their colleagues has behaved in a way that discredits the profession.

Consider the case of a social worker who has inherited a client from another social worker. The client, who has a history of lying to make himself the centre of attention, hints to the new social worker that his relationship with the previous social worker was more than purely professional. The client will neither confirm nor deny the innuendos. The new therapist doubts the client's allegations and does not know if he should report this to the College. He ultimately chooses to file a report. This leads to a disciplinary investigation with unpleasant professional, emotional, and financial consequences for the innocent social worker. Did the social worker who lodged the report act ethically in this case?

IV.   Self-Determination

The issues surrounding a client's right to self-determination also can give rise to conflicting values. As has been discussed throughout this book, there are some situations, such as reporting of therapist-client sexual relationships, in which social work ethics and legislation deny clients the right to follow a particular course of action, despite the fact that the concept of client self-determination is held dear by the profession of social work. Again, the social worker is forced to balance competing rights. As Bisman aptly points out,

> respect for the client as an individual with free will and the inherent right to self-determination is a given. At the same time, social workers must work toward client change, so there *is* an inherent manipulation in the social work endeavor. Social workers are presented as experts, professing to know better than the client [regarding] certain matters. *Balancing the act of offering expert help with respect for a client's autonomy remains a challenge for every practising social worker.*[2]

Is it ethical to support a client who wants to do something that the social worker knows is not in the client's best interest? What if a client wants to return home to a violently abusive husband? And if a social worker believes in the value of self-determination for individuals who rationally choose to commit suicide, why is the social worker not allowed to accept a client's decision to commit suicide?

---

2.   C. Bisman, *Social Work Practice: Cases and Principles* (Pacific Grove, CA: Brooks/Cole Publishing Company, 1994) at 49.

V. The Supervisory Relationship

It has been established that the supervisory relationship should provide a safe and supportive atmosphere for social workers to discuss concerns about transference. Yet certain disclosures, such as that the social worker is sexually attracted to a client, can lead to adverse consequences for the social worker. There are cases where professionals working in the area of child sexual abuse have been fired for disclosing feelings of arousal with regard to child sexuality. Sex-related disclosures can create particularly difficult quandaries for supervisors, who are charged with providing an atmosphere that encourages open discussion of a supervisee's feelings while at the same time safeguarding the welfare of clients. Supervisors are thus called on to balance the competing demands of compassion, discretion, and the law.

What should a supervisor do in the following scenario? A supervisee who outwardly appears to be doing a competent job admits that she is experiencing many of the symptoms of burnout — depression, poor decision making, blurred boundaries, and disturbed sleep patterns. The supervisor, knowing that she might be held liable if the supervisee in the course of her work makes a mistake that harms a third party, reports the supervisee to the College. The supervisee feels betrayed because she was looking to the supervisor for help in resolving her difficulties. Moreover, the two social workers must continue to work together while the investigation proceeds. The supervisor is left in a quandary as neither option, reporting or not reporting, turned out to provide a satisfactory outcome.

VI. Divided Loyalties — Agency versus College

The *Standards of Practice Handbook* tells us that College principles supersede agency policy in cases where they conflict. Some people, however, would argue that it is the College member's obligation to abide by the policies and regulations of the agency that employs him or her, especially since accepting employment presumes an agreement to abide by those policies and regulations.

Consider the case of a social service agency that matches fatherless children with adult volunteer mentors. A match has been made and significant positive changes have been noted in every aspect of the child's life. The child has bonded well to the adult and has developed a trusting relationship. All is going well until the mentor, who is gay, learns of an agency policy forbidding gays and lesbians from acting as volunteers. Although the volunteer is in no way a threat to the child, he feels obligated to disclose his sexual orientation to his supervisor, who is a social worker. What should the supervisor do? Should she follow agency policy and terminate the volunteer's service, or comply with the College requirement that a member will not discriminate on the basis of sexual orientation? What if adhering to College policy costs the supervisor her job? And perhaps most importantly, what if following the agency policy and finding another mentor causes further disruption in the child's life?

VII. Confidentiality

Consider a situation in which a social worker is counselling a client who has allegedly abused both his wife and his children. The client is angry at being denied access to his family and begins harassing the social worker. He makes veiled threats regarding her family and sexually inappropriate comments about the social worker, as well as suggesting that they meet socially. The social worker feels threatened and frightened. How should she protect herself? Seek supervision? Change her home telephone number? Move? Can she report the client to the police, or does this violate client confidentiality? If she takes this case to supervision, will she be supported or will she be seen as weak and unable to set appropriate boundaries?

Another case in the same vein involves a social worker who is seeing a client for the first time to help him deal with sexual difficulties. The client, who had asked for a female therapist, appears to be becoming sexually aroused as he discusses his problems. The social worker begins to believe that this client's only reason for seeking counselling is to achieve sexual gratification by discussing his sex life with a virtual stranger. Can the social worker refuse to counsel this client? What is the proper termination procedure? Barker and Branson advise social workers to "discontinue treatment only after the client's needs have been met or he has been appropriately referred."[3] Does the social worker have to give the client reasonable notice or refer him to another therapist, who would be placed in the same dangerous situation? Can she warn the next therapist he visits without breaching confidentiality? Is there a duty to warn? If there is a duty to warn or report, and the social worker fails to abide by it, he or she could face legal repercussions. On the other hand, warning or reporting could endanger the social worker if the client learns of her actions and chooses to retaliate.

VIII. Children and Confidentiality

Confidentiality is a particularly difficult issue where children are concerned. At what age is a young client entitled to confidentiality? Can a child provide a legally valid consent, and if so at what age? Who has the right to review the

---

3.   Barker, R.L., and D.M. Branson, *Forensic Social Work: Legal Aspects of Professional Practice* (New York: Haworth Press, 1993) at 39.

child's file? How does the social worker ascertain that the person requesting access to the file is in fact the child's legal guardian or biological parent? Social workers are legally obligated to tell parents when a child is suicidal, but does this obligation apply to children who are anorexic or self-mutilators? Who use drugs or alcohol, steal, skip school, or engage in inappropriate sexual behaviours? Concerned parents want to know these things about their children, but if the child is not guaranteed confidentiality, he or she may refuse needed counselling.

IX.　Dual Relationships

In smaller cities, rural communities, and especially in isolated communities it is not uncommon for social workers to be involved in dual relationships; frequently it is impossible to avoid such relationships. The dual relationships issue can be especially difficult with regard to romantic and sexual relationships, because the social worker may have some sort of professional relationship with a large proportion of the limited number of available partners or members of their families. Or take the hypothetical case of a potential client, a businessman with numerous involvements in community life. The businessman and the social worker belong to the same service club and sit on the local hospital's board of directors. The businessman's daughter is dating the social worker's son; his wife, whom he is thinking of divorcing, is a friend of the social worker's wife and runs the daycare centre where the social worker sends his youngest child. Should the social worker refuse to take on the businessman as a client? If he becomes a client, should the social worker forbid his teenage children to date the client's children? If the answer to that question is yes, how does the social worker explain to his children, without violating client confidentiality, why the children cannot date the businessman's children?

X.　Termination of Service

There has been much discussion about the proper procedure to follow when terminating service. If a client cancels or fails to show up for an appointment, and it appears that the client does not want to continue counselling, experts advise attempting to reach the client by telephone or letter to arrange a termination session. But what if, in attempting to contact the client, the social worker tries to reach the client through family members who are unaware that the client was in counselling? Is this a violation of client confidentiality? If the client agrees to attend a termination session, is it ethical to charge the client the usual session fee?

In cases where a social worker is sexually attracted to a client, there may be an ethical obligation to terminate service. But will the client see this as a rejection? If the social worker explains the reason for termination, will the client inappropriately blame himself or herself for causing the end of the relationship?

C.   Conclusion

Being a responsible social worker means learning about the legislation governing one's profession, understanding its repercussions, and thinking about areas of ethical conflict and confusion. Each topic that has been discussed in this book is connected to all of the others, and it is the social worker's responsibility to avoid viewing any one topic in isolation from the others, and instead to recognize that each action he or she takes as a social worker can have many consequences.

The best way for a social worker to minimize the chances of being accused of an ethical or professional transgression is to keep current with the applicable legislation. Laws are always changing, and it is imperative to be aware of not only the changes themselves but also their repercussions. The social worker must also be prepared to act as an advocate for changes in the law when necessary.

Social work is a profession of high ideals. It is unique in its all-encompassing and humanitarian view of human nature and in its belief that people can achieve self-actualization when given the opportunity. It is the only profession that subscribes to a biopsychosocial view of humanity that recognizes the interconnectedness of the biological, psychological, and social influences on individuals. Social work does not see the client as sick and does not rely on the medical model; rather, it views the client as a capable individual who occasionally needs guidance and information. It subscribes to the view that we are all our brother's keepers and, as such, should support each other in achieving our maximum individual and collective potential. This is a wonderfully optimistic view of humanity, and one that makes the profession of social work deserving of its recently enhanced status.

As in medicine, the foremost rule of social work is "first, do no harm." There is no social worker who would challenge this as a guiding principle. But how do we know what causes harm? Unless our attitudes are continually challenged, how do we know they are valid? Until the sixteenth century, humanity was certain that the sun revolved around the earth, but this seemingly unchallengeable fact was, of course, proved wrong. Like the scientific reformers of that earlier age, we must always be prepared to question and reevaluate our beliefs.

The purpose of this book has been to prepare Ontario social workers and social service workers to take their place in a world of regulated professions. As a result of the passage of the *Social Work and Social Service Work Act,* and the creation of the Ontario College of Social Workers and Social Service Workers, public confidence in the profession will build and the true value of social work will finally be recognized. Ontario social workers and social service workers have now joined the ranks of professionals who have long enjoyed the benefits of legislation. To maintain these benefits, all of us must accept the challenge of living by the ideals embodied in the legislation. The future is up to you!

Chapter 19

Sample Forms and Agreements

The proper use of standardized forms and agreements protects both the social worker and the client. Indeed, the regular use of such documents can be the social worker's best defence against unfounded accusations of negligence, failure to obtain informed consent, and other kinds of unprofessional behaviour. Every social work agency and private practitioner should have on hand a set of standardized consent forms, confidentiality agreements, and so forth that covers most of the eventualities of social work practice. These documents should be written in language that the average client can readily understand and be presented in a clear and simple format which incorporates print that is large enough to be easily read. Employing standardized forms and agreements helps ensure that all relevant issues are discussed with the client, that the client understands the issues, and that the discussions are thoroughly documented in the client's file. In particular, standardized consent forms should be used whenever the client is about to undergo an unusual type of treatment such as hypnosis or a type of treatment that he or she has never experienced. Needless to say, however, a social worker who engages in unethical or illegal behaviour cannot hide behind a client's signed consent form or agreement.

The following pages provide templates for forms and agreements that the social worker can use in his or her practice. These have been created by the authors of this book or taken from publicly available sources such as the books by Bernstein,[1] Houston-Vega,[2] Austin,[3] and their co-authors and

1. B.E. Bernstein and T.L. Hartsell, *The Portable Lawyer for Mental Health Professionals* (New York: John Wiley & Sons, 1998).
2. M.K. Houston-Vega and E.M. Nuehring, *Prudent Practice: A Guide for Managing Malpractice Risk* (Washington, DC: National Association of Social Workers, 1997).
3. K. Austin, M. Moline, and G. Williams, *Confronting Malpractice: Legal and Ethical Dilemmas in Psychotherapy* (Newbury Park, CA: Sage Publications, 1990).

adapted for use by Ontario social workers. These templates should not be treated as sacrosanct, however. It is up to the social worker, with legal assistance if necessary, to revise them when revision is required to meet the needs of his or her practice, and to create new documents when circumstances dictate. Finally, it is crucial for the social worker to understand that the templates presented here are not provided as substitutes for independent legal advice.

Please note that each of the forms included in the following pages can be accessed digitally at www.irwinlaw.com. Select Managing a Legal and Ethical Social Work Practice and click on print online forms. The password is ir653p72.

A.   AGREEMENT TO PROVIDE SERVICES

CLIENT NAME: _____

CLIENT DOB:_____

I, _____ confirm _____
will be providing therapy and/or counselling to me, which may also include
Assessment, Diagnostic, Treatment and Evaluation services.

I have been informed and understand that the aforementioned services are
being provided to me, subject to the terms and conditions of this agreement.

CONFIDENTIALITY:

Confidentiality will be strictly maintained whenever possible. Please note,
however, that there are some situations in which confidentiality may not be
guaranteed. These are:

1.   It is against the law to maintain confidentiality in situations where
on-going child abuse is disclosed and/or there is reason to believe
that child abuse is occurring. I am required by law to immediately
report these cases to the authorities. I will, however, be prepared
to assist you through any resultant investigation.

2.   If your file is subpoenaed to court all information in the file is
subject to review by the court and its representatives. In addition,
anything that you give me to add to the file, such as writing that
I might suggest you do, becomes a part of the file and by law,
cannot be returned. In cases where the file is subpoenaed, this
information must accompany the file.

3.   If you tell me that you intend to kill or harm yourself or others, I
will not maintain confidentiality. I will not, however, disclose
thoughts of such things where, in my professional opinion, I have
no indication of imminent intent.

ACCESS AND DISCLOSURE:

If you request it, you may have reasonable, supervised access to your file
at my office. I will not provide access to your file or segments of your file if,
in my professional opinion, to do so would be detrimental to your well-being.
If I refuse access I will advise you of my reason for refusing so that we may
discuss it.

I cannot disclose or release any information about you or your file to any third parties unless I receive your signed authorization in writing permitting me to do so. This does not apply if disclosure is required or allowed by law.

FEES:

My fee for therapy and counselling services is _____ an hour. I am required by law to charge GST. A higher hourly rate may be charged if I provide specialized services such as Hypnosis or EMDR (Eye Movement & Desensitization Reprocessing). This will be discussed and agreed to at the time these services are provided.

I normally do not charge for missed or cancelled appointments if I receive reasonable notice and it is not a regular occurrence.

I will provide services on a sliding scale, if you request it and if in my opinion, it is warranted.

CLIENT'S ACKNOWLEDGMENT: I have read and fully understand this agreement. I understand that I should not sign this form if all items, including all my questions, have not been explained or answered to my satisfaction or if I do not understand any of the terms or words contained in this consent form.

DO NOT SIGN UNLESS YOU HAVE READ AND THOROUGHLY UNDERSTAND THIS FORM!

I have read and understand this agreement, my questions have been answered and I sign this form, freely and without undue influence. By signing this agreement I acknowledge and understand that I am bound by the terms and conditions contained therein.

Client

_____

Address

_____

Date _____

B. CLIENT WAIVER OF FULL DISCLOSURE PROVISION

I, *(client's name)* have been advised that I have a right to review and obtain copies of my entire file in the possession of *(therapist's name)*. I have been advised and understand that some information contained in my records may not be in my best interest to review. In the event my therapist in (her/his) professional opinion believes that the information in my file may be injurious to me, I waive my right to review and/or obtain copies of my file. I agree to release *(therapist's name)* from any and all claims, damages and actions that I could assert for (her/his) refusal to provide me with the information requested. I acknowledge and agree that my therapist's discretion shall prevail.

SIGNED _____ day of _____ , 2002

_____

Client's Name

_____

Address

_____

City/Province

C. FORM 14, MENTAL HEALTH ACT

Consent to the Disclosure, Transmittal or Examination of a Clinical Record under Section 35 of the Ontario Mental Act.

I, *(client's name)* of *(client's full address)* hereby consent to the disclosure or transmittal to or the examination by *(therapist's name)* of the clinical record completed in *(name of facility, clinic or therapist's name)* in respect of *(name of client, date of birth)*

_____   _____

Witness   Client's Signature

Dated the _____ day of _____ , 2002.

D.   GROUP CONFIDENTIALITY FORM

I, (client's name) hereby agree to participate in group therapy with the under-signed therapist. I agree to abide by the following group rules:

- **First,** I will attend all of the *(number)* _____ group sessions and be on time. I understand that if I am late or absent the effectiveness of the group process is diminished.
- **Second,** I understand that I am expected to be an active group partici-pant, although I can choose what and how much information I want to discuss in the group. I understand that my responsibilities include being truthful about what I say in the group, not monopolizing the group, and making certain that I resolve any unfinished business before the end of the session.
- **Third,** I understand that confidentiality and privacy are basic to build-ing trust among group members. I agree to keep confidential what other group members share, and I will not talk about what is shared during the group with others outside the group.
- **Fourth,** I understand that I have the right to leave the group. However, I understand that it is very important not to leave any unfinished busi-ness with other group members. Hence, it is my responsibility to explain to other members my reasons for wanting to leave the group before I leave.
- **Fifth,** I agree that I will not socialize with group members outside our sessions.

I understand that with group therapy, there is a risk of disclosure of confi-dential information by persons in the group to outside individuals. I agree that the undersigned therapist is not responsible for any information dis-closed by members of the group to outside individuals and I agree to hold the undersigned therapist from any and all claims or liability resulting from such disclosure.

SIGNED this _____ day of _____ , 2002

_____
Therapist's Name

SIGNED this _____ day of _____ , 2002

_____
Client's Name

E. PARENTAL WAIVER OF RIGHT TO CHILD'S RECORDS

I hereby waive my right as parent/guardian to obtain information and/or copies of any records from *(therapist's name)* relating to the treatment and/or counselling of my child *(name)*, age_____. I acknowledge and understand that *(therapist's name)* will not provide access to the file or segments of the file if, in *(her/his)* professional opinion, to do so would be detrimental to my child's well-being. If access is refused I understand I will be advised of the reason for refusing so that we may discuss it. I hereby release *(therapist's name)* from any and all liability for refusing to disclose my child's records if the refusal is made in good faith.

_____   _____
Date   Parent/Guardian

_____   _____
Date   Parent/Guardian

_____   _____
Date   Witness/ (Therapist)

F.   CONSENT TO DISCLOSURE OF CLIENT RECORDS/INFORMATION TO A THIRD PARTY

I, *(client's name),* hereby consent to and authorize *(therapist's name)* to release or disclose to *(name of third party)*, any and/or all of my records, documents or information *(therapist's name)* may have in *(her/his)* possession pertaining to my treatment with *(therapist's name)* for the period *(put in time frame).* I acknowledge and agree that I am waiving my right to confidentiality with respect to the records and information that are being disclosed pursuant to this consent.

I hereby release *(therapist's name)* from any and all liability arising from the release and disclosure of my records to *(name of third party)*.

This consent is subject to revocation at any time except to the extent that the person instructed to make the disclosure has already taken action in reliance on it. If not previously revoked, this consent will terminate on *(date, event, or condition)* _____ .

SIGNED this _____ day of _____2002.

Witnessed by: _____
                                 Client

_____
Print name

                                 _____
                                 Address

                                 _____
                                 City/Province

                                 _____
                                 Date of Birth

G. INFORMED CONSENT FOR HYPNOSIS

CLIENT NAME: _____

CLIENT DOB:_____

I, _____ confirm that I have requested and
agreed to undergo hypnosis with (therapist's name) for the purpose of
_____.

I acknowledge that (therapist's name) advised me, prior to my first session
of Hypnosis, of the following:

1. Hypnosis is not dangerous to my physical or emotional well
   being.
2. I cannot be hypnotized against my will.
3. While I am hypnotized, I am not and will not, at any time be
   under the control of (therapist's name), nor can I be made to do
   anything by her I do not wish to do.
4. I can terminate the process at anytime, without danger to my self.
5. While I am hypnotized, I will be able to hear and remember what
   is said during the session.
6. I understand that, if at any time (therapist's name) stops the
   process, my hypnotic state will terminate and that I will naturally
   return to my normal consciousness.
7. I understand, if in the professional opinion of (therapist's name),
   a post-hypnotic suggestion is to be used, that this will be agreed
   upon prior to the start. I further understand that due to the nature
   of a post hypnotic suggestion, I will not be told what it is ahead
   of time.

CLIENT'S CONSENT: I have read and fully understand this consent form,
and I consent to allow (therapist's name) to hypnotize me. I understand that
I should not sign this form if all items, including all my questions, have not
been explained or answered to my satisfaction or if I do not understand any
of the terms or words contained in this consent form.

IF YOU HAVE ANY QUESTIONS AS TO THE RISKS OR HAZARDS OF
HYPNOSIS, GIVEN YOUR MEDICAL HISTORY, ASK YOUR DOCTOR
NOW BEFORE SIGNING THIS CONSENT FORM.

DO NOT SIGN UNLESS YOU HAVE READ AND THOROUGHLY
UNDERSTAND THIS FORM!

I have read and understand this consent form, and my questions have been answered and I sign this consent form, freely and without undue influence.

Client _____

Time _____

Date _____

I have explained the contents of this document to the client and have answered all the client's questions, and to the best of my knowledge, I feel the client has been adequately informed and has consented.

(Therapist's signature) _____

Date _____

H.   INFORMED CONSENT FOR EMDR
(Eye Movement Desensitization & Reprocessing)

CLIENT NAME: _____

CLIENT DOB:_____

I, _____ confirm that I have requested and
agreed to undergo EMDR with (therapist's name) for the purpose of
_____.

I have been advised by (therapist's name) and understand that Eye Movement Desensitization and Reprocessing (EMDR) is a new treatment
approach that has not been widely validated by research. I have been
informed that initial studies have shown EMDR has produced promising
results in reducing anxiety and in reducing post-traumatic stress symptoms,
such as intrusive thoughts, nightmares, and flashbacks.

I have also been advised that, although there are currently no known serious
side effects to EMDR, there is minimal data as to its efficacy or safety.

I have been specifically advised that the following may occur during or after
a treatment:

(a)   Distressing, unresolved memories may surface through the use of
the EMDR procedure.

(b)   Some clients have experienced reactions during the treatment sessions that neither they nor the administering clinician may have
anticipated, including a high level of emotional or physical sen-
sations.

(c)   Subsequent to the treatment session, the processing of inci-
dents/material may continue, and other dreams, memories, flashbacks, feelings may surface.

If in the professional opinion of (therapist/s name), it is determined that the
client is experiencing a reaction to the EMDR treatment, which may impair
his or her ability to function safely, she will take whatever reasonable steps
she deems appropriate to assist the client.

CLIENT'S CONSENT: I have read and fully understand this consent form,
and I consent to allow (therapist's name) to treat me with EMDR. I understand that I should not sign this form if all items, including all my questions,
have not been explained or answered to my satisfaction or if I do not understand any of the terms or words contained in this consent form.

IF YOU HAVE ANY QUESTIONS AS TO THE RISKS OR HAZARDS OF EMDR, GIVEN YOUR MEDICAL HISTORY, ASK YOUR DOCTOR NOW BEFORE SIGNING THIS CONSENT FORM.

DO NOT SIGN UNLESS YOU HAVE READ AND THOROUGHLY UNDERSTAND THIS FORM!

I have read and understand this consent form, and my questions have been answered and I sign this consent form, freely and without undue influence.

Client _____

Time _____

Date _____

I have explained the contents of this document to the client and have answered all the client's questions, and to the best of my knowledge, I feel the client has been adequately informed and has consented.

(Therapist's signature) _____

Date _____

I. THERAPY PLAN

Name:_____

Problem Area:

1.
2.
3.
4.

Behavioural Objective:

1.
2.
3.
4.

Time Frame:

1.
2.
3.
4.

Concepts/Skills to Develop:

1.
2.
3.
4.

Materials/Activities:

1.
2.
3.
4.

INFORMED CONSENT

I, *(client's name)*, acknowledge that I have discussed the goals, objectives, methods and time frame of my Treatment Plan with *(therapist's name)*. I understand that the above may be changed, altered or modified as my therapy/counselling progresses. I have been told that I may terminate my therapy at any time should I choose. I acknowledge that my therapist has explained and I fully understand the risks, alternatives and the nature of the treatment to be used.

At this time, I consent to work toward the achievement of the objectives stated in my Treatment Plan. I sign this consent without pressure or coercion and of my own free will.

SIGNED_____day of_____, 2002

_____
Client's Signature

_____
Witness

J. CONFIDENTIALITY AGREEMENT AND
NOTICE TO EMPLOYEES/VOLUNTEERS

The identities of our current and former clients, their personal communications to us, and their records are confidential by law. This office requires that confidentiality laws be strictly followed. We cannot expect to treat our clients effectively unless they feel that they can talk freely without concern that their confidences will be revealed to others. Any employee or volunteer of this organization who violates a client's confidentiality is subject to immediate dismissal. Further, that employee or volunteer, as well as the organization, might be subject to a lawsuit brought by a client.

Do Not
- reveal a client's identity in any way
- address a client by name when others are in the office
- disclose that a person is a client to anyone, including a client's spouse
- leave a client's file unattended on your desk or anywhere else in the workplace
- have files or appointment books on your desk or anywhere else in the workplace in a manner that allows a client's name to be seen by others
- have a client's information visible on a computer screen when you are away from your desk
- leave computers and file cabinets that store client information unsecured when you are not in the work area
- remove client files from the workplace for reasons other than authorized functions (for example, a home visit or court appearance)
- repeat anything a client tells you to anyone other than your supervisor
- disclose anything in a client's chart to anyone other than your supervisor
- talk about a client with anyone other than your supervisor in a private situation, even if you do not use the client's name
- talk about a client with your spouse or other members of your family or friends
- give copies of anything in a client's chart to anyone other than your supervisor
- retrieve messages from your voice mail or answering machine within earshot of others.

Do
- address clients in the workplace by "Sir" or "Ma'am" or other courteous address without the use of a client's name when other people are present

- keep files and appointment books face down or otherwise out of view on your desk and throughout the workplace so that a client's name cannot be seen by others
- safeguard your computer password to prevent unauthorized people from accessing client information
- strictly comply with a client's permission to disclose identity, confidences, or records when permission has been properly obtained in writing
- observe all limits and conditions a client places on any permission to disclose confidential information
- discard confidential materials properly by shredding them
- consider a client's confidentiality on the receiving end of fax communications, e-mail, and telephone message-taking devices; ensure that the intended recipient is the only recipient of such communications.

It is possible that requests for information—including subpoenas—about our clients may come to you from the police or other law enforcement personnel, lawyers, or the courts. Tell your supervisor immediately when you receive these types of requests and determine with your supervisor how to proceed. Note that "following orders" may not be sufficient justification in a court of law for breaching confidentiality.

Some exceptions to confidentiality may require or authorize certain disclosures about our clients. Immediately inform your supervisor of any information you obtain about our clients that leads you to believe that you, the client, or anyone else may be endangered by the client. Immediately inform your supervisor of any information you obtain that leads you to believe that a client may be involved in some way, directly or indirectly, in the abuse or neglect of a child, elderly person, or disabled person. Meet with your supervisor at once and determine how to proceed. Note that "following orders" may not be sufficient justification in a court of law for breaching confidentiality.

I, _____, hereby acknowledge that I have read this confidentiality agreement and notice to employees/-volunteers. I understand it fully, and I will strictly follow its terms.

Signature _____

Date_____

K. WORKING AGREEMENT FOR PARENTS WHEN A CHILD IS THE PRIMARY CLIENT

We, *(names of parents)* _____ ,

hereby agree to our child, *(name of child)* _____ ,

beginning service with *(name of therapist)* _____ .

We have read the *(client handbook, practice brochure, or fact sheets)*. We have discussed with our child's social worker the role and responsibilities of our child's social worker, and our roles and responsibilities as parents. We understand that we are consenting to begin our child's treatment, not our own, and that although our consent is important and necessary, our role is to help provide information, to plan, to assist in measuring progress, and to coordinate our child's treatment.

We understand that after our child is assessed, our child and our child's social worker will develop a service plan and that we will make another agreement to follow through with the service plan.

We understand that our child's social worker will protect our privacy and that confidential information about us will be revealed only if we give our written consent, if our child's safety or the safety of someone else is threatened, or if a court orders the information released.

We also understand that our child's social worker will keep discussions he or she has with us in the absence of our child confidential and will keep material discussed with our child in our absence confidential. However, we understand that the social worker may breach confidentiality with our child if our child talks about harming himself or herself and *(specify any conditions about which social workers are required by law to inform the parents or that you believe should be shared with them)*. We will be encouraged, as a family, to talk about our respective sessions with the social worker. However, our child's social worker will not transmit information from one of us to the other(s).

We realize that, although service is recommended for our child and will probably be helpful, there are no guarantees that any or all of his or her problems will be remedied. We further understand that service involves possible risks as well as benefits. Hence, we and our child may experience stress, strained relationships, or other difficulties as a result of the service process.

We understand that service will terminate when the goals of the service plan have been fulfilled. However, we also understand that we may end service at any time we wish or feel that we and/or our child need to do so. We further understand that our child's social worker may also end service if our child does not make progress or has needs that the social worker cannot meet. If our child's service is ended before the goals of the service plan have been accomplished, we understand that the social worker will do all possible to refer our child to an alternative source of care.

Name of legally responsible parent or guardian (please print)

_____

Signature_____

Date_____

Name of legally responsible parent or guardian (please print)

_____

Signature_____

Date_____

Name and title of witness_____

Signature_____

Date_____

By signing below, I, *(name of therapist)* _____ ,
am indicating that I agree to begin the process of assessment and service with *(names of clients)* _____ , who I believe have read and comprehended the *(client handbook, practice brochure, or fact sheets)*. I have discussed the content of our written client information thoroughly with them and am satisfied, by their comments and questions, that they are clear in their understanding and are prepared to begin service.

Signature_____

Date_____

L.   AGREEMENT FOR COUPLES OR FAMILIES

We, *(names of clients)* _____ ,

hereby agree to begin service in *(name of setting)* _____ ,

with *(name of clinician)*_____ .

We have read the *(client handbook, practice brochure, or fact sheets)*. We have discussed with our social worker the role and responsibilities of our social worker, and our roles and responsibilities as clients. We understand our rights to privacy and confidentiality. We understand that our social worker will protect our privacy and that confidential information about us will be revealed only if we give our written consent, if our safety or the safety of someone else is threatened, or if a court orders the information released.

We understand that the social worker will not keep secrets with individual family members. Hence, we are expected as a family to talk about our respective individual sessions.

We understand our financial responsibilities and arrangements with our insurance payer or payers, the rules about notifying our social worker if we have to miss an appointment or will be late, the charges for broken appointments and late arrivals without prior notification, and the consequences if our account is past due.

We understand that staff in this setting other than our social worker must have access to confidential information about us because of *(give reasons)*. In granting consent for the release of confidential information about us from one professional to another or to our health plan, we stipulate that

_____ We each wish to sign our own release of information and, if we are legal adults, each reserve the right to withhold permission to release part or all of the information sought that is specifically about us as individuals; or

_____ We grant to one party, *(name)* _____ ,
the right to consent to the release of confidential information about us as a family.

We understand that we will be asked to furnish the name of someone close to us to be contacted in the event of an emergency. We understand that in contacting that person, our social worker will have to identify his or her relationship to us and our whereabouts and condition. However, we are assured that no details of our service will be provided to that person. Our contact person is *(name, address, and telephone number)* _____ .

We understand that our relationship with our social worker is now and will be in the future solely a professional relationship and that we will have no shared interests or activities outside our service.

We realize that, although service is recommended for us and will probably be helpful, there are no guarantees that any or all of our problems will be remedied. We further understand that service involves possible risks as well as benefits. We understand that as individuals we may have to set aside our individual goals and needs to achieve the goals of the family and to resolve our family problems. Hence, we know that we may experience stress, strained relationships, or other difficulties as a result of the service process.

We understand that service will terminate when the goals of the service plan that we agree to have been fulfilled. However, we also understand that we may end service at any time we wish or feel that we need to do so. If one or some of us wish to continue while the other or others wish to end service, we understand that our social worker will initiate a new working agreement and a new service plan and contract with the one or those of us wishing to continue. We further understand that our social worker may also end service if we do not make progress, if our relationship becomes too strained to continue our work, or if we and/or our insurer are no longer able to pay for services. If our service is ended before the goals of our service plan have been fulfilled, we understand that our social worker will do everything possible to refer us to an alternate source of care.

Client name (please print) _____

Signature_____

Date_____

Client name (please print) _____

Signature_____

Date_____

Client name (please print) _____

Signature_____

Date_____

Client name (please print) _____

Signature_____

Date_____

Client name (please print) _____

Signature _____

Date _____

Name of legally responsible parent or guardian (where required)

_____

Signature _____

Date _____

Name and title of witness _____

Signature _____

Date _____

By signing below, I, *(name of clinician)* _____ ,
am indicating that I agree to begin the process of assessment and service with
(names of clients) _____ , who I believe have
read and comprehended the *(client handbook, practice brochure, or fact
sheets).* I have discussed the content of our written client information thoroughly with the clients and am satisfied, by their comments and questions,
that they are clear in their understanding and are prepared to begin service.

Signature _____

Date _____

M. AUTHORIZATION TO A CURRENT PROVIDER FOR RELEASE OF CONFIDENTIAL INFORMATION

I, *(name of client)* _____, ( ) request ( ) authorize *(name of clinician and setting)* _____

_____

to disclose *(type, amount of, and time period of information to be disclosed)*

_____

_____

to *(name and organization to which disclosure is to be made)*

_____

_____

for the purpose of *(purpose)* _____

_____

The designated information about me ( ) may ( ) may not be transmitted by fax, electronic mail, or other electronic file transfer mechanisms. The provider of the information and the recipient designated above ( ) may ( ) may not discuss by telephone the content of the information released.

This request and authorization to release information is based on my understanding of the content of my records, the use of the information once it is released, and my understanding that the source providing the information cannot be responsible for the protection of my privacy once the information is conveyed. I release the source of information from all liability arising from the release. I understand that the willingness to treat me of the party requesting information is not affected by the response of the source of the requested information. I understand that this release of information is intended to allow me to provide my informed consent for an exception to my confidentiality. This consent is subject to revocation at any time except to the extent that the program instructed to make the disclosure has already taken action in reliance on it. If not previously revoked, this consent will terminate on *(date, event, or condition)* _____

_____ .

Signature of client _____

Date _____

Signature of parent or guardian (where required)

_____

Date _____

Signature of person authorized to sign in lieu of the client (where required)

_____

Date _____

Signature of witness _____

Date _____

N.   REQUEST FOR INFORMATION

Name of client _____

Date of birth _____

Address _____

Dear Colleague:

The above-named client is currently receiving services from *(name of setting)*. In the best interests of client care, it would be appreciated if you would release to us the information specified below pertaining to care and services received from your organization between *(give month/year to month/year)*. Attached is a signed authorization for release of this information. Thank you for your prompt attention and response.

Sincerely,

O. TERMINATION

Note to Practitioners:
When you terminate service consensually because service goals have been met and further services are not needed, send a brief letter to the client, if appropriate, that includes the following points:

- Briefly summarize the service that has taken place, including when you began and ended, central goals, interventions, accomplishments, and final recommendations.
- Thank the client for the opportunity to serve him or her. Indicate you will be available in the future should the need for service arise again, and invite the client to refer others to your setting.
- Remind the client that you will retain his or her clinical record *(state where)* for *(state period of time)* and that those records or parts of them will be provided to another entity only if you receive a legal release of information signed by the client, if you receive a court order, or if you are required by law to release information.
- Include as an attachment a final statement of the satisfied account or a final invoice if appropriate.

When the client terminates service against professional advice, your letter should include the following points:

- Briefly summarize the service that has been completed, including when you began and ended, central goals, interventions, accomplishments, unrealized objectives, final recommendations, and referrals.
- Emphasize your judgment that continued service is advisable, and encourage the client to consider returning to treatment. Indicate you would be pleased to resume your work with the client or to discuss alternative sources of care and referrals.
- If you believe that not receiving service seriously jeopardizes the client or endangers others, say so.
- If the client refused a final session with you, encourage him or her to make a final appointment so that you both can be satisfied that you achieved closure.
- Thank the client for the opportunity to serve him or her, indicate that you regret the circumstances that have interrupted your relationship, and reiterate that you will be available in the future should he or she reconsider and wish to resume service.
- Remind the client that you will retain his or her records *(state where)* for *(state period of time)* and that those records or parts of them will be provided to another entity only if you receive a legal release of information signed by the client, if you receive a court order, or if you are required by law to release information.

- Include as an attachment a final statement of the satisfied account or a final invoice if appropriate.

When you terminate service with the client against her or his wishes, your letter should include the following points:

- Briefly summarize the service that has been completed, including when you began and ended, central goals, interventions, accomplishments, unrealized objectives, reasons for your decision to terminate the relationship, final recommendations, and referrals.
- Emphasize your judgment that continued service is either advisable *(or not indicated),* and encourage the client to consider your final recommendations for alternative services or use of other resources. Provide explicit information about other appropriate sources of service. Offer to discuss alternative sources of service and additional referrals by telephone, but remain clear that the service relationship has ended.
- If you believe that not receiving service seriously jeopardizes the client or endangers others, say so.
- Thank the client for the opportunity to serve him or her, and indicate that you regret the circumstances that have interrupted your relationship.
- Remind the client that his or her records will be retained by you *(state where)* for *(state period of time)* and that those records or parts of them will be provided to another entity only if you receive a legal release of information signed by the client, if you receive a court order, or if you are required by law to release information.
- Include as an attachment a final statement of the satisfied account or a final invoice if appropriate.

P. CONSENT TO PROFESSIONAL USE OF CLINICAL RECORD DATA AND AUDIO VISUAL RECORDINGS OF SERVICE

By checking items that are acceptable to me and signing below I, _____ , am agreeing to the indicated procedures associated with my service in *(name of setting)* by *(name of clinician)*.

I am agreeable to my clinician making audiotapes of our sessions for his or her use in

_____ supervision, case consultation, and routine staffings in this setting

_____ consultation about my case with an expert outside this setting

_____ in-service training of other professionals or interns in this setting

_____ scientific presentations or publications as long as the data are presented anonymously and in a manner that would completely protect my identity.

I am agreeable to my clinician making videotapes of our sessions, as long as the camera focuses on my clinician and I cannot be viewed or identified by sight, for his or her use in

_____ supervision, case consultation, and routine staffings in this setting

_____ consultation about my case with an expert outside this setting

_____ in-service training of other professionals or interns in this setting

_____ scientific presentations or publications as long as the data are presented anonymously and in a manner that would completely protect my identity.

I am agreeable to my clinician using information from my written clinical record for purposes of

_____ supervision, case consultation, and routine staffings in this setting

_____ consultation about my case with an expert outside this setting

_____ in-service training of other professionals or interns in this setting

_____ scientific presentations or publications as long as the data are presented in grouped statistical form, so that no individual information is reported, or individual data are presented anonymously and in a manner that would completely protect my identity.

I understand that anyone who hears and views material from my clinical record and tapes of our sessions made by my clinician is a professional or trainee in a bona fide profession and that these individuals are ethically obligated to protect my confidentiality just as rigorously as my clinician is bound.

Any further use of audiotaped, videotaped, or written material from my treatment for other professional, scholarly, or research purposes or by professionals other than my clinician will require separate discussion with me and additional informed consent.

Name (please print) _____

Signature_____

Date_____

Name of legally responsible parent or guardian (please print)

_____

Signature_____

Date_____

Name and title of witness (please print)

_____

_____

Signature_____

Date_____

Q. CLIENT INFORMATION AND CONSENT

Therapist:

The undersigned therapist is a registered social worker engaged in private practice providing mental health care services to clients directly and as an independent contractor/provider for various EAP providers.

Mental Health Services:

While it may not be easy to seek help from a mental health professional, it is hoped that you will be better able to understand your situation and feelings and move toward resolving your difficulties. The therapist, using his/her knowledge of human development and behaviour, will make observations about situations as well as suggestions for new ways to approach them. It will be important for you to explore your own feelings and thoughts and to try new approaches in order for change to occur. You may bring other family members to a therapy session if you feel it would be helpful or if your therapist recommends this.

Appointments:

Appointments are made by calling _____ Monday through Friday between the hours of 9:00 A.M. and 6:00 P.M. Please call to cancel or reschedule at least 24 hours in advance, or you will be charged for the missed appointment.

Number of Visits:

The number of sessions needed depends on many factors and will be discussed by the therapist.

Length of Visits:

Therapy sessions are usually 60 minutes in length but can take longer if specialized treatment is being used.

Relationship:

Your relationship with the therapist is a professional and therapeutic relationship. In order to preserve this relationship, it is imperative that the therapist not have any other type of relationship with you. Personal and/or business relationships undermine the effectiveness of the therapeutic relationship. The therapist cares about helping you but is not in a position to be your friend or to have a social or personal relationship with you.

Gifts, bartering and trading services are not appropriate and should not be shared between you and the therapist.

Cancellations:

Cancellations must be received at least 24 hours before your scheduled appointment otherwise you will be charged the customary fee for that missed appointment. You are responsible for calling to cancel or reschedule your appointment.

Payment for Service:

The charge for your initial session is _____ and the charge for any subsequent sessions is _____. Payment is expected at the end of each session. Although it is the goal of the undersigned therapist to protect the confidentiality of your records, there may be times when disclosure of your records or testimony will be compelled by law. Confidentiality and exceptions to confidentiality are discussed below. In the event disclosure of your records or testimony is required by law, you will be responsible for and shall pay the costs involved in producing the records and the therapist's normal hourly rate for the time involved in preparing for and giving testimony. Such payments are to be made at the time or prior to the time the therapist renders the services.

Confidentiality:

Discussions between a therapist and a client are confidential. No information will be released without the client's written consent unless mandated by law. Possible exceptions to confidentiality include but not limited to the following situations: child abuse; abuse of the elderly or disabled; abuse of patients in mental health facilities; sexual exploitation; AIDS/HIV infection and possible transmission, child custody cases; lawsuits in which the mental health of a party is an issue; situations where the therapist has a duty to disclose, or where, in the therapist's judgment, it is necessary to warn or disclose; fee disputes between the therapist and the client; negligence suit brought by the client against the therapist; or the filing of a complaint with the Social Work regulatory body.

If you have any questions regarding confidentiality, you should bring them to the attention of the therapist when you and the therapist discuss this matter further. By signing this information and consent form, you are giving your consent to the undersigned therapist to share confidential information with all persons and/or service providers responsible for providing your mental health care services and payment for those services, and you are also releasing and holding harmless the undersigned therapist from any departure from your right of confidentiality that may result.

Duty to Warn:

In the event that the undersigned therapist reasonably believes that I am a danger, physically or emotionally, to myself or another person, I specifically consent for the therapist to warn the person in danger and to contact the following persons, in addition to medical and law enforcement personnel:

Name:_____

Telephone Number:_____

Risks of Therapy:

Therapy is the Greek word for change. You may learn things about yourself that you don't like. Often, growth cannot occur until you experience and confront issues that induce you to feel sadness, sorrow, anxiety, or pain. The success of our work together depends on the quality of the efforts on both our parts, and the realization that you are responsible for lifestyle choices/changes that may result fro therapy. Specifically, one risk or marital therapy is the possibility of exercising the divorce option.

Therapist's Incapacity or Death:

I acknowledge that, in the event the undersigned therapist becomes incapacitated or dies, it will become necessary for another therapist to take possession of my file and records. By signing this information and consent form, I give my consent to allowing another mental health professional selected by the undersigned therapist to take possession of my file and records and provide me with copies upon request, or deliver them to a therapist of my choice.

Consent to Treatment:

I, voluntarily, agree to receive mental health services, assessment, care or treatment, and authorize the undersigned therapist to provide such care, treatment or services as are considered necessary and advisable. I understand and agree that I will participate in the planning of my care, treatment or services, and that I may stop such care, treatment or services that I receive through the undersigned therapist at any time.

By signing this Client Information and Consent form, I, the undersigned client acknowledge that I have both read and understood all the terms and information contained herein. Ample opportunity has been offered to me to ask questions and seek clarification of anything unclear to me.

_____   _____
Client   Date

_____   _____
Witness   Date

R.   REQUEST FOR ACCESS TO CLIENT RECORDS

I, _____, am hereby requesting access to my clinical record.

In requesting this review, I understand that I am releasing (therapist's name) from liability for any damages, material or psychological, resulting from my request.

I understand that some of the information in my clinical record may be sensitive and that there is risk that it may invoke strong emotions on my part. Therefore, if my therapist judges it to be beneficial, he or she will meet with me in person before the review to prepare me. I understand that I will be allowed to read all or any portion of my record only while in the presence of my therapist. I understand that my therapist will be present to discuss my file or answer any questions I may have. I understand that portions of my record may be withheld from me if allowing my access would breach the confidentiality of someone else who has not given consent to my reading the information they have provided.

If my request is granted, access will be scheduled within 14 working days of the date of this signed request at a time convenient for my therapist and me.

I understand the process described above, and I agree to abide by the requirements set forth by the records access policy of my therapist.

Signature_____

Date of Request _____

Witnessed by _____

S.   SAMPLE PROGRESS NOTES

Name: _____   Date:_____

1.   Observations/Appearance/Affect:

2.   Significant/Recent Events:

3.   Content/Topics:

4.   Assignments/Homework:

5.   Diagnosis (Same/Different):

6.   Treatment Plan: Same or Replace:

Suicidal: Y   N   Violence: Y   N

References: Medical:
                   Psychiatric:
                   Neurological:

Next Session: Therapist's Initials:

Appendix 1

Code of Ethics

Ontario College of Social Workers and Social Service Workers Code of Ethics

The Ontario College of Social Workers and Social Service Workers regulates two professions, social workers and social service workers. The following sets out the Code of Ethics for members of the College.

1) A social worker or social service worker shall maintain the best interest of the client as the primary professional obligation;

2) A social worker or social service worker shall respect the intrinsic worth of the persons she or he serves in her or his professional relationships with them;

3) A social worker or social service worker shall carry out her or his professional duties and obligations with integrity and objectivity;

4) A social worker or social service worker shall have and maintain competence in the provision of a social work or social service work service to a client;

5) A social worker or social service worker shall not exploit the relationship with a client for personal benefit, gain or gratification;

6) A social worker or social service worker shall protect the confidentiality of all professionally acquired information. He or she shall disclose such information only when required or allowed by law to do so, or when clients have consented to disclosure;

7) A social worker or social service worker who engages in another profession, occupation, affiliation or calling shall not allow these outside interests to affect the social work or social service work relationship with the client;

8)   A social worker or social service worker shall not provide social work or social service work services in a manner that discredits the profession of social work or social service work or diminishes the public's trust in either profession;

9)   A social worker or social service worker shall advocate for workplace conditions and policies that are consistent with this Code of Ethics and the Standards of Practice of the Ontario College of Social Workers and Social Service Workers;

10) A social worker or social service worker shall promote excellence in his or her respective profession;

11) A social worker or social service worker shall advocate change in the best interest of the client, and for the overall benefit of society, the environment and the global community.

The mandatory observance of an ethical code is necessary for a profession to carry out its self-regulation. Codes of ethics place both the social worker and the public on notice that a certain standard of behaviour is expected and that behaviour deemed to be below a standard will be punished.

Appendix 2

Standards of Practice Handbook

ONTARIO COLLEGE OF SOCIAL WORKERS
AND
SOCIAL SERVICE WORKERS

Standards of Practice Handbook

First Edition, 2000

SCOPES OF PRACTICE

This Standards of Practice Handbook applies to the profession of social work and the profession of social service work.

The scope of practice of the profession of social work means the assessment, diagnosis, treatment and evaluation of individual, interpersonal and societal problems through the use of social work knowledge, skills, interventions and strategies, to assist individuals, dyads, families, groups, organizations and communities to achieve optimum psychosocial and social functioning and includes, without limiting the generality of the foregoing, the following:

i) The provision of assessment, diagnostic, treatment and evaluation services within a relationship between a social worker and client;

ii) The development, promotion, management, administration, delivery and evaluation of human service programs, including that done in collaboration with other professionals;

iii) The provision of professional supervision to a social worker, social work student or other supervisee;

iv) The provision of consultation services to other social workers or professionals in relation to the activities described in paragraph (i) above;

v) The development, promotion, implementation and evaluation of social policies aimed at improving social conditions and equality;

vi) The conduct of research or provision of education regarding the practice of social work, as defined in paragraphs (i) to (v) above and (vii) below; and

vii) Any other activities recognized by the College.

The scope of practice of the profession of social service work means the assessment, treatment and evaluation of individual, interpersonal and societal problems through the use of social service work knowledge, skills, interventions and strategies, to assist individuals, dyads, families, groups, organizations and communities to achieve optimum social functioning and includes, without limiting the generality of the foregoing, the following:

a) The provision of assessment, treatment and evaluation services within a relationship between a social worker and client;

b) The development, promotion, management, administration, delivery and evaluation of human service programs, including that done in collaboration with other professionals;

c) The provision of professional supervision to a social service worker, social service work student or other supervisee;

d)   The provision of consultation services to other social service workers or professionals in relation to the activities described in paragraph (a) above;

e)   The development, promotion, implementation and evaluation of social policies aimed at improving social conditions and equality;

f)   The conduct of research or provision of education regarding the practice of social service work, as defined in paragraphs (a) to (e) above and (g) below; and

g)   Any other activities recognized by the College.

The Principles and Interpretations set out below are to be applied in the context of the scope of practice of each profession.

RELATIONSHIP WITH CLIENTS

Principle I

The social work relationship and the social service work relationship, as a component of professional service, are each a mutual endeavour between active participants in providing and using social work or social service work expertise, as the case may be. Clients and College members jointly address relevant social and /or personal problems of concern to clients. The foundation of this professional orientation is the belief that clients have the right and capacity to determine and achieve their goals and objectives. The social work relationship and the social service work relationship are each grounded in and draw upon theories of the social sciences and social work or social service work practice, as the case may be.

Interpretation

Clients and client systems with whom College members are involved include individuals, couples, families, groups, communities, organizations and government. The following fundamental practice principles arise from basic professional values. College members adhere to these principles in their relationships with clients.

1.1   College members and clients participate together in setting and evaluating goals. A purpose for the relationship between College members and clients is identified.

        1.1.1   Goals for relationships between College members and clients include the enhancement of clients' functioning and the strengthening of the capacity of clients to adapt and make changes.

1.2   College members observe, clarify and inquire about information presented to them by clients.

1.3   College members respect and facilitate self-determination in a number of ways including acting as resources for clients and encouraging them to decide which problems they want to address as well as how to address them.[1]

1.4   Although not compelled to accept clients' interpretation of problems, College members demonstrate acceptance of each client's uniqueness.

1.5   College members are aware of their values, attitudes and needs and how these impact on their professional relationships with clients.

1.6   College members distinguish their needs and interests from those of their clients to ensure that, within professional relationships, clients' needs and interests remain paramount.

1.7   College members employed by organizations maintain an awareness and consideration of the purpose, mandate and function of those organizations and how these impact on and limit professional relationships with clients.

COMPETENCE AND INTEGRITY

Principle II

College members maintain competence and integrity in their practice and adhere to the College standards in the "Ontario College of Social Workers and Social Service Workers Code of Ethics" and the "Standards of Practice Handbook".

Interpretation

2.1   Competence

College members are committed to ongoing professional development and maintaining competence in their practice.

---

1.   Limitations to self-determination may arise from the client's incapacity for positive and constructive decision-making, from civil law and from agency mandate and function.

2.I.I   College members are responsible for being aware of the extent and parameters of their competence and their professional scope of practice and limit their practice accordingly. When a client's needs fall outside the College member's usual area of practice, the member informs the client of the option to be referred to another professional. If, however, the client wishes to continue the professional relationship with the College member and have the member provide the service, the member may do so provided that:

   i)   he or she ensures that the services he or she provides are competently provided by seeking additional supervision, consultation and/or education; and

   ii)   the services are not beyond the member's professional scope of practice.

   Recommendations for particular treatment services, referrals to other professionals or a continuation of the professional relationship are guided by the client's interests as well as the College member's clinical judgment and knowledge.

2.I.2   College members remain current with emerging social work or social service work knowledge and practice relevant to their areas of professional practice. Members demonstrate their commitment to ongoing professional development by engaging in any continuing education and continuing competence measures required by the College.

2.1.3   College members maintain current knowledge of policies, legislation, programs and issues related to the community, its institutions and services in their areas of practice.

2.1.4   College members ensure that any professional recommendation or opinions they provide are appropriately substantiated by evidence and supported by a credible body of professional social work knowledge or a credible body of professional social service work knowledge.[1] [2]

---

1.   "Evidence" refers to information tending to establish facts. For College members, evidence can include, but is not limited to: direct observation; information collected in clinical sessions and professional meetings; collateral information; information from documents and information gathered from the use of clinical tools (e.g. questionnaires, diagnostic assessment measures, rating scales).

2.   Each of the phrases "Body of professional social work knowledge" and "body of professional social service work knowledge" relates to both theoretical and practical understanding. A body of knowledge can be attained through education, clinical experience, consultation and supervision, professional development and a review of relevant research and literature. Professional social work knowledge and professional social service work knowledge draw upon the knowledge base of other professions including

2.1.5   As part of maintaining competence and acquiring skills in social work or social service work practice, College members engage in the process of self review and evaluation of their practice and seek consultation when appropriate.

2.2   Integrity

College members are in a position of power and responsibility with respect to all clients. This necessitates that care be taken to ensure that all clients are protected from the abuse of such power during and after the provision of professional services.

College members establish and maintain clear and appropriate boundaries in professional relationships for the protection of clients. Boundary violations include sexual misconduct and other misuse and abuse of the member's power.

2.2.1   College members do not engage in professional relationships that constitute a conflict of interest or in situations in which members ought reasonably to have known that the client would be at risk in any way. College members avoid or declare conflict of interest situations. College members do not provide a professional service to the client while the member is in a conflict of interest. (See also Interpretation 3.7.)

2.2.2   College members do not have sexual relations with clients (See footnote 1 under Principle VIII Sexual Misconduct.) In other professional relationships, College members do not have sexual relations with any person where these relations, combined with the professional relationship, would create a conflict of interest.

2.2.3   College members do not use information obtained in the course of a professional relationship, and do not use their professional position of authority, to coerce, improperly influence, harass, abuse or exploit a client, former client, student, trainee, employee, colleague or research subject.

2.2.4   College members do not solicit or use private or confidential information from clients to acquire, either directly or indirectly, advantage or material benefits.

---

sociology, psychology, anthropology, medicine, law and economics as well as their own respective distinct bodies of knowledge.

2.2.5 When a complaint investigation is underway or a matter has been referred to the Discipline Committee or the Fitness to Practise Committee for a hearing, College members co-operate fully with all policies and procedures of the Complaints, Discipline and Fitness to Practise Committees, and conduct themselves in a manner which demonstrates respect for both the complainant and the College.[3]

2.2.6 College members do not engage in the practice of social work or social service work,

i) While under the influence of any substance, or
ii) While suffering from illness or dysfunction,

which the member knows or ought reasonably to know impairs the member's ability to practise.

2.2.7 College members do not misrepresent professional qualifications, education, experience or affiliation. (See also Principle VI Fees and Principle VII Advertising)

2.2.8 In the practice of social work or social service work, College members avoid conduct which could reasonably be perceived as reflecting negatively on the professions of social work or social service work.

2.2.9 College members promote social justice and advocate for social change on behalf of their clients. College members are knowledgeable and sensitive to cultural and ethnic diversity and to forms of social injustice such as poverty, discrimination and imbalances of power that exist in the culture and that affect clients. College members strive to enhance the capacity of clients to address their own needs and problems in living. College members assist clients to access necessary information, services and resources wherever possible. College members promote and facilitate client participation in decision making.

2.2.10 If there is a conflict between College standards of practice and a College member's work environment, the College member's obligation is to the "Ontario College of Social Workers and

---

3. College members are cognizant of their influential position with respect to witnesses or complainants in complaint, discipline and fitness to practise proceedings.

Social Service Workers Code of Ethics" and the "Standards of Practice Handbook".

RESPONSIBILITY TO CLIENTS

Principle III

College members ensure that professional services are provided responsibly to those persons, groups or organizations seeking their assistance.

Interpretation

3.1   College members provide clients with accurate and complete information regarding the extent, nature and limitations of any services available to them.[1] (See also Principle VII Advertising.)

3.2   College members deliver client services and respond to client queries, concerns, and/or complaints in a timely and reasonable manner.

3.3   College members do not solicit their employers' clients for private practice.[1,2]

3.4   College members do not discriminate against anyone based on race, ethnicity, language, religion, marital status, gender, sexual orientation, age, ability, economic status, political affiliation or national origin.[3]

3.5   College members assist potential clients to obtain services if members are unable or unwilling, for appropriate reasons, to provide the requested professional help.[4,5]

---

1.   The term employer also includes a person or organization with whom the member has an independent service contract.
2.   College members may accept referrals from their employers.
3.   College members adhere to the "Ontario Human Rights Code" and the "Charter of Rights and Freedoms" in the provision of services.
4.   Appropriate reasons for refusing to provide service include but are not limited to:
   i)   complying with the potential client's request for service would require the member to violate ethical and legal requirements including, but not limited to: the "Ontario College of Social Workers and Social Service Workers Code of Ethics"; the "Standards of Practice Handbook"; the "Criminal Code of Canada"; the "Ontario Human Rights Code", and the "Charter of Rights and Freedoms";
   ii)   complying with the potential client's request would violate the member's values, beliefs and traditions to the extent that the member would not be able to provide appropriate professional service;
   iii) the member is aware of extenuating circumstances (e.g. a planned absence from the office, serious health problems, relocation of practice, etc.) that would make compliance with the potential client's request for service impossible and/or not in the potential client's best interests;

3.6   College members inform clients of foreseeable risks as well as rights, opportunities, and obligations associated with the provision of professional services.

3.7   College members avoid conflicts of interest and/or dual relationships with clients or former clients, or with students, employees and supervisees that could impair members' professional judgment or increase the risk of exploitation or harm to clients.[6]

3.8   In a situation where a personal relationship does occur between the member and a client or former client, it is the member, not the client or former client, who assumes full responsibility for demonstrating that the client or former client, has not been exploited, coerced or manipulated, intentionally or unintentionally.

3.9   College members may provide services and/or products so long as the provision of these services and/or products are relevant and conform to College standards. College members do not provide a service and/or product that the member knows or ought reasonably to know is not likely to benefit the client.

3.10   College members terminate professional services to clients when such services are no longer required or requested. It is professional misconduct to discontinue professional services that are needed unless:

---

iv)   the potential client is unable or unwilling to reimburse the member or the member's employer for services rendered, wherever such reimbursement is both appropriate and required as a condition of providing service;

v)   the potential client has repeatedly, and without adequate explanation, cancelled or changed the interview or meeting time to the extent that the member experiences or believes that financial hardship and/or service disruption will occur; and

vi)   the potential client behaves in a threatening or abusive manner such that the member believes that the safety of the member or anyone with whom the member has a personal or professional relationship would be in jeopardy.

5.   When a client is refused further service, the client should be provided with an explanation.

6.   "Dual Relationship" is defined as a situation in which a College member, in addition to his/her professional relationship, has one or more other relationships with the client, regardless of whether this occurs prior to, during, or following the provision of professional services. A dual relationship does not necessarily constitute a conflict of interest; however, where dual relationships exist, there is a strong potential for conflict of interest and there may be an actual or perceived conflict of interest. Relationships beyond the professional one include, but are not limited to, those in which the College member receives a service from the client, the College member has a personal, familial or business relationship with the client, or the College member provides therapy to students, employees or supervisees.

  i) the client requests the discontinuation,

  ii) the client withdraws from the service,

  iii) reasonable efforts are made to arrange alternative or replacement services,

  iv) the client is given a reasonable opportunity to arrange alternative or replacement services, or

  v) continuing to provide the services would place the member at serious risk of harm,

and in the circumstances described in subparagraph I, ii, iii, or iv, the member makes reasonable efforts to hold a termination session with the client.

3.11 College members who anticipate the termination or interruption of service to clients notify clients promptly and arrange the termination, transfer, referral, or continuation of service in accordance with clients' needs and preferences.

3.12 Where appropriate, College members advocate for and/or with clients and inform clients of any action taken and its outcome. Members adhere to Principle V Confidentiality of this Standards of Practice Handbook when providing advocacy services.[7]

3.13 Members may provide appropriate services as a courtesy without remuneration, so long as these services adhere to College standards and do not constitute a conflict of interest.

RECORD KEEPING

Principle IV

The creation and maintenance of records by social workers and social service workers is an essential component of professional practice. The process of preparation and organization of material for the record provides a means to understanding the client and planning the social work and social service work intervention. The purpose of the social work and social service work record is to document services in a recognizable form in order to ensure the conti-

---

7. "Advocacy" is defined as, "The act of directly representing or defending others; in social work, championing the rights of individuals or communities through direct intervention or through empowerment. According to the NASW Code of Ethics, it is a basic obligation to the profession and its members." *The Social Work Dictionary*, 2nd edition, Robert L. Barker, 1991. This definition applies equally to social service work.

nuity and quality of service, to establish accountability for and evidence of the services rendered, to enable the evaluation of service quality, and to provide information to be used for research and education. College members ensure that records are current, accurate, contain relevant information about clients and are managed in a manner that protects client privacy.[1,2]

Interpretation

4.1   Record Content and Format

4.1.1   College members keep systematic, dated, and legible records for each client or client system served.

4.1.2   The record reflects the service provided and the identity of the service provider.

4.1.3   College members document their own actions. College members do not sign records or reports authored by any other person. The exception is the co-signing of records or reports when the College member is acting in a supervisory capacity.

4.1.4   Information is recorded when the event occurs or as soon as possible thereafter.

4.1.5   Recorded information conforms with accepted service or intervention standards and protocols and is in a format that facili-

---

1.   Social work and social service work records include any or all of the following: narrative reports (handwritten, typed, or electronic); progress notes; checklists; correspondence; minutes; process logs; journals or appointment records; films and audio or video tapes. The tools or data used by the College member in developing a professional opinion may be or need not be included in the record. Such tools may be personal notes, memos or messages, test results, sociograms, genograms, etc. Once placed in the record, however, they become an integral part of that record. If they are kept separate from the record, the College member observes the same standards with respect to confidentiality, security and destruction as with the social work and social service work record.

2.   An accurate record will:
   a)   Document the client's situation/ problem exactly and contain only information that is appropriate and useful to the understanding of the situation and the management of the case;
   b)   Report impartially and objectively the factors relevant to the client's situation. The record clearly distinguishes the College member's observations and opinions from the information reported by the client;
   c)   Be easily understandable, avoid vague, unclear or obscure language and symbols;
   d)   Identify corrections;
   e)   Be free of prejudice and discriminatory remarks;
   f)   Identify sources of data.

tates the monitoring and evaluation of the effects of the service/intervention.[3]

4.1.6 College members may use a documentation by exception system provided that the system permits the total record to capture the minimum content as set out in Footnote 3.

4.1.7 College members do not make statements in the record, or in reports based on the record, or issue or sign a certificate, report or other document in the course of practicing either profession that the member knows or ought reasonably to know are false, misleading, inaccurate or otherwise improper.

4.1.8 College members preserve the integrity of client records. If a client disagrees with the accuracy of a record and wishes the

---

3.   Information in the social work and social service work record with respect to each client includes not less than:
   a)   Identifying information regarding the recipient of services (individual, family, couple, group, agency, organization, community);
        In the case of clinical practice, identifying information includes:
        i) name, address, telephone number, date of birth of the client (s); and
        ii) where indicated in risk situations, name, address, and telephone number of a person to be contacted in case of emergency;
        In the case of non-clinical practice, identifying information includes;
        i) name, address, telephone number of the client(s);
        ii) name, address, telephone number(s) of the main contact person or position, if different from i); and
        iii) Sponsors, funders, accountability.
   b)   The date, initiator and purpose of the social work or social service work referral;
   c)   The date, initiator, purpose and, if significant, the setting of the first professional encounter with the client;
   d)   Where applicable, the key elements of the contract or working agreement, namely: client, contracted services, provider of services, fee, reimbursement schedule, and time period for completion of services;
   e)   The time period of involvement if not specified in (d)
   f)   The date of completion/termination, and if significantly different from (d), an explanation for the difference;
   g)   Particulars of the social work or social service work process, as applicable;
        i) the history obtained by the member;
        ii) assessment, diagnosis, formulation and plan;
        iii) treatment and other interventions, e.g. facilitation, advocacy, transfer of skills;
        iv) outcome or results and evaluation;
        v) referrals made by the member;
        vi) recommendations; and
        vii) other services, e.g. verbal and/or written reports/briefs/analyses, research studies and/or their individual components, presentations/speeches/lectures, management related services, stakeholder consultations and professional opinions.
   h)   Consents, releases or authorizations pertaining to the intervention or the communication of information about the client;
   i)   Fees and charges administered, if any.

record altered, the member may incorporate into the record a signed statement by the client specifying the disagreement and the client's correction.

4.2   Record Maintenance

4.2.1   College members employed by an organization acquire and maintain a thorough understanding of the organization's policies with regard to the retention, storage, preservation and security of records. Self-employed College members establish clear policies relating to record retention, storage, preservation and security.

4.2.2   College members take necessary steps to protect the confidentiality and security of paper records, faxes and electronic records.[4]

4.2.3   College members ensure that each client record is stored and preserved in a secure location for a period of time not less than seven years from the date of the last entry. Longer periods of storage time may be defined by the policies of a member's employing organization or by the policies of a self-employed member. Such policies should be developed with a view to the potential future need for the record.[5]

4.2.4   College members who cease independent practice may (i) maintain their client records in accordance with Interpretation

---

4.   Client records, whether they are paper files or electronic files such as computer diskettes, are kept in an area that is not accessible to persons who have no legitimate interest in the records, and where the privacy of the records may be secured by lock and key.

When sending faxes that contain client information, the College member ensures that the information is marked confidential and that the information has been received by the people for whom it was intended.

An electronic system containing social work and social service work records has the following security features:

a)   In the event of a shared system, the College member has a private access code or password that provides reasonable protection against unauthorized access;

b)   The system maintains an audit trail that:
        i)   records the date and time of each entry of information for each client;
        ii) indicates any changes in the recorded information; and
        iii) preserves the original content of the recorded information when changed or updated;

c)   The system allows for the recovery of files, or otherwise provides reasonable protection against loss of, damage to, and inaccessibility of information;

d)   The system provides for a paper print-out of the record.

5.   Examples of situations in which records may be retained for longer periods include cases such as sexual abuse, accidents involving minors and situations where litigation may be ongoing or may arise in the future.

4.2.3, or (ii) make arrangements to transfer the records to another College member and advise their clients of the future location of their records. The College member to whom such records have been transferred complies with the principles regarding retention, storage, preservation and security with respect to the transferred records.

4.2.5   Client records may be destroyed following the time frames outlined in Interpretation 4.2.3. College members dispose of record contents in such a way that ensures that the confidentiality of the information is not compromised.

4.3   Access and Disclosure

4.3.1   College members employed by an organization acquire and maintain an understanding of the organization's policies regarding access to confidential client information. Such policies pertain to access requests by the clients themselves as well as by other parties. Self-employed College members establish clear policies regarding access to and disclosure of confidential client information.

4.3.2   College members inform clients, upon request, of their policies regarding access to information. Members furthermore inform clients early in their relationship of any limits of record confidentiality.

4.3.3   College members provide clients or their authorized representatives with reasonable, supervised access to their records or such part or parts of the clients' records as is reasonable in the circumstances. Such access may include providing the client with a copy of a segment of his or her record or of the record in its entirety subsequent to the client's and the member's joint review of the record's contents. The client has the right to receive appropriate explanations by the College member of the content of the member's reports concerning him or her.

4.3.4   A client's general access to information contained in the record may be restricted for valid reasons. The College member may deem that such access would be extremely detrimental to the client. In such cases, the College member informs the client of the reason for refusal of access and of the recourse available to the client if he or she disagrees. When the work has involved different members of a family, group or community, and access to a record could therefore mean divulging confidential information received from others, or when recorded language could be misunderstood and prejudicial to one of those members, access may also be restricted. In such instances, College members allow individuals to review recorded information that pertains to those individuals only.

4.3.5 When authorized in writing by clients or their authorized representatives, College members release information from the record to third parties within a reasonable time. The authorization must specify, (i) the information that is to be released, for example a partial record, the entire record, or a summary of the member's contact with the client, (ii) the party or parties to whom the information is to be released and (iii) the term of validity of the authorization. Members may release information from the record to third parties without the client's authorization only if disclosure is required or allowed by law or if the member believes, on reasonable grounds, that the disclosure is essential to the prevention of physical injury to self or others. Members may decide not to release information to a third party if, in the member's professional judgment, such a release could result in harm to the client. (See also Interpretation 5.1.6)

4.3.6 Prior to releasing information from a record that pertains to more than one client, for example a couple, family, group, community agency, government department, or other organization/business, College members receive authorization from each individual client.

4.3.7 College members who are served with a formal notice or subpoena to produce client records before a court and who are of the opinion that disclosure would be detrimental to the client, should themselves, or through legal counsel, advocate for nondisclosure to the court.

4.3.8 College members may permit client records to be used in a non-identifying manner for the purpose of research, teaching, or general evaluation of service delivery. (See also Interpretation 5.4) if the removal of identifying information does not adequately protect clients' anonymity, e.g. where clients' roles/activities are highly specialized and/or publicized, or where confidentiality is compromised in cases of consultation, research, or policy analysis, the member does not permit access to the record for these purposes.

4.3.9 College members to whom another member's client records have been transferred, comply with the aforementioned standards regarding access and disclosure with respect to the transferred records.

CONFIDENTIALITY

Principle V

College members respect the privacy of clients by holding in strict confidence all information about clients. College members disclose such information only when required or allowed by law to do so or when clients have consented to disclosure.[1]

Interpretation

5.1   College members shall not disclose confidential information concerning or received from clients, subject to any exceptions contained in the following interpretation.

    5.1.1   When College members are employed by an agency, or organization, College standards of confidentiality may conflict with the organization's policies and procedures concerning confidentiality. When there is a conflict, College standards take precedence.[2]

    5.1.2   When in a review, investigation or proceeding under the Act in which the professional conduct, competency or capacity of a College member is in issue, the member may disclose such confidential information concerning or received from a client as is reasonably required by the member or the College for the purposes of the review, investigation or proceeding, without the client's authorization. College members do not divulge more information than is reasonably required.

    5.1.3   When disclosure is required or allowed by law or by order of a court, College members do not divulge more information than is required or allowed.

---

1.   See "Ontario College of Social Workers Code of Ethics", "A social worker or social service worker shall protect the confidentiality of all professionally acquired information. He or she shall disclose such information only when required or allowed by law to do so, or when clients have consented to disclosure."
2.   See "Ontario College of Social Workers and Social Service Workers Code of Ethics", "A social worker or social service worker shall maintain the best interest of the client as the primary professional obligation."

5.1.4 College members wishing to use collection agencies or legal proceedings to collect unpaid fees may release, in the context of legal proceedings, only the client's name, the contract for service, statements of accounts and any records related to billing. This release would not extend to the content of the services provided. (See also Interpretation 6.1.3.)

5.1.5 College members inform clients of the parameters of information to be disclosed and make reasonable efforts to advise clients of the possible consequences of such disclosure.[3]

5.1.6 College members in clinical practice do not disclose the identity of and/or information about a person who has consulted or retained them unless the nature of the matter requires it. Unauthorized disclosure is justified if the disclosure is obligated legally or allowed by law or if the member believes, on reasonable grounds, that the disclosure is essential to the prevention of physical injury to self or others. (See also Interpretation 4.3.5.)

5.1.7 In clinical practice, College members have clients sign completed consent forms prior to the release of information. A separate consent form is required to cover each authorization for releasing client information. In urgent circumstances, a verbal consent by the client to the disclosure of information may constitute proper authorization. The member should document that this consent was obtained.

5.1.8 College members make reasonable efforts to ensure that the information disclosed is pertinent and relevant to the professional service for which clients have contracted.

5.2 College members inform clients early in their relationship of the limits of confidentiality of information. In clinical practice, for example, when social work service or social service work service is delivered

---

3.   In clinical practice the College member informs the client of at least the following:
   a)   who wants the information (name, title, employer and address);
   b)   why the information is desired;
   c)   how the receiving party plans to use the information;
   d)   if the receiving party may pass the information on to yet a third party without the client's consent;
   e)   exactly what information is to be disclosed;
   f)   the repercussions of giving consent or refusing permission for the disclosure
   g)   the expiration date of the consent;
   h)   how to revoke the consent.

in the context of supervision or multi-disciplinary professional teams, College members explain to clients the need for sharing pertinent information with supervisors, allied professionals and para professionals, administrative co-workers, social work or social service work students, volunteers and appropriate accreditation bodies.[4] (See also Principle IV The Social Work And Social Service Work Record.)

5.3   College members in non-clinical practice distinguish between public and private information related to their clients. Public information, as defined below, may be disclosed in the appropriate circumstances.

5.3.1   'Public information' is any information about clients and/or their activities that is readily available to the general public and the disclosure of which could not harm the client. When in doubt, the College member obtains permission from the client or a duly authorized representative before disclosing or otherwise using such information.[5]

5.3.2   When working with community groups, government agencies and other organizations, the College member keeps confidential any information about the personal lives, personalities, and personal behaviour of the individuals involved.

5.3.3   The College member also keeps confidential any other sensitive information about such clients, including human resources, financial, managerial, strategic and/or politically sensitive material, the disclosure of which could harm the client.

5.4   College members obtain clients' informed consent before photographing, audio or videotaping or permitting third party observation of clients' activities.[6] Where case scenarios are presented for research, educational or publication purposes, client confidentiality is ensured

---

4.   College members in clinical or non-clinical practice anticipate circumstances which may limit confidentiality. Clear discussion of these limits and contracting for confidentiality with the team, group or community should be undertaken. Individual clients should be aware, however, that there is no legal recourse if their confidentiality is violated by another group member.

5.   For example, in non-clinical practice College members should obtain the client's verbal permission before:
   a)   publishing reports about their work with the client;
   b)   referring to their work with the client in their advertising;
   c)   speaking with media, funders, potential funders and other individuals/groups about the organization; and
   d)   bringing guests, observers, or media to meetings involving the client.

6.   Exceptions may be allowed under law, for example, in child abuse investigations.

through the alteration and disguise of identifying information.(See also Interpretation 4.3.8.)

5.5 College members may use public information and/or non-identifying information for research, educational and publication purposes.

5.6 College members are aware of the distinction between consultation and supervision as it pertains to sharing client information. In consultation, clients are not identified.

FEES

Principle VI

When setting or administering fee schedules for services performed, College members inform clients fully about fees, charges and collection procedures.

Interpretation

6.1 College members do not charge or accept any fee which is not fully disclosed.

6.1.1 College members explain in advance or at the commencement of a service the basis of all charges, giving a reasonable estimate of projected fees and disbursements, pointing out any uncertainties involved, so that clients may make informed decisions with regard to using a member's services.[1]

6.1.2 College members discuss and renegotiate the service contract with clients when changes in the fee schedule are anticipated.

6.1.3 College members ensure that fee schedules clearly describe billing procedures, reasonable penalties for missed and cancelled appointments or late payment of fees, the use of collection agencies or legal proceedings to collect unpaid fees and third party fee payments.[2] (See also Interpretation 5.1.4)

6.1.4 College members may reduce, waive or delay collecting fees in situations where there is financial hardship to clients, or

---

1. These charges may be based on such factors as the amount of time and effort required and spent, the complexity of the matter and whether a special skill, expertise or service has been required and provided.
2. Interest on late payments should be expressed as an annualized rate.

they may refer clients to appropriate alternative agencies so that clients are not deprived of professional social work or social service work services.[3, 4]

6.1.5   College members do not charge fees on the basis of material or financial benefits accruing to clients as a result of services rendered or fees which are excessive in relation to the service performed.

6.1.6   College members in clinical practice, or in charitable or publicly funded settings, do not accept or give commissions, rebates, fees, other benefits or anything of value for receiving or making a referral of a client to or from another person.

6.1.7   College members seek an agreement, preferably in writing, dealing with the provision of Interpretations 6.1.1 to 6.1.5 inclusive, at the time of contracting for services with a client.

ADVERTISING

Principle VII

Advertising is intended to inform and educate the public about available social work and social service work services. College members ensure that advertisements are compatible with the standards and ethics of the social work and social service work professions.

Interpretation

7.1   College members may advertise their services through public statements, announcements, advertising media and promotional activities provided that these:

7.1.1   are not false or misleading, and that any factual information is verifiable;

---

3.   College members who accept barter payments are aware of the potential conflict of interest and taxation issues that this style of payment may create. College members avoid this method of payment if it constitutes a conflict of interest.

4.   College members are not expected to reduce their fees unless required to do so by the policy of the agency by whom they are employed. College members may request that the client notify the member immediately if any circumstances arise that may interfere with the normal payment of fees.

7.1.2   do not bring the professions or College into disrepute;

7.1.3   do not compare services with other College members;

7.1.4   do not include any endorsements or testimonials;

7.1.5   do not display any affiliations with an organization or association in a manner that falsely implies that organization's sponsorship or certification;

7.1.6   do not claim uniqueness or special advantage unsupported by professional or scientific evidence; and

7.1.7   are in keeping with standards of good taste and discretion.

7.2   College members may advertise fees charged for their services provided that advertised fees clearly relate to proposed services and include disclosure or possible limits, uncertainties or circumstances whereby additional fees may be charged. (See also Principle VI Fees.)

7.3   College members' education, training, and experience, as well as areas of competence, professional affiliations and services are described in an honest and accurate manner.[1,2]

---

1.   The following alternatives are acceptable forms for individual vocational designation on business cards, letterheads stationary, forms, business telephone listings, directories, signs and identification of business premises, etc.:

a)   College members who are social workers identify themselves by using the designation "RSW" following their names. College members who are social service workers identify themselves by using the designation "RSSW" following their names. College members may add an optional one line description of the College member's area of limited practice or specialty; or

b)   "RSW", in the case of a social worker, or "RSSW", in the case of a social service worker, following the highest academic degree or diploma;

c)   where a doctoral degree has been earned, either the degree or the prefix "Doctor" or "Dr.", but not both, in addition to the designations in either clauses a) or b);

d)   where the College member is a consultant or advisor in the public or private sector, the phrase "Consultant in ." or "Advisor in .", when contained in professional materials, is used only in connection with such position and as an addition to the designation in either clauses a) or b); and

e)   where the College member is an employee in the public or private sector, such affiliation with an accurate and appropriate indication of rank, title or nature of function may be displayed on a professional card and used only in connection with such employment in addition to the designation in clauses a) or b).

2.   College members organized within a business, partnership, or corporation may use one of the following acceptable alternatives:

a)   a list of the names of the business partners, with College members designated as in Footnote 1;

b)   a partnership title containing;

i) the surnames or full names of two or more actual partners; or

ii) where there are three or more actual partners, the surnames or full names may be used with the term "and Associate" or "and Associates" as appropriate;

c)   a partnership title as above with an individual listing of the College members' names and acceptable vocational designations; and

7.3.1 College members cite educational degrees only when they have been received from an accredited university or educational diplomas only when they have been received from a college of applied arts and technology.

7.3.2 College members may represent themselves as specialists in certain areas of practice only if they can provide evidence of specialized training, extensive experience or education;

7.3.3 College members do not make false, misleading or exaggerated claims of efficacy regarding past or anticipated achievements with respect to clients, scholarly pursuits or contributions to society.

7.3.4 College members correct, whenever possible, false, misleading, or inaccurate information and representations made by others concerning College members' qualifications or services.

7.4 College members do not solicit prospective clients in ways that are misleading, that disadvantage fellow members or that discredit the professions of social work or social service work.

SEXUAL MISCONDUCT

Principle VIII

The influence of the helping relationship upon clients is pervasive and may endure long after the relationship has terminated. College members are aware of the potential for conflict of interest and abusive treatment of clients within the helping relationship. Behaviour of a sexual nature by a College member toward a client represents an abuse of power in the helping relationship. College members do not engage in behaviour of a sexual nature with clients.

Interpretation

8.1 College members are solely responsible for ensuring that sexual misconduct does not occur.

8.2 College members do not engage in the following actions with clients:

---

d) a business or corporation name with an individual listing of the College members' names and acceptable vocational designations. (See also Footnote 1)

8.2.1 Sexual intercourse or another form of physical sexual relations between member and the client.[1]

8.2.2 Touching, of a sexual nature, of the client by the member,[2] and

8.2.3 Behaviour or remarks of sexual nature by the member towards the client, other than behaviour or remarks of a clinical nature appropriate to the service provided.[3]

8.3 If a College member develops sexual feelings toward a client that could, in the member's judgment, put the client at risk, the member seeks consultation/supervision and develops an appropriate clinical plan.[4]

8.4 If a client initiates behaviour of a sexual nature, the member states clearly that this behaviour is inappropriate by virtue of the professional relationship.

8.4.1 If overtures or provocative sexual behaviour by a client toward a College member become intrusive to the counselling or therapy process, the College member may choose to terminate the relationship and may offer to assist the client to seek alternative services.

8.5 College members do not provide clinical services to individuals with whom they have had a prior relationship of a sexual nature.

---

1. Physical sexual relations whether or not initiated by the client, include, but are not limited to, kissing of a sexual nature, touching of breasts or genital contact and sexual intercourse.

2. Touching is defined as physical contact of a sexual nature. It includes hugging, holding, patting, stroking, rubbing and any form of contact which is unnecessary to the helping process.

3. Behaviour or remarks of a sexual nature include but are not limited to amorous, romantic, seductive and sexual behaviours or remarks. These may include: expressing amorous and/or romantic feelings, e.g.. being "in love"; requests to date; inappropriate gift giving; unnecessarily arranging sessions in off-site locations, e.g. in restaurants or the client's or the member's home, or beyond normal business hours; unnecessary comments about the client's body or clothing; requesting details of sexual history or sexual preferences not pertinent to the service that is being provided; initiation by the College member of conversations regarding the College member's sexual problems, preferences or fantasies; the wearing of sexually suggestive clothing or adornment; displaying pornographic or other offensive material and jokes or remarks that are sexually provocative or sexually demeaning.
Behaviour or remarks of a sexual nature do not include behaviour or remarks of a clinical nature appropriate to the service being provided.

4. In such cases it may be appropriate for the College member to seek alternative services for the client and terminate the relationship as soon as possible, in keeping with the client's interests.

8.6   Sexual relationships between College members and clients at the time of referral, assessment, counselling, psychotherapy, or other professional services are prohibited.

8.7   Sexual relationships between College members and clients to whom the members have provided psychotherapy and /or counselling services are prohibited at any time following termination of the professional relationship.[5, 6]

8.8   Sexual relationships between College members and clients to whom the members have provided social work or social work services, other than psychotherapy or counselling services, are prohibited for a period of one (1) year following termination of the professional relationship.[5, 6]

8.9   College members do not engage in sexual activities with client's relatives or other individuals with whom clients maintain a close personal relationship when there is a risk of exploitation or potential harm to the client or when such activities would compromise the appropriate professional boundaries between the member and the client.

---

5.   "Psychotherapy Services" are defined as any form of treatment for psycho-social or emotional difficulties, behavioural maladaptions and/or other problems that are assumed to be of an emotional nature, in which a social worker establishes a professional relationship with a client for the purposes of promoting positive personal growth and development.

6.   "Counselling Services" are defined as services provided within the context of a professional relationship with a goal of assisting clients in dealing with issues in their lives by such activities as giving advice, identifying alternatives, problem solving and the provision of information and not as defined in footnote 5.

Appendix 3

Regulations

Social Work and Social Service Work Act, 1998

ONTARIO REGULATION 383/00

No Amendments

REGISTRATION

Certificates of Registration

1. (1) The following are prescribed as classes of certificates of registration for social work:

1. General.

2. Provisional. O. Reg. 383/00, s. 1 (1).

(2) The following are prescribed as classes of certificates of registration for social service work:

1. General.

2. Provisional. O. Reg. 383/00, s. 1 (2).

2. In this Regulation,

"member" means a member of the College. O. Reg. 383/00, s. 2.

3. A person may apply for a certificate of registration by submitting a completed application in the form provided by the Registrar, together with the application fee prescribed by the by-laws. O. Reg. 383/00, s. 3.
4. It is a requirement for the issuing of a certificate of registration of any class that the applicant pay the fees prescribed by the by-laws. O. Reg. 383/00, s. 4.

5. (1) This section applies for the purposes of sections 18, 59 and 63 of the Act. O. Reg. 383/00, s. 5 (1).

(2) The following are registration requirements for a certificate of registration of any class:

1. The applicant must disclose, at the time the application is made and at the time the certificate of registration is issued, the following information relating to the applicant and to the practice of social work, social service work or any other profession, whether in Ontario or in any other jurisdiction:

    i.   Every finding of professional misconduct, incompetence or incapacity and every other similar finding, including a finding of professional misconduct, incompetence or incapacity made by a professional association or other body that has self-regulatory responsibility.

    ii. Every current proceeding in relation to professional misconduct, incompetence or incapacity and every other similar proceeding, including a proceeding relating to professional misconduct, incompetence or incapacity held by a professional association or other body that has self-regulatory responsibility.

2. The applicant must disclose, at the time the application is made and at the time the certificate of registration is issued, every finding of guilt in relation to a criminal offence, an offence under the *Controlled Drugs and Substances Act* (Canada) or the *Food and Drugs Act* (Canada) or any other offence relevant to the applicant's suitability to practise social work or social service work, as the case may be.

3. The applicant's past and present conduct must afford reasonable grounds for the belief that the applicant,

    i.   is mentally competent to practise social work or social service work, as the case may be,

    ii. will practise social work or social service work, as the case may be, with decency, integrity and honesty and in accordance with the law, including but not limited to the Act, the regulations and the by-laws, and

    iii. has sufficient knowledge, skill and judgment to practise social work or social service work, as the case may be.

4. The applicant must demonstrate the ability to speak and write either English or French with reasonable fluency.

5. The applicant must be a Canadian citizen or a permanent resident of Canada or be authorized under the *Immigration Act* (Canada) to engage

in the practice of social work or social service work, as the case may be. O. Reg. 383/00, s. 5 (2).

(3) Despite any other provision in this Regulation, an applicant who makes a false or misleading statement, representation or declaration in or in connection with his or her application, by commission or omission, shall be deemed thereafter, with respect to the application, not to satisfy, and not to have satisfied, the requirements for a certificate of registration of any class. O. Reg. 383/00, s. 5 (3).

(4) An applicant who, after having applied for but before being issued a certificate of registration, becomes the subject of a finding or a proceeding described in subparagraph 1 i or ii of subsection (2) or is found guilty of an offence described in paragraph 2 of subsection (2), shall immediately inform the Registrar. O. Reg. 383/00, s. 5 (4).

6. The following are conditions of a certificate of registration of any class:

1. The member must disclose the following information relating to the member and to the practice of social work, social service work or any other profession, whether in Ontario or in any other jurisdiction:

    i. Every finding of professional misconduct, incompetence or incapacity and every other similar finding, if the finding is made after the initial registration of the member, including a finding of professional misconduct, incompetence or incapacity made by a professional association or other body that has self-regulatory responsibility.

    ii. Every proceeding in relation to professional misconduct, incompetence or incapacity and every other similar proceeding, if the proceeding is held after the initial registration of the member, including a proceeding relating to professional misconduct, incompetence or incapacity held by a professional association or other body that has self-regulatory responsibility.

2. The member must disclose every finding of guilt against the member in relation to a criminal offence, an offence under the *Controlled Drugs and Substances Act* (Canada) or the *Food and Drugs Act* (Canada) or any other offence relevant to the applicant's suitability to practise social work or social service work, as the case may be, if the finding is made after the initial registration of the member.

3. The member must provide evidence satisfactory to the College of the member's continuing competence to practise social work or social service work, as the case may be, in accordance with the guidelines approved by Council from time to time and published and distributed by the College to the members of the College. O. Reg. 383/00, s. 6.

General Certificates of Registration

7. (1) In addition to the requirements set out in sections 4 and 5, the following are registration requirements for a general certificate of registration for social work to be issued under subsection 18 (1) of the Act:

1. The applicant must produce documentation satisfactory to the Registrar that shows that the applicant,

    i.   has obtained a degree in social work from a social work program accredited by the Canadian Association of Schools of Social Work, or a degree from a social work program or an equivalent program offered in Canada and approved by Council as equivalent to a social work program accredited by the Canadian Association of Schools of Social Work,

    ii. has obtained a degree from a social work program or an equivalent program offered outside Canada and approved by Council as equivalent to a social work program accredited by the Canadian Association of Schools of Social Work, or

    iii. has a combination of academic qualifications and practical experience that the Registrar determines is substantially equivalent to the qualifications required for a degree in social work from a social work program accredited by the Canadian Association of Schools of Social Work.

2. The applicant must have successfully completed the examination or examinations in social work, if any, set or approved by Council. O. Reg. 383/00, s. 7 (1).

(2) An applicant for a general certificate of registration for social work whose application and the fees prescribed by the by-laws are received by the College before the day that is three years after the day the first duly elected and appointed Council takes office is exempt from the examination requirement set out in paragraph 2 of subsection (1). O. Reg. 383/00, s. 7 (2).

(3) In addition to the requirements set out in sections 4 and 5, the following are registration requirements for a general certificate of registration for social work to be issued under subsection 59 (1) of the Act, if the application and the fees prescribed by the by-laws are received by the College before March 1, 2001:

1. The applicant must produce documentation satisfactory to the Registrar that shows that the applicant,

    i.   has obtained a degree in social work from a social work program accredited by the Canadian Association of Schools of Social

Work, or a degree from a social work program or an equivalent program offered in Canada and approved by Council as equivalent to a social work program accredited by the Canadian Association of Schools of Social Work, or

ii. has obtained a degree from a social work program or an equivalent program offered outside Canada and approved by Council as equivalent to a social work program accredited by the Canadian Association of Schools of Social Work. O. Reg. 383/00, s. 7 (3).

8. (1) In addition to the requirements set out in sections 4 and 5, the following are registration requirements for a general certificate of registration for social service work to be issued under subsection 18 (2) of the Act:

1. The applicant must produce documentation satisfactory to the Registrar that shows that the applicant,

   i. has obtained a diploma in social service work from a social service work program offered in Ontario at a College of Applied Arts and Technology,

   ii. has obtained a diploma from a program offered in Ontario at a College of Applied Arts and Technology that is equivalent to a social service work program and approved by Council as equivalent to a social service work program offered in Ontario at a College of Applied Arts and Technology,

   iii. has obtained a diploma from a social service work program or an equivalent program offered outside Ontario and approved by Council as equivalent to a social service work program offered in Ontario at a College of Applied Arts and Technology, or

   iv. has a combination of academic qualifications and practical experience that the Registrar determines is substantially equivalent to the qualifications required for a diploma in social service work from a social service work program offered in Ontario at a College of Applied Arts and Technology.

2. The applicant must have successfully completed the examination or examinations in social service work, if any, set or approved by Council. O. Reg. 383/00, s. 8 (1).

(2) An applicant for a general certificate of registration for social service work whose application and the fees prescribed by the by-laws are received by the College before the day that is three years after the day the first duly elected and appointed Council takes office is exempt from the examination requirement set out in paragraph 2 of subsection (1). O. Reg. 383/00, s. 8 (2).

(3) In addition to the requirements set out in sections 4 and 5, the following are registration requirements for a general certificate of registration for social service work to be issued under subsection 59 (2) of the Act, if the application and the fees prescribed by the by-laws are received by the College before March 1, 2001:

1.   The applicant must produce documentation satisfactory to the Registrar that shows that the applicant,

    i.   has obtained a diploma in social service work from a social service work program offered in Ontario at a College of Applied Arts and Technology, or

    ii.   has obtained a diploma from a social service work program or an equivalent program offered outside Ontario and approved by Council as equivalent to a social service work program offered in Ontario at a College of Applied Arts and Technology. O. Reg. 383/00, s. 8 (3).

Provisional Certificates of Registration

9. (1) In this section,

"role of a social worker" means the role of a person who assesses, diagnoses, treats and evaluates individual, interpersonal and societal problems through the use of social work knowledge, skills, interventions and strategies, to assist individuals, dyads, families, groups, organizations and communities to achieve optimum psychosocial and social functioning. O. Reg. 383/00, s. 9 (1).

(2) In addition to the requirements set out in sections 4 and 5, the following are conditions to be met by an applicant before a provisional certificate of registration for social work is issued to the applicant in accordance with subsections 18 (1) and 63 (1) of the Act:

1.   Before the day that is two years after the day the first duly elected and appointed Council takes office, the applicant must submit a completed application for a provisional certificate of registration for social work in the form provided by the Registrar and pay the fees prescribed by the by-laws.

2.   The applicant must produce documentation satisfactory to the Registrar that shows that,

    i.   the applicant has obtained a baccalaureate degree from a Canadian university, or

    ii.   the applicant,

    A.   has obtained an Ontario secondary school diploma or has successfully completed educational training or testing that has been approved by Council as equivalent to an Ontario secondary school diploma, and

    B.   has successfully completed one or more training programs in human services that the Registrar determines is or are sufficient in content, length and intensity to enable the applicant to perform the role of a social worker.

3.   The applicant must be employed in the role of a social worker in Ontario on the date of application.

4.   The applicant must be performing the role of a social worker as his or her principal occupation.

5.   The applicant must produce documentation from the applicant's current employer in the form required by the College in which the applicant's current employer confirms, to the satisfaction of the Registrar,

    i.   the applicant's current duties and responsibilities,

    ii.   that the applicant practises social work safely and ethically, and

    iii.   that the employer remunerates the applicant for the services performed by the applicant.

6.   The applicant must produce documentation from the applicant's current employer in the form required by the College that demonstrates to the satisfaction of the Registrar that the applicant's current duties and responsibilities constitute performing the role of a social worker.

7.   The applicant must provide evidence satisfactory to the Registrar,

    i.   that the applicant performed the role of a social worker for at least 2,000 hours within the two years immediately preceding the date of application, or

    ii.   if the applicant had an authorized leave of absence within the two years immediately preceding the date of application, that the applicant performed the role of a social worker for at least 2,000 hours within the three years immediately preceding the date of application.

8.   The applicant must provide evidence satisfactory to the Registrar,

    i.   that the applicant was employed in the role of a social worker for at least five years within the seven years immediately preceding the date of application, or

    ii.   if the applicant had an authorized leave of absence within the seven years immediately preceding the date of application, that the applicant was employed in the role of a social worker for at least five years within the period of time immediately preceding the date of application that is equal to seven years plus the length of the authorized leave of absence.

9.   The applicant must sign an undertaking to the College in which the applicant agrees to successfully complete, to the satisfaction of the Registrar, additional training approved by the College in social work ethics and social work standards of practice, within three years after the day the College notifies the applicant of the additional training. O. Reg. 383/00, s. 9 (2).

(3) If the applicant's current employer unreasonably refuses to provide the documentation described in paragraphs 5 and 6 of subsection (2), the Registrar may consider documentation produced by the applicant from a previous employer for whom the applicant has worked within the seven years immediately preceding the date of the application and which is otherwise in accordance with those paragraphs. O. Reg. 383/00, s. 9 (3).

10. (1) In this section,

"role of a social service worker" means the role of a person who assesses, treats and evaluates individual, interpersonal and societal problems through the use of social service work knowledge, skills, interventions and strategies, to assist individuals, dyads, families, groups, organizations and communities to achieve optimum social functioning. O. Reg. 383/00, s. 10 (1).

(2) In addition to the requirements set out in sections 4 and 5, the following are conditions to be met by an applicant before a provisional certificate of registration for social service work is issued to the applicant in accordance with subsections 18 (2) and 63 (2) of the Act:

1.   Before the day that is two years after the day the first duly elected and appointed Council takes office, the applicant must submit a completed application for a provisional certificate of registration for social service work in the form provided by the Registrar and pay the fees prescribed by the by-laws.

2.   The applicant must produce documentation satisfactory to the Registrar that shows that the applicant has obtained an Ontario secondary school diploma or has successfully completed educational training or testing that has been approved by Council as equivalent to an Ontario secondary school diploma.

3.   The applicant must be employed in the role of a social service worker in Ontario on the date of application.

4.   The applicant must be performing the role of a social service worker as his or her principal occupation.

5.   The applicant must produce documentation from the applicant's current employer in the form required by the College in which the applicant's current employer confirms, to the satisfaction of the Registrar,

    i.   the applicant's current duties and responsibilities,

    ii.   that the applicant practises social service work safely and ethically, and

    iii.   that the employer remunerates the applicant for the services performed by the applicant.

6.   The applicant must produce documentation from the applicant's current employer in the form required by the College that demonstrates to the satisfaction of the Registrar that the applicant's current duties and responsibilities constitute performing the role of a social service worker.

7.   The applicant must provide evidence satisfactory to the Registrar,

    i.   that the applicant performed the role of a social service worker for at least 2,000 hours within the two years immediately preceding the date of application, or

    ii.   if the applicant had an authorized leave of absence within the two years immediately preceding the date of application, that the applicant performed the role of a social service worker for at least 2,000 hours within the three years immediately preceding the date of application.

8.   The applicant must provide evidence satisfactory to the Registrar,

    i.   that the applicant was employed in the role of a social service worker for at least five years within the seven years immediately preceding the date of application, or

    ii.   if the applicant had an authorized leave of absence within the seven years immediately preceding the date of application, that the applicant was employed in the role of a social service worker for at least five years within the period of time immediately preceding the date of application that is equal to seven years plus the length of the authorized leave of absence.

9.   The applicant must sign an undertaking to the College in which the applicant agrees to successfully complete, to the satisfaction of the Registrar, additional training approved by the College in social service work ethics and social service work standards of practice, within three

years after the day the College notifies the applicant of the additional training. O. Reg. 383/00, s. 10 (2).

(3) If the applicant's current employer unreasonably refuses to provide the documentation described in paragraphs 5 and 6 of subsection (2), the Registrar may consider documentation produced by the applicant from a previous employer for whom the applicant has worked within the seven years immediately preceding the date of the application and which is otherwise in accordance with those paragraphs. O. Reg. 383/00, s. 10 (3).

11. In sections 12, 13 and 14,

"additional training" means,

(a) in the case of a member who holds a provisional certificate of registration for social work, the additional training approved by the College in social work ethics and social work standards of practice that the member has undertaken under paragraph 9 of subsection 9 (2) to successfully complete, to the satisfaction of the Registrar, within three years after the day the College notifies the member of the additional training, and

(b) in the case of a member who holds a provisional certificate of registration for social service work, the additional training approved by the College in social service work ethics and social service work standards of practice that the member has undertaken under paragraph 9 of subsection 10 (2) to successfully complete, to the satisfaction of the Registrar, within three years after the day the College notifies the member of the additional training. O. Reg. 383/00, s. 11.

12. (1) In addition to the conditions set out in section 6, the following are conditions of a provisional certificate of registration:

1. The member must successfully complete the additional training within three years after the day the College notifies the member of the additional training.

2. Until such time as the member provides evidence satisfactory to the Registrar that the member has successfully completed the additional training, the member must, at each of the following times, provide evidence satisfactory to the Registrar that the member has enrolled and is participating in the additional training:

   i. A day that is on or before the first anniversary of the day the member is notified of the additional training.

   ii. A day that is at least six months after the first anniversary and on or before the second anniversary of the day the member is notified of the additional training.

iii.   A day that is at least six months after the second anniversary and before the third anniversary of the day the member is notified of the additional training. O. Reg. 383/00, s. 12 (1).

(2) A member who, when notified of the additional training, provides evidence satisfactory to the Registrar that the member has successfully completed training that the Registrar determines is equivalent to the additional training shall be deemed to have satisfied the conditions set out in subsection (1). O. Reg. 383/00, s. 12 (2).

13. (1) Subject to subsection (2), a provisional certificate of registration expires on the day that is three years after the day the College notifies the member of the additional training. O. Reg. 383/00, s. 13 (1).

(2) If, before the day that is three years after the day the College notifies the member of the additional training, the member applies for a general certificate of registration, on the basis that he or she has successfully completed the additional training or has been deemed under subsection 12 (2) to have satisfied the conditions set out in subsection 12 (1), the member's provisional certificate of registration expires on the day the Registrar issues, or determines not to issue, the general certificate of registration to the member in accordance with section 14. O. Reg. 383/00, s. 13 (2).

14. (1) A member who holds a provisional certificate of registration for social work is entitled to a general certificate of registration for social work if, at the time of application for a general certificate of registration for social work, the member provides evidence satisfactory to the Registrar that,

(a) the member satisfies the requirements set out in section 5; and

(b) the member,

(i)   has successfully completed the additional training within three years after the day the College notified the member of the additional training, or

(ii)   is deemed under subsection 12 (2) to have satisfied the conditions set out in subsection 12 (1). O. Reg. 383/00, s. 14 (1).

(2) A member who holds a provisional certificate of registration for social service work is entitled to a general certificate of registration for social service work if, at the time of application for a general certificate of registration for social service work, the member provides evidence satisfactory to the Registrar that,

(a)   the member satisfies the requirements set out in section 5; and

(b)   the member,

    (i)   has successfully completed the additional training within three years after the day the College notified the member of the additional training, or

    (ii)   is deemed under subsection 12 (2) to have satisfied the conditions set out in subsection 12 (1). O. Reg. 383/00, s. 14 (2).

Titles and Designations

15. (1) A holder of a certificate of registration for social work shall use at least one of the following titles in connection with his or her practice of social work:

1.   Social Worker.

2.   Registered Social Worker.

3.   Travailleur social.

4.   Travailleur social inscrit. O. Reg. 383/00, s. 15 (1).

(2) A holder of a certificate of registration for social work shall use the designation RSW or TSI in documentation used in connection with his or her practice of social work. O. Reg. 383/00, s. 15 (2).

16. (1) A holder of a certificate of registration for social service work shall use at least one of the following titles in connection with his or her practice of social service work:

1.   Social Service Worker.

2.   Registered Social Service Worker.

3.   Technicien en travail social.

4.   Technicien en travail social inscrit. O. Reg. 383/00, s. 16 (1).

(2) A holder of a certificate of registration for social service work shall use the designation RSSW or TTSI in documentation used in connection with his or her practice of social service work. O. Reg. 383/00, s. 16 (2).

17. Omitted (revokes other Regulations). O. Reg. 383/00, s. 17.

18. Omitted (provides for transition). O. Reg. 383/00, s. 18.

19. Omitted (provides for coming into force of provisions of this Regulation). O. Reg. 383/00, s. 19.

Note: Despite the revocation of Ontario Regulation 579/99 by section 17 of Ontario Regulation 383/00, a person who, immediately before Ontario Regulation 579/99 was revoked, held a certificate of registration for social work issued under that regulation shall be deemed to hold a general certificate of registration for social work issued under Ontario Regulation 383/00. See: O. Reg. 383/00, s. 18 (1).

Note: Despite the revocation of Ontario Regulation 579/99 by section 17 of Ontario Regulation 383/00, a person who, immediately before Ontario Regulation 579/99 was revoked, held a certificate of registration for social service work issued under that regulation shall be deemed to hold a general certificate of registration for social service work issued under Ontario Regulation 383/00. See: O. Reg. 383/00, s. 18 (2).

Note: If an application for a certificate of registration was made, but not finally dealt with, before Ontario Regulation 579/99 was revoked,

    (a)   the requirements set out in that Regulation continue, despite the revocation, to apply to the application and not those set out in Ontario Regulation 383/00; and

    (b)   a person who is issued a certificate of registration pursuant to the requirements set out in Ontario Regulation 579/99 shall be deemed to hold a general certificate of registration for social work or social service work, as the case may be, issued under Ontario Regulation 383/00. See: O. Reg. 383/00, s. 18 (3).

Social Work and Social Service Work Act, 1998

ONTARIO REGULATION 384/00

No Amendments

Note: **This Regulation comes into force on the day subsection 26(2) of the Act comes into force. This day has been named as August 15, 2000. See: O. Reg. 384/00, s.3.**

PROFESSIONAL MISCONDUCT

1. In this Regulation,

"member" means a member of the College;

"profession" means the profession of social work or the profession of social service work. O. Reg. 384/00, s. 1.

2. The following are acts of professional misconduct for the purposes of clause 26 (2) (c) of the Act:

THE PRACTICE OF THE PROFESSION AND THE CARE OF, AND RELATIONSHIP WITH CLIENTS

1.   Contravening a term, condition or limitation imposed on the member's certificate of registration.

2.   Failing to meet the standards of the profession.

3.   Doing anything to a client in the course of practicing the profession in a situation in which consent is required by law, without such a consent.

4.   Failing to supervise adequately a person who is under the professional responsibility of the member and who is providing a social work service or a social service work service.

5.   Abusing a client physically, sexually, verbally, psychologically or emotionally, including sexually abusing a client within the meaning of subsection 43 (4) of the Act.

6.   Using information obtained during a professional relationship with a client or using one's professional position of authority to coerce, improperly influence, harass or exploit a client or former client.

7. Practising the profession,

    i)   while under the influence of any substance, or

    ii) while suffering from illness or dysfunction,

    which the member knows or ought reasonably to know impairs the member's ability to practise.

8. Discontinuing professional services that are needed unless,

    i)   the client requests the discontinuation,

    ii)   the client withdraws from the service,

    iii) reasonable efforts are made to arrange alternative or replacement services,

    iv)   the client is given a reasonable opportunity to arrange alternative or replacement services, or

    v)   continuing to provide the services would place the member at serious risk of harm,

    and, in the circumstances described in subparagraph i, ii, iii, or iv, the member makes reasonable efforts to hold a termination session with the client.

9. Providing a service that the member knows or ought reasonably to know is not likely to benefit the client.

10. Providing a professional service while the member is in a conflict of interest.

11. Giving information about a client to a person other than the client or his or her authorized representative except,

    i.   with the consent of the client or his or her authorized representative,

    ii.   as required or allowed by law, or

    iii. in a review, investigation or proceeding under the Act in which the professional conduct, competency or capacity of the member is in issue and only to the extent reasonably required by the member or the College for the purposes of the review, investigation or proceeding.

12. Breaching a term of an agreement with a client relating to,

    i.   the fees for professional services, or

    ii.   professional services for the client

13. Failing to provide a truthful and appropriate explanation of the nature of a professional service following a client's request for an explanation.

14. Failing, without reasonable cause, to provide access to the client or his or her authorized representative to the client's record or such part or parts of the client's record as is reasonable in the circumstances.

REPRESENTATIONS ABOUT MEMBERS AND THEIR QUALIFICATIONS

15. Inappropriately using a term, title or designation in respect of the member's practice.

16. Failing to identify oneself as a social worker or social service worker to a client when providing social work or social service work.

17. Failing to advise the College promptly of a change in the name used by the member in providing or offering to provide social work or social service work services.

18. Using a name other than the member's name as set out in the register in the course of practicing the profession except where the use of another name is necessary for personal safety, the member's employer and the College have been made aware of the pseudonym and the pseudonym is distinctive.

RECORD KEEPING AND REPORTS

19. Falsifying a record relating to the member's practice.

20. Failing to keep records as required by the regulations and standards of the profession.

21. Making a record, or issuing or signing a certificate, report or other document in the course of practicing the profession that the member knows or ought reasonably to know is false, misleading or otherwise improper.

22. Failing, without reasonable cause, to provide a report or certificate relating to a service performed by the member, within a reasonable time, to the client or his or her authorized representative after a client or his or her authorized representative has made a written request for such a report or certificate.

BUSINESS PRACTICES

23. Failing to inform the client, before or at the commencement of a service, of the fees and charges to be levied for the service, and for late cancellations or missed appointments.

24. Submitting an account or charge for services that the member knows is false or misleading.

25. Charging a fee that is excessive in relation to the service performed.

26. Receiving or conferring a rebate, fee or other benefit by reason of the referral of a client to or from another person.

27. Failing to provide an itemized account of professional services within a reasonable time, if requested to do so by the client or person or agency who is to pay, in whole or in part, for the services.

MISCELLANEOUS MATTERS

28. Contravening the Act or regulations or by-laws.

29. Contravening a federal, provincial or territorial law or a municipal by-law if,

    i.   the purpose of the law or by-law is to protect public health, or

    ii. he contravention is relevant to the member's suitability to practise.

30. Influencing a client to change his or her will or other testamentary instrument.

31. Failing to comply with an order of a panel of the Complaints Committee, Discipline Committee or Fitness to Practise Committee of the College.

32. Failing to comply with a written undertaking given to the College or to carry out an agreement entered into with the College.

33. Failing to co-operate in a College investigation.

34. Failing to take reasonable steps to ensure that the requested information is provided in a complete and accurate manner where a member is required to provide information to the College pursuant to the Act, regulations or by-laws.

35. In the case of a member whose certificate of registration is suspended, engaging in the practice of social work or social service work while the certificate is suspended.

36. Engaging in conduct or performing an act relevant to the practice of the profession that, having regard to all circumstances, would reasonably be regarded by members as disgraceful, dishonourable or unprofessional. O. Reg. 384/00, s.2.

Bibliography

Albert, R. *Law and Social Work Practice*. New York, NY: Springer Publishing Company, 1986.

Andreae, D. "Social Work Legislation — A Reality." (1999) 26 *OASW Newsmagazine* 1.

Austin, K., M. Moline, and G. Williams. *Confronting Malpractice: Legal and Ethical Dilemmas in Psychotherapy*. Newbury Park, CA: Sage Publications, 1990.

Barker, R.L., and D.M. Branson. *Forensic Social Work: Legal Aspects of Professional Practice*. New York, NY: Haworth Press, 1993.

Bernstein, B.E., and T.L. Hartsell. *The Portable Lawyer for Mental Health Professionals*. New York, NY: John Wiley & Sons, 1998.

Bersharov, D. *The Vulnerable Social Worker: Liability for Serving Children & Families*. Washington, DC: National Association of Social Workers, 1985.

Bersoff, D. *Ethical Conflicts in Psychology*. Washington, DC: American Psychological Association, 1999.

Bisbing, S., L. Jorgenson, and P. Sutherland. *Sexual Abuse by Professionals: A Legal Guide*. Charlottesville, VA: The Michie Company, 1997.

Bisman, C. *Social Work Practice: Cases and Principles*. Pacific Grove, CA: Brooks/Cole Publishing Company, 1994.

Black's Law Dictionary. St. Paul, MN: West Publishing Company, 1979.

Bond, T. *Standards and Ethics for Counselling in Action*. London: Sage Publications, 1993.

Brieland, D., and J. Lemmon. *Social Work and the Law*. St. Paul: West Publishing Company, 1977.

Bullis, R.K. *Clinical Social Worker Misconduct Law, Ethics and Personal Dynamics*. Chicago, Ill: Nelson-Hall Publishers, 1995.

Canadian Association of Social Workers, *CASW National Scope of Practice Statement* (2000).

Carniol, B. *Case Critical: Challenging Social Work in Canada.* Toronto,
    ON: Between the Lines, 1990.
Dryden, W. *Questions and Answers on Counselling in Action.* London: Sage
    Publications, 1993.
Evans, D.R. *The Law, Standards of Practice, and Ethics in the Practice of
    Psychology.* Toronto: Emond Montgomery, 1997.
Furrow, B. *Malpractice in Psychotherapy.* Toronto: Lexington Books, 1982.
Gabbard, G., and E. Lester. *Boundaries and Boundary Violations in Psycho-
    analysis.* Washington, DC: American Psychiatric Press, 1993.
Gambrill, E., and R. Pruger. *Controversial Issues in Social Work.* Needham
    Heights, MA: Allyn and Bacon, 1992.
Government of Ontario. Health Professions Legislation Review. *Striking a
    New Balance: A Blueprint for the Regulation of Ontario's Health Pro-
    fessions.* Toronto: Health Professions Legislation Review, 1989.
Graham, J., and A. Al-Krenawi. "Contested Terrain." (2000) 17 *Canadian
    Social Work Review* 245.
Gutheil, T., and P. Applebaum. *Clinical Handbook of Psychiatry and the
    Law.* New York: McGraw-Hill, 1991.
Hainey, G., and E. Cole. *Professional Vulnerability: Social Work Account-
    ability before the Criminal Justice System.* Toronto, ON: (unpub-
    lished), 2001.
Harris, J. "Social Workers and the Law: Are You Protected?" (Summer
    1999) *OASW Newsmagazine* 9.
Houston-Vega, M.K., and E.M. Nuehring. *Prudent Practice: A Guide for
    Managing Malpractice Risk.* Washington, DC: National Association of
    Social Workers, 1997.
Hunt, G. A. *Whistleblowing in the Social Services: Public Accountability &
    Professional Practice.* London: Arnold, 1998.
Jehu, D. *Patients as Victims: Sexual Abuse in Psychotherapy and Coun-
    selling.* New York: John Wiley & Sons, 1994.
Jenkins, P. *Counselling, Psychotherapy and the Law.* London: Sage Publica-
    tions, 1997.
Jones, C. *Questions of Ethics in Counselling and Therapy.* Buckingham,
    England: Open University Press, 2000.
*Judicial Inquiry into the Care of Kim Anne Popen by the Children's Aid Soci-
    ety of the City of Sarnia and the County of Lambton.* Toronto: Queen's
    Printer, 1982.
Kruk, E. *Mediation and Conflict Resolution in Social Work and the Human
    Services.* Chicago, Ill: Nelson-Hall Publishers, 1997.
Koocher G.P. & P. Keith-Spiegel. *Ethics in Psychotherapy, Professional
    Standards & Cases.* New York, NY: Oxford University Press, 1998.
Lens, V. "Protecting the Confidentiality of the Therapeutic Relationship: Jaf-
    fee v. Redmond." (2000) 45 *Social Work* 273.

Linzer, N. *Resolving Ethical Dilemmas in Social Work Practice*. New York: Allyn & Bacon, 1999.

McCorquodale, S. "The Role of Regulators In Practice," in F.J. Turner, ed., *Social Work Practice: A Canadian Perspective*. Scarborough, ON: Prentice-Hall Canada, 1999.

Nagy, T.F. *Ethics in Plain English*. Washington, DC: American Psychological Association, 2000.

Ontario Association of Social Workers. *Guidelines for Social Work Record-Keeping* (1999).

Ontario College of Social Workers and Social Service Workers. *Standards of Practice Handbook* (2000).

Pope, K. *Sexual Involvement With Therapists*. Washington, DC: American Psychological Association, 1994.

——, and M. Vasquez. *Ethics in Psychotherapy and Counselling*. San Francisco: Jossey-Bass Publishers. 1998.

Pryzwansky, W.and R. Wendt. *Professional and Ethical Issues in Psychology*. New York, NY: W.W. Norton & Company, 1999.

Reamer, F.G. *Ethical Dilemmas in Social Se*rvice. New York: Columbia University Press, 1990.

——. *Ethical Standards in Social Work: A Critical Review of the NASW Code of Ethics*. Washington, DC: NASW Press, 1998.

——. *Social Work Malpractice and Liability*. New York: Columbia University Press, 1994.

——. *Tangled Relationships: Managing Boundary Issues in the Human Services*. New York: Columbia University Press, 2001.

——, and M. Abramson. *The Teaching of Social Work Ethics*. Hastings, NY: The Institute of Society, Ethics and the Life Sciences, 1982.

Regehr, C. "Confidentiality of Social Work Records." (Spring 2000) *OASW Newsmagazine* 23.

Ross, L., and M. Roy. *Cast the First Stone: Ethics in Analytical Practice*. Wilmette, IL: Chiron Publications; 1995.

Russell, J. *Out of Bounds: Sexual Exploitation in Counselling and Therapy*. London: Sage Publications, 1993.

Sales, B.D. *The Professional Psychologists Handbook*. New York, NY: Plenum Press, 1983.

Saltzman, A., and K. Proch. *Law and Social Work Practice*. Chicago: Nelson-Hall, 1994.

Schutz, B. *Legal Liability in Psychotherapy: A Practitioner's Guide to Risk Management*. San Francisco: Jossey-Bass Publishers, 1982.

Sharwell, G.R. "Learn'em Good: The Threat of Malpractice." (1979) 6 *Journal of Social Welfare* 39.

Steinecke, R. *A Complete Guide to the Regulated Health Professions Act*. Aurora, ON: Canada Law Book, 1995.

Taylor, A. "Hostages to fortune: the abuse of children in care," in G. Hunt, ed., *Whistleblowing in the Social Services: Public Accountability & Professional Practice*. London: Arnold, 1998 at 45.

Turner, F.J. *Psychosocial Therapy: A Social Work Perspective*. New York: The Free Press, 1978.

Vayda, E., and M. Satterfield. *Law for Social Workers: A Canadian Guide*. Toronto: Carswell, 1989.

5 Wigmore on Evidence, 3rd ed., s. 2285.

Table of Cases

Index

About the Authors

Marilyn J. Samuels, B.A., B.P.H.E., LL.B., is in private practice just outside of Toronto, Ontario. In addition to practicing law for the past 12 years, in a variety of areas, she also offers mediation and legal seminars in association with Elayne Tanner, a registered social worker. Through their unique association they are able to offer a combination of services that meet the personal and legal needs of the individuals that attend the counselling and conference centre.

Elayne M. Tanner B.A., B.S.W., M.S.W., R.S.W., is a private practitioner offering individual, family and couple counselling. She has been working in private practice for 11 years from her office located on her farm property west of Toronto, Ontario. In the past year the office has been rebuilt to include a conference room where she and her associates provide seminars on a wide variety of topics to this underserved rural area. The office expansion now also includes the full time law practice of Marilyn J. Samuels. The beautiful 60 acre escarpment location adds to the client experience.